C

LIGHT

In the Good News Bible

Compiled by Geoffrey Baskett

HarperCollins*Publishers*

HarperCollins Publishers
P. O. Box, Glasgow G4 0NB

First published in 1990 by Marshall Pickering,
an imprint of HarperCollins Publishers

This edition first published 1993

Reprint 10 9 8 7 6 5 4 3 2 1 0

© HarperCollins Publishers 1993

ISBN 0 00 470279 4
Printed in Great Britain by
HarperCollins Manufacturing, Glasgow

I am the light of the world.
Whoever follows me will have
the light of life and will
never walk in darkness.
                    – John 8:12

FOREWORD

This remarkable book of devotions contains Bible Readings for each day. This arrangement of Scripture selections is truly "Daily Light on the Daily Path".

The Scripture passages for each day revolve around a single theme. In one year you will have read portions from Genesis to Revelation. We commend this heartily for your daily reading.

Keep this book by your side. In the Bible is to be found "everything we need to live a truly religious life" (2 Peter 1:3).

The regular reading of the Word of God is important to our daily growth in the meaning and power of the Christian life. In times like these it is well to be grounded in a Book that is a lamp to our feet, and a light to our path (Psalm 119:105).

Billy Graham

THE STORY OF DAILY LIGHT

The origin of *Daily Light* is so closely bound up with the family of Bagster and the publishing firm of that name, that the proper background of the compilation of this most popular of all daily devotional books must necessarily include some account of Samuel Bagster, his antecedents and life.

Samuel Bagster was born on December 26, 1772, the second son of George and Mary Bagster of a Lyme Regis, Dorsetshire, family. Samuel Bagster's father, George Bagster, was a member of the congregation which assembled for worship under the pastorship of Dr Andrew Gifford, a Baptist minister, notable antiquarian and assistant librarian at the British Museum. It was at these prayer meetings that George Bagster met his friend Mr John Birch, whose daughter, Eunice Birch, became Samuel Bagster's wife.

When Samuel Bagster was seven years of age, his father sent him to school with the Rev. John Ryland, a Baptist minister who was the father of the well-known Dr Ryland, of Bristol. From his parents and from Rev. John Ryland, Samuel Bagster learned the precepts and practice of a devout Christian which sustained him throughout his life and which in turn he passed on to his children.

Samuel Bagster was indentured to a bookseller in the Strand and on completion of his apprenticeship he opened his own bookshop at No. 81 Strand, London, on April 19, 1794, when twenty-one years of age. As one might expect from a high-principled and religious-minded man, he made it a rule that he would never sell any book which might be considered questionable in taste or subject. An attitude of mind by no means common in those days.

Samuel Bagster and Eunice Birch were married at the Parish Church of St Giles in the Field on December 19, 1797. She was a brave woman of high principles and steadfast faith, a real helpmeet to her husband throughout their long married life. She died the day before her hundredth birthday on August 22, 1877, a few months after she had been honoured by a personal visit from Queen Victoria, who, it is said, knelt at Mrs Bagster's bedside to receive the blessing of this, her revered and venerable subject.

Samuel and Eunice Bagster were blessed with twelve children, and it was Jonathan, their tenth child, who was mainly responsible for the idea and for the method by which *Daily Light* was compiled. He was the Editor-in-Chief, and his daughter Ann was his chief assistant.

The practice of corporate daily worship had always been followed in the family, and it was the daily text that Jonathan Bagster selected that the family, joined together in prayer, were asked to illustrate by further applicable texts. The resultant Scripture quotations were then carefully considered, discussed and arranged by common consent of all those present, after which the manuscript would be laid aside for prayer and meditation to see if there would be any guidance for its further improvement. Sometimes it was weeks before it was felt that the reading for a particular day could not be improved and then that page would be sent to the printer to be set in type. Later it would be read and corrected and all the references would be verified. Each day for over two years the readings were compiled, corrected and improved in this way until the whole book was ready for publication in two volumes, one of morning readings and the other of evening readings.

Robert Bagster, one of Jonathan's sons, who as a lad was present with the family at these daily prayers, wrote these words many years after: "Few are able to appreciate the heart-searching care with which every text was selected, the days, nay the weeks, of changes, alterations and improvements, until at last each page was passed on to the printer. It has been said that each page was prayed over. This is true enough, but far less than the fact that portions were left over for weeks to see if any further guidance came. So this book stands today quite unrivalled, with not one word altered since those devoted people put it forth to the world. It has struck me as a wonderful thought that hundreds of thousands of Christians throughout the world, to its remotest corners, are each day reading the same page with its message of comfort and help."

The truth of this last statement is amply borne out by the many letters that are still received which tell of the help that *Daily Light* has been, and still is, to the Missionaries from the frozen wastes of Canada and Alaska to the steaming heat of the jungles of Assam, Burma and tropical Africa and every climate between these extremes.

Thus the spirit of God-fearing devotion, passed down through successive generations, bears fruit which increases year by year and spreads to the very ends of the earth. The parable of the grain of mustard seed was never so aptly illustrated as by the story of *Daily Light*.

In 1970 Samuel Bagster Ltd. was incorporated with Marshall Morgan & Scott, whose successor, Marshall Pickering, is now part of the Religious Division of HarperCollins Publishers.

BOOKS OF THE BIBLE

Gen.	Genesis	S. of S.	Song of Solomon
Exod.	Exodus	Isa.	Isaiah
Lev.	Leviticus	Jer.	Jeremiah
Num.	Numbers	Lam.	Lamentations
Deut.	Deuteronomy	Ezek.	Ezekiel
Josh.	Joshua	Dan.	Daniel
Judg.	Judges	Hos.	Hosea
Ruth	Ruth	Joel	Joel
1 Sam.	1st Samuel	Amos	Amos
2 Sam.	2nd Samuel	Obad.	Obadiah
1 Kgs.	1st Kings	Jonah	Jonah
2 Kgs.	2nd Kings	Mic.	Micah
1 Chr.	1st Chronicles	Nahum	Nahum
2 Chr.	2nd Chronicles	Hab.	Habakkuk
Ezra	Ezra	Zeph.	Zephaniah
Neh.	Nehemiah	Hag.	Haggai
Esther	Esther	Zech.	Zechariah
Job	Job	Mal.	Malachi
Ps.	Psalms	Matt.	Matthew
Prov.	Proverbs	Mark	Mark
Eccles.	Ecclesiastes	Luke	Luke

John	John	2 Tim.	2nd Timothy
Acts	Acts	Titus	Titus
Rom.	Romans	Philem.	Philemon
1 Cor.	1st Corinthians	Heb.	Hebrews
2 Cor.	2nd Corinthians	Jas.	James
Gal.	Galatians	1 Pet.	1st Peter
Eph.	Ephesians	2 Pet.	2nd Peter
Phil.	Philippians	1 John	1st John
Col.	Colossians	2 John	2nd John
1 Thess.	1st Thessalonians	3 John	3rd John
2 Thess.	2nd Thessalonians	Jude	Jude
1 Tim.	1st Timothy	Rev.	Revelation

HOW TO USE REFERENCES

In each of the daily readings the first text is given in italic type and each paragraph that follows represents a new text. Sometimes a paragraph contains more than one text. When this occurs, the texts within a paragraph are separated by a long dash. References for the texts are given at the foot of each page, where they appear in sequence, each reference being separated by a dash.

JANUARY 1

The one thing I do, however, is to forget what is behind me ... so I run straight towards the goal in order to win the prize, which is God's call through Christ Jesus to the life above.

Father! You have given them to me, and I want them to be with me where I am, so that they may see my glory, the glory you gave me; for you loved me before the world was made. —I am still full of confidence, because I know whom I have trusted, and I am sure that he is able to keep safe until that Day what he has entrusted to me.—God, who began this good work in you, will carry it on until it is finished on the Day of Christ Jesus.

You know that many runners take part in a race, but only one of them wins the prize. Run, then in such a way as to win the prize. Every athlete in training submits to strict discipline, in order to be crowned with a wreath that will not last; but we do it for one that will last for ever.—Let us rid ourselves of everything that gets in the way, and of the sin which holds on to us so tightly, and let us run with determination the race that lies before us. Let us keep our eyes fixed on Jesus, on whom our faith depends from beginning to end.

PHIL. 3.13, 14.—JOHN 17.24.—2 TIM. 1.12.—
PHIL. 1.6.—1 COR. 9.24, 25.—HEB. 12.1, 2.

Sing a new song to the LORD.

Shout for joy to God our defender; sing praise to the God of Jacob! Start the music and beat the tambourines; play pleasant music on the harps and the lyres.—He taught me to sing a new song, a song of praise to our God. Many who see this will take warning and will put their trust in the LORD.

Remember that I have commanded you to be determined and confident! Don't be afraid or discouraged, for I, the LORD your God, am with you wherever you go.—The joy that the LORD gives you will make you strong.—Paul … thanked God and was greatly encouraged.

You know that the time has come for you to wake up from your sleep. For the moment when we will be saved is closer now than it was when we first believed. The night is nearly over, day is almost here. Let us stop doing the things that belong to the dark, and let us take up weapons for fighting in the light. Let us conduct ourselves properly, as people who live in the light of day – no orgies or drunkenness, no immorality or indecency, no fighting or jealousy. But take up the weapons of the LORD Jesus Christ, and stop paying attention to your sinful nature and satisfying its desires.

ISA. 42.10.—PS. 81.1, 2.—PS. 40.3.—JOSH. 1.9.—
NEH. 8.10.—ACTS 28.15.—ROM. 13.11–14.

He led them by a straight road to a city where they could live.

He found them wandering through the desert, a desolate, wind-swept wilderness. He protected them and cared for them, as he would protect himself. Like an eagle teaching its young to fly, catching them safely on its spreading wings, the LORD kept Israel from falling. The LORD alone led his people without the help of a foreign god.—I am your God and will take care of you until you are old and your hair is grey. I made you and will care for you; I will give you help and rescue you.

He gives me new strength. He guides me in the right paths, as he has promised. Even if I go through the deepest darkness, I will not be afraid, LORD, for you are with me. Your shepherd's rod and staff protect me.

I will always guide you and satisfy you with good things. I will keep you strong and well. You will be like a garden that has plenty of water, like a spring of water that never runs dry.—This God is our God for ever and ever; he will lead us for all time to come.—He is the greatest teacher of all.

PS. 107.7.—DEUT. 32.10–12.—ISA. 46.4.—
PS. 23.3, 4.—ISA. 58.11.—PS. 48.14.—
JOB 36.22.

You have not yet entered the land that the LORD your God is giving you, where you can live in peace.

There is no safety here any more.—There still remains for God's people a rest like God's resting on the seventh day.—This hope ... is safe and sure, and goes through the curtain of the heavenly temple into the inner sanctuary. On our behalf Jesus has gone in there before us, and has become a high priest for ever.

There are many rooms in my Father's house, and I am going to prepare a place for you. I would not tell you this if it were not so. And after I go and prepare a place for you, I will come back and take you to myself, so that you will be where I am.—I want very much to leave this life and be with Christ, which is a far better thing.

He will wipe away all tears from their eyes. There will be no more death, no more grief or crying or pain. The old things have disappeared.—In the grave wicked men stop their evil, and tired workmen find rest at last.

Store up riches for yourselves in heaven, where moths and rust cannot destroy, and robbers cannot break in and steal. For your heart will always be where your riches are.—Set your hearts on the things that are in heaven ... Keep your minds fixed on things there, not on things here on earth.

DEUT. 12.9.—MIC. 2.10.—HEB. 4.9.—
HEB. 6.19, 20.—JOHN 14.2, 3.—PHIL. 1.23.—
REV. 21.4.—JOB 3.17.—MATT. 6.20, 21.—
COL. 3.1, 2.

JANUARY 5

We who believe, then, do receive that rest which God promised.

They ... will not give up their sinning.—I see a different law at work in my body—a law that fights against the law which my mind approves of. It makes me a prisoner to the law of sin which is at work in my body. What an unhappy man I am! Who will rescue me from this body that is taking me to death?

Come to me, all of you who are tired from carrying heavy loads, and I will give you rest.—Now that we have been put right with God through faith, we have peace with God through our Lord Jesus Christ. He has brought us by faith into this experience of God's grace, in which we now live. And so we boast of the hope we have of sharing God's glory!

Whoever receives that rest which God promised will rest from his own work.—I no longer have a righteousness of my own, the kind that is gained by obeying the Law. I now have the righteousness that is given through faith in Christ, the righteousness that comes from God and is based on faith.—He offered rest and comfort to all of you, but you refused to listen to him.

HEB. 4.3.—JER. 9.5.—ROM. 7.23, 24.—
MATT. 11.28.—ROM. 5.1, 2.—HEB. 4.10.—
PHIL. 3.9.—ISA. 28.12.

*LORD our God, may your blessings be with us. Give us
success in all we do!*

You became famous in every nation for your perfect
beauty, because I was the one who made you so lovely.—All
of us, then, reflect the glory of the Lord with uncovered
faces; and that same glory, coming from the LORD, who is
the Spirit, transforms us into his likeness in an ever greater
degree of glory.

Happy are those who obey the LORD, who live by his
commands. Your work will provide for your needs; you will
be happy and prosperous.—Ask the LORD to bless your
plans, and you will be successful in carrying them out.

Keep on working with fear and trembling to complete
your salvation, because God is always at work in you to
make you willing and able to obey his own purpose.—May
our LORD Jesus Christ himself and God our Father, who
loved us and in his grace gave us unfailing courage and a
firm hope, encourage you and strengthen you to always do
and say what is good.

PS. 90.17.—EZEK. 16.14.—2 COR. 3.18.—
PS. 128.1, 2.—PROV. 16.3.—PHIL. 2.12, 13.—
2 THESS. 2.16, 17.

JANUARY 7

I pray you, O God, remember to my credit everything that I have done.

The LORD [said] ... "I remember how faithful you were when you were young, how you loved me when we were first married; you followed me through the desert."—I will honour the covenant I made with you when you were young, and I will make a covenant with you that will last for ever.—I will show my concern for you and keep my promise to bring you back home. I alone know the plans I have for you, plans to bring you prosperity and not disaster, plans to bring about the future you hope for.

As high as the heavens are above the earth, so high are my ways and thoughts above yours.—I would turn to God and present my case to him. We cannot understand the great things he does, and to his miracles there is no end.—You have done many things for us, O LORD our God; there is no one like you! You have made many wonderful plans for us. I could never speak of them all—their number is so great!

NEH. 5.19.—JER. 2.2.—EZEK. 16.60.—
JER. 29.10, 11.—ISA. 55.9.—JOB 5.8, 9.—PS. 40.5.

JANUARY 8

Those who know you, LORD, will trust you; you do not abandon anyone who comes to you.

The LORD is like a strong tower, where the righteous can go and be safe.—God is my saviour; I will trust him and not be afraid. The LORD gives me power and strength; he is my saviour.

I am an old man now; I have lived a long time, but I have never seen a good man abandoned by the LORD or his children begging for food.—For the LORD loves what is right and does not abandon his faithful people. He protects them for ever, but the descendants of the wicked will be driven out.—The LORD has made a solemn promise, and he will not abandon you, for he has decided to make you his own people.—From such terrible dangers of death he saved us, and will save us; and we have placed our hope in him that he will save us again.

Be satisfied with what you have. For God has said, "I will never leave you; I will never abandon you." Let us be bold, then, and say, "The Lord is my helper, I will not be afraid. What can anyone do to me?"

PS. 9.10.—PROV. 18.10.—ISA. 12.2.—PS. 37.25.—
PS. 37.28.—1 SAM. 12.22.—2 COR. 1.10.—
HEB. 13.5, 6.

JANUARY 9

*You have warned those who show you reverence, so that they
might escape destruction.*

The LORD is my Banner.—From east to west everyone will
fear him and his great power. He will come like a rushing
river, like a strong wind.

Then we will shout for joy over your victory and celebrate your triumph by praising our God.—The LORD has
shown that we are in the right. Let's go and tell the people
in Jerusalem what the LORD our God has done.—In all
these things we have complete victory through him who
loved us!—Thanks be to God who gives us the victory
through our Lord Jesus Christ!—Jesus is the one who leads
them to salvation.

Finally, build up your strength in union with the Lord
and by means of his mighty power.—Serve me as a brave
and loyal soldier, and fight the LORD's battles.—Don't be
discouraged, any of you. Do the work, for I am with you …
do not be afraid.—Take a good look at the fields; the crops
are now ripe and ready to be harvested!—Just a little while
longer, and he who is coming will come; he will not delay.

PS. 60.4.—EXOD. 17.15.—ISA. 59.19.—PS. 20.5.—
JER. 51.10.—ROM. 8.37.—1 COR. 15.57.—
HEB. 2.10.—EPH. 6.10.—1 SAM. 18.17.—
HAG. 2.4, 5.—JOHN 4.35.—HEB. 10.37.

May the God who gives us peace make you holy in every way and keep your whole being – spirit, soul, and body – free from every fault at the coming of our LORD Jesus Christ.

Christ loved the church and gave his life for it ... in order to present the church to himself in all its beauty – pure and faultless, without spot or wrinkle or any other imperfection.—So we preach Christ to everyone. With all possible wisdom we warn and teach them in order to bring each one into God's presence as a mature individual in union with Christ.

God's peace, which is far beyond human understanding, will keep your hearts and minds safe in union with Christ Jesus.—The peace that Christ gives is to guide you in the decisions you make; for it is to this peace that God has called you together in the one body.

May our Lord Jesus Christ himself and God our Father, who loved us and in his grace gave us unfailing courage and a firm hope, encourage you and strengthen you to always do and say what is good.—He will also keep you firm to the end, so that you will be faultless on the Day of our Lord Jesus Christ.

1 THESS. 5.23.—EPS. 5.25, 27.—COL. 1.28.—
PHIL. 4.7.—COL. 3.15.—2 THESS. 2.16, 17.—
1 COR. 1.8.

JANUARY 11

O God, it is right for us to praise you in Zion and keep our promises to you.

There is for us only one God, the Father, who is the Creator of all things and for whom we live; and there is only one Lord, Jesus Christ, through whom all things were created and through whom we live.—So that all will honour the Son in the same way as they honour the Father. Whoever does not honour the Son does not honour the Father who sent him. Let us, then, always offer praise to God as our sacrifice through Jesus, which is the offering presented by lips that confess him as Lord.—Giving thanks is the sacrifice that honours me, and I will surely save all who obey me.

After this I looked, and there was an enormous crowd – no one could count all the people! They were from every race, tribe, nation, and language, and they stood in front of the throne and of the Lamb, dressed in white robes and holding palm branches in their hands. They called out in a loud voice: "Salvation comes from our God, who sits on the throne, and from the Lamb!" They worshipped God, saying, "Amen! Praise, glory, wisdom, thanksgiving, honour, power, and might belong to our God for ever and ever! Amen!"

PS. 65.1.—1 COR. 8.6.—JOHN 5.23.—HEB. 13.15.—
PS. 50.23.—REV. 7.9–12.

God our Saviour, through Jesus Christ.

God has brought you into union with Christ Jesus, and God has made Christ to be our wisdom. By him we are put right with God; we become God's holy people and are set free.— Can you discover the limits and bounds of the greatness and power of God? The sky is no limit for God, but it lies beyond your reach. God knows the world of the dead, but you do not know it.

The wisdom I proclaim is God's secret wisdom, which is hidden from mankind, but which he had already chosen for our glory even before the world was made.—God, who is the Creator of all things, kept his secret hidden through all the past ages, in order that at the present time, by means of the church, the angelic rulers and powers in the heavenly world might learn of his wisdom in all its different forms.

If any of you lacks wisdom, he should pray to God, who will give it to him; because God gives generously and graciously to all.—The wisdom from above is pure first of all; it is also peaceful, gentle, and friendly; it is full of compassion and produces a harvest of good deeds; it is free from prejudice and hypocrisy.

JUDE 25.—1 COR. 1.30.—JOB 11.7, 8.—
1 COR. 2.7.—EPH. 3.9, 10.—JAS 1.5.—JAS 3.17.

JANUARY 13

*You, LORD, give perfect peace to those who keep their
purpose firm and put their trust in you.*

Leave your troubles with the LORD, and he will defend you;
he never lets honest men be defeated.—God is my saviour;
I will trust him and not be afraid. The LORD give me power
and strength; he is my saviour.

Why are you so frightened? How little faith you have!—
Don't worry about anything, but in all your prayers ask God
for what you need, always asking him with a thankful heart.
And God's peace, which is far beyond human understanding, will keep your hearts and minds safe in union with
Christ Jesus.—Come back and quietly trust in me. Then you
will be strong and secure.

Because everyone will do what is right, there will be
peace and security for ever.—Peace is what I leave with you;
it is my own peace that I give you. I do not give it as the
world does. Do not be worried and upset; do not be
afraid.—Grace and peace be yours from God, who is, who
was, and who is to come.

ISA. 26.3.—PS. 55.22.—ISA. 12.2.—MATT. 8.26.—
PHIL. 4.6, 7.—ISA. 30.15.—ISA 32.17.—
JOHN 14.27.—REV. 1.4.

The Father … is greater than I.

When you pray, say this: Father: may your holy name be honoured.—My Father and their Father, my God and their God.

I love the Father; that is why I do everything as he commands me.—The words that I have spoken to you do not come from me. The Father, who remains in me, does his own work.

The Father loves his Son and has put everything in his power.—For you gave him authority over all mankind, so that he might give eternal life to all those you gave him.

"Lord, show us the Father; that is all we need." Jesus answered, "For a long time I have been with you all; yet you do not know me, Philip? Whoever has seen me has seen the Father. Why, then, do you say, 'Show us the Father'? Do you not believe that I am in the Father and the Father is in me?"—The Father and I are one.—I love you just as the Father loves me; remain in my love. If you obey my commands, you will remain in my love, just as I have obeyed my Father's commands and remain in his love.

JOHN 14.28.—LUKE 11.2.—JOHN 20.17.—
JOHN 14.31.—JOHN 14.10.—JOHN 3.35.—
JOHN 17.2.—JOHN 14.8-10.—JOHN 10.30.—
JOHN 15.9, 10.

I lie defeated in the dust; revive me, as you have promised.

You have been raised to life with Christ, so set your hearts on the things that are in heaven, where Christ sits on his throne at the right-hand side of God. Keep your minds fixed on things there, not on things here on earth. For you have died, and your life is hidden with Christ in God.—We, however, are citizens of heaven, and we eagerly wait for our Saviour, the Lord Jesus Christ, to come from heaven. He will change our weak mortal bodies and make them like his own glorious body, using that power by which he is able to bring all things under his rule.

For what our human nature wants is opposed to what the Spirit wants, and what the Spirit wants is opposed to what our human nature wants. These two are enemies, and this means that you cannot do what you want to do.—So then, my brothers, we have an obligation, but it is not to live as our human nature wants us to. For if you live according to your human nature, you are going to die; but if by the Spirit you put to death your sinful actions, you will live.—I appeal to you, my friends, as strangers and refugees in this world! Do not give in to bodily passions, which are always at war against the soul.

PS. 119.25.—COL. 3.1-3.—PHIL. 3.20, 21.—
GAL. 5.17.—ROM. 8.12, 13.—1 PET. 2.11.

It was by God's own decision that the Son has in himself the full nature of God.

The Father loves his Son and has put everything in his power.—God raised him to the highest place above and gave him the name that is greater than any other name. And so, in honour of the name of Jesus all beings in heaven, on earth, and in the world below will fall on their knees, and all will openly proclaim that Jesus Christ is Lord, to the glory of God the Father.—Christ rules there above all heavenly rulers, authorities, powers, and lords; he has a title superior to all titles of authority in this world and in the next.—For through him God created everything in heaven and on earth, the seen and the unseen things, including spiritual powers, lords, rulers, and authorities. God created the whole universe through him and for him.

Christ died and rose to life in order to be the Lord of the living and of the dead.—You have been given full life in union with Him. He is supreme over every spiritual ruler and authority.—Out of the fullness of his grace he has blessed us all, giving us one blessing after another.

COL. 1.19.—JOHN 3.35.—PHIL. 2.9–11.—
EPH. 1.21.—COL. 1.16.—ROM. 14.9.—COL. 2.10.—
JOHN 1.16.

You save my life from all danger; you forgive all my sins.

God showed his love for us by sending his only Son into the world, so that we might have life through him. This is what love is: it is not that we have loved God, but that he loved us and sent his Son to be the means by which our sins are forgiven.

There is no other god like you, O LORD; you forgive the sins of your people who have survived. You do not stay angry for ever, but you take pleasure in showing us your constant love. You will be merciful to us once again. You will trample our sins underfoot and send them to the bottom of the sea!—I cried to you for help, O LORD my God, and you healed me; you kept me from the grave. I was on my way to the depths below, but you restored my life.—When I felt my life slipping away, then, O LORD, I prayed to you, and in your holy Temple you heard me.—I waited patiently for the LORD's help; then he listened to me and heard my cry. He pulled me out of a dangerous pit, out of the deadly quicksand. He set me safely on a rock and made me secure.

ISA. 38.17.—1 JOHN 4.9, 10.—MIC. 7.18, 19.—
PS. 30.2, 3.—JONAH 2.7.—PS. 40.1, 2.

JANUARY 18

The one who was to come.

Jesus ... was made lower than the angels ... now crowned with glory and honour because of the death he suffered.— Christ ... died for everyone.—Just as all people were made sinners as the result of the disobedience of one man, in the same way they will all be put right with God as the result of the obedience of the one man.

The first man, Adam, was created a living being; but the last Adam is the life-giving Spirit. It is not the spiritual that comes first, but the physical, and then the spiritual.—God said, "And now we will make human beings; they will be like us and resemble us. They will have power over the fish, the birds, and all animals, domestic and wild, large and small." So God created human beings, making them to be like himself.—In these last days [God] has spoken to us through his Son ... He reflects the brightness of God's glory and is the exact likeness of God's own being.—You gave him authority over all mankind.

The first Adam, made of earth, came from the earth; the second Adam came from heaven. Those who belong to the earth are like the one who was made of earth; those who are of heaven are like the one who came from heaven.

ROM. 5.14.—HEB. 2.9.—2 COR. 5.14.—
ROM. 5.19.—1 COR. 15.45, 46.—GEN. 1.26, 27.—
HEB. 1.1–3.—JOHN 17.2.—1 COR. 15.47, 48.

32

With all humility and many tears I did my work as the Lord's servant.

If one of you wants to be great, he must be the servant of the rest; and if one of you wants to be first, he must be your slave – like the Son of Man, who did not come to be served, but to serve and to give his life to redeem many people.

If someone thinks he is somebody when really he is nobody, he is only deceiving himself.—Because of God's gracious gift to me I say to every one of you: Do not think of yourself more highly than you should. Instead, be modest in your thinking, and judge yourself according to the amount of faith that God has given you.—When you have done all you have been told to do, say, "We are ordinary servants; we have only done our duty."

We are proud that our conscience assures us that our lives in this world … have been ruled by God-given frankness and sincerity, by the power of God's grace and not by human wisdom.—We who have this spiritual treasure are like common clay pots, in order to show that the supreme power belongs to God, not to us.

ACTS 20.19.—MATT. 20.26-28.—GAL. 6.3.—
ROM. 12.3.—LUKE 17.10.—2 COR. 1.12.—
2 COR. 4.7.

He will be called, "Wonderful ..."

The Word became a human being and, full of grace and truth, lived among us. We saw his glory, the glory which he received as the Father's only Son.—Your name and your commands are supreme.

He will be called Immanuel, which means "God is with us".—You will name him Jesus – because he will save his people from their sins.

All will honour the Son in the same way as they honour the Father.—For this reason God raised him to the highest place above and gave him the name that is greater than any other name.—Christ rules there above all heavenly rulers, authorities, powers, and lords; he has a title superior to all titles of authority in this world and in the next. God put all things under Christ's feet.—He had a name written on him, but no one except himself knows what it is ... "King of kings and Lord of lords."

God's power is so great that we cannot come near him.—Who is he, if you know? Who is his son?

ISA. 9.6.—JOHN 1.14.—PS. 138.2.—MATT. 1.23.—
MATT. 1.21.—JOHN 5.23.—PHIL. 2.9.—
EPH. 1.21, 22.—REV. 19.12, 16.—
JOB 37.23.—PROV. 30.4.

JANUARY 21

He prunes every branch that does bear fruit, so that it will be clean and bear more fruit.

He will be like a strong soap, like a fire that refines metal. He will come to judge like one who refines and purifies silver. As a metal-worker refines silver and gold, so the LORD's messenger will purify the priests, so that they will bring to the LORD the right kind of offerings.

We also boast of our troubles, because we know that trouble produces endurance, endurance brings God's approval, and his approval creates hope. This hope does not disappoint us, for God has poured out his love into our hearts by means of the Holy Spirit, who is God's gift to us.—Endure what you suffer as being a father's punishment; your suffering shows that God is treating you as his sons. Was there ever a son who was not punished by his father? If you are not punished, as all his sons are, it means you are not real sons. When we are punished, it seems to us at the time something to make us sad, not glad. Later, however, those who have been disciplined by such punishment reap the peaceful reward of a righteous life. Lift up your tired hands, then, and strengthen your trembling knees!

JOHN 15.2.—MAL. 3.2, 3.—ROM. 5.3–5.—
HEB. 12.7, 8, 11, 12.

This God is our God for ever and ever; he will lead us for all time to come.

LORD, you are my God; I will honour you and praise your name. You have done amazing things; you have faithfully carried out the plans you made long ago.—You, LORD, are all I have, and you give me all I need; my future is in your hands.

He gives me new strength. He guides me in the right paths, as he has promised. Even if I go through the deepest darkness, I will not be afraid, LORD, for you are with me. Your shepherd's rod and staff protect me.—I always stay close to you, and you hold me by the hand. You guide me with your instruction and at the end you will receive me with honour. What else have I in heaven but you? Since I have you, what else could I want on earth? My mind and my body may grow weak, but God is my strength; he is all I ever need.—We are glad because of him; we trust in his holy name.—You will do everything you have promised; LORD, your love is eternal. Complete the work that you have begun.

PS. 48.14.—ISA. 25.1.—PS. 16.5.—PS. 23.3, 4.—
PS. 73.23–26.—PS. 33.21.—PS. 138.8.

This hope does not disappoint us.

I am the LORD; no one who waits for my help will be disappointed.—I will bless the person who puts his trust in me.—You, LORD, give perfect peace to those who keep their purpose firm and put their trust in you. Trust in the LORD for ever; he will always protect us.—I depend on God alone; I put my hope in him. He alone protects and saves me; he is my defender, and I shall never be defeated.—I am still full of confidence, because I know whom I have trusted.

To those who were to receive what he promised, God wanted to make it very clear that he would never change his purpose; so he added his vow to the promise. There are these two things, then, that cannot change and about which God cannot lie. So we who have found safety with him are greatly encouraged to hold firmly to the hope placed before us. We have this hope as an anchor for our lives. It is safe and sure, and goes through the curtain of the heavenly temple into the inner sanctuary. On our behalf Jesus has gone in there before us.

ROM. 5.5.—ISA. 49.23.—JER. 17.7.—ISA. 26.3, 4.—
PS. 62.5, 6.—2 TIM 1.12.—HEB. 6.17-20.

The Lord is coming soon.

There will be the shout of command, the archangel's voice, the sound of God's trumpet, and the Lord himself will come down from heaven. Those who have died believing in Christ will rise to life first; then we who are living at that time will be gathered up along with them in the clouds to meet the Lord in the air. And so we will always be with the Lord. So then, encourage one another with these words.— He who gives his testimony to all this says, "Yes indeed! I am coming soon!" So be it. Come, Lord Jesus!

My friends, as you wait for that Day, do your best to be pure and faultless in God's sight and to be at peace with him.—Avoid every kind of evil. May the God who gives us peace make you holy in every way and keep your whole being – spirit, soul, and body – free from every fault at the coming of our Lord Jesus Christ. He who calls you will do it, because he is faithful.

Be patient. Keep your hopes high, for the day of the Lord's coming is near.

PHIL. 4.5.—1 THESS. 4.16-18.—REV. 22.20.—
2 PET. 3.14.—1 THESS. 5.22-24.—JAS 5.8.

God puts people right through their faith in Jesus Christ.
God does this to all who believe in Christ.

Christ was without sin, but for our sake God made him share our sin in order that in union with him we might share the righteousness of God.—By becoming a curse for us Christ has redeemed us from the curse that the Law brings.—God has brought you into union with Christ Jesus, and God has made Christ to be our wisdom. By him we are put right with God; we become God's holy people and are set free.—He saved us. It was not because of any good deeds that we ourselves had done, but because of his own mercy that he saved us, through the Holy Spirit, who gives us new birth and new life by washing us. God poured out the Holy Spirit abundantly on us through Jesus Christ our Saviour.

I reckon everything as complete loss for the sake of what is so much more valuable, the knowledge of Christ Jesus my Lord. For his sake I have thrown everything away; I consider it all as mere refuse, so that I may gain Christ and be completely united with him. I no longer have a righteousness of my own, the kind that is gained by obeying the Law. I now have the righteousness that is given through faith in Christ, the righteousness that comes from God and is based on faith.

ROM. 3.22.—2 COR. 5.21.—GAL. 3.13.—
1 COR. 1.30.—TITUS 3.5, 6.—PHIL. 3.8, 9.

JANUARY 26

Let us, then, go to him outside the camp and share his shame. For there is no permanent city for us here on earth; we are looking for the city which is to come.

My dear friends, do not be surprised at the painful test you are suffering, as though something unusual were happening to you. Rather be glad that you are sharing Christ's sufferings, so that you may be full of joy when his glory is revealed.—As you share in our sufferings, you also share in the help we receive.

Happy are you if you are insulted because you are Christ's followers; this means that the glorious Spirit, the Spirit of God, is resting on you.

As the apostles left the Council, they were happy, because God had considered them worthy to suffer disgrace for the sake of Jesus.—He [Moses] preferred to suffer with God's people rather than to enjoy sin for a little while. He reckoned that to suffer scorn for the Messiah was worth far more than all the treasures of Egypt, for he kept his eyes on the future reward.

HEB. 13.13, 14.—1 PET. 4.12, 13.—2 COR. 1.7.—
1 PET. 4.14.—ACTS 5.41.—HEB. 11.25, 26.

*You know that Christ appeared in order to take away sins,
and that there is no sin in him.*

In these last days [God] has spoken to us through his Son.
He reflects the brightness of God's glory and is the exact
likeness of God's own being, sustaining the universe with
his powerful word. After achieving forgiveness for the sins
of mankind, he sat down in Heaven at the right-hand side
of God, the Supreme Power.—Christ was without sin, but
for our sake God made him share our sin in order that in
union with him we might share the righteousness of God.

Spend the rest of your lives here on earth in reverence
for him. For you know what was paid to set you free from
the worthless manner of life handed down by your ancestors. It was not something that can be destroyed, such as
silver or gold; it was the costly sacrifice of Christ, who was
like a lamb without defect or flaw. He had been chosen by
God before the creation of the world and was revealed in
these last days for your sake.—We are ruled by the love of
Christ, now that we recognize that one man died for everyone, which means that all share in his death. He died for all,
so that those who live should no longer live for themselves,
but only for him who died and was raised to life for their
sake.

1 JOHN 3.5.—HEB. 1.1–3.—2 COR. 5.21.—
1 PET. 1.17–20.—2 COR. 5.14, 15.

May he always live secure.

And when you are arrested and taken to court, do not worry beforehand about what you are going to say; when the time comes, say whatever is then given to you. For the words you speak will not be yours; they will come from the Holy Spirit.—So do not worry about tomorrow; it will have enough worries of its own. There is no need to add to the troubles each day brings.

The God of Israel … gives strength and power to his people.—He strengthens those who are weak and tired.

"My grace is all you need, for my power is greatest when you are weak." I am most happy, then, to be proud of my weaknesses, in order to feel the protection of Christ's power over me. I am content with weaknesses, insults, hardships, persecutions, and difficulties for Christ's sake. For when I am weak, then I am strong.—I have the strength to face all conditions by the power that Christ gives me.—I shall march, march on, with strength!

DEUT. 33.25.—MARK 13.11.—MATT. 6.34.—
PS. 68.35.—ISA. 40.29.—2 COR. 12.9, 10.—
PHIL. 4.13.—JUDG. 5.21.

A God Who Sees.

LORD, you have examined me and you know me. You know everything I do; from far away you understand all my thoughts. You see me, whether I am working or resting; you know all my actions. Even before I speak, you already know what I will say. Your knowledge of me is too deep; it is beyond my understanding.

The LORD sees what happens everywhere; he is watching us, whether we do good or evil.—The LORD sees everything you do. Wherever you go, he is watching.—God knows your hearts. For the things that are considered of great value by man are worth nothing in God's sight.—The LORD keeps close watch over the whole world, to give strength to those whose hearts are loyal to him.

Jesus ... knew them all. There was no need for anyone to tell him about them, because he himself knew what was in their hearts.—Lord, you know everything; you know that I love you.

GEN. 16.13.—PS. 139.1-4, 6.—PROV. 15.3.—
PROV. 5.21.—LUKE 16.15.—2 CHRN. 16.9.—
JOHN 2.24, 25.—JOHN 21.17.

Let us run with determination the race that lies before us.
Let us keep our eyes fixed on Jesus, on whom our faith
depends from beginning to end.

If anyone wants to come with me, he must forget self, take up his cross every day, and follow me.—None of you can be my disciple unless he gives up everything he has.—Let us stop doing the things that belong to the dark.

Every athlete in training submits to strict discipline. I run straight for the finishing-line; that is why I am like a boxer who does not waste his punches. I harden my body with blows and bring it under complete control, to keep myself from being disqualified after having called others to the contest.—I do not claim that I have already succeeded or have already become perfect. The one thing I do, however, is to forget what is behind me and do my best to reach what is ahead. So I run straight towards the goal in order to win the prize, which is God's call through Christ Jesus to the life above.—Let us try to know the LORD.

**HEB. 12.1, 2.—LUKE 9.23.—LUKE 14.33.—
ROM. 13.12.—1 COR. 9.25-27.—PHIL. 3.12-14.—
HOS. 6.3.**

*If you do not drive out the inhabitants of the land, those that
are left will be as troublesome as splinters in your eyes and
thorns in your sides, and they will fight against you.*

Run your best in the race of faith.—The weapons we use
in our fight are not the world's weapons but God's powerful
weapons, which we use to destroy strongholds. We destroy
false arguments; we pull down every proud obstacle that is
raised against the knowledge of God; we take every thought
captive and make it obey Christ.

We have an obligation, but it is not to live as our human
nature wants us to. For if you live according to your human
nature, you are going to die; but if by the Spirit you put to
death your sinful actions, you will live.

For what our human nature wants is opposed to what
the Spirit wants, and what the Spirit wants is opposed to
what our human nature wants. These two are enemies, and
this means that you cannot do what you want to do.—I see
a different law at work in my body – a law that fights against
the law which my mind approves of.—In all these things
we have complete victory through him who loved us!

NUM. 33.55.—1 TIM 6.12.—2 COR. 10.4, 5.—
ROM. 8.12, 13.—GAL. 5.17.—ROM. 7.23.—
ROM. 8.37.

You love him, although you have not seen him.

Our life is a matter of faith, not of sight.—We love because God first loved us.—We ourselves know and believe the love which God has for us. God is love, and whoever lives in love lives in union with God and God lives in union with him.—You also became God's people when you heard the true message, the Good News that brought you salvation. You believed in Christ, and God put his stamp of ownership on you by giving you the Holy Spirit he had promised.—God's plan is to make known his secret to his people, this rich and glorious secret which he has for all peoples. And the secret is that Christ is in you, which means that you will share in the glory of God.

If someone says he loves God, but hates his brother, he is a liar. For he cannot love God, whom he has not seen, if he does not love his brother, whom he has seen.

Jesus said to him, "Do you believe because you see me? How happy are those who believe without seeing me!"—Happy are all who go to him for protection.

1 PET. 1.8.—2 COR. 5.7.—1 JOHN 4.19.—
1 JOHN 4.16.—EPH. 1.13.—COL. 1.27.—
1 JOHN 4.20.—JOHN 20.29.—PS. 2.12.

FEBRUARY 2

Keep me from anything evil that might cause me pain.

Why are you sleeping? Get up and pray that you will not fall into temptation.—The spirit is willing, but the flesh is weak.

I ask you, God, to let me have two things before I die: keep me from lying, and let me be neither rich nor poor. So give me only as much food as I need. If I have more, I might say that I do not need you. But if I am poor, I might steal and bring disgrace on my God.

The LORD will protect you from all danger; he will keep you safe.—I will rescue you from the power of wicked and violent men. I, the LORD, have spoken.—No child of God keeps on sinning, for the Son of God keeps him safe, and the Evil One cannot harm him.

Because you have kept my command to endure, I will also keep you safe from the time of trouble which is coming upon the world to test all the people on earth.—The Lord knows how to rescue godly people from their trials.

1 CHR. 4.10.—LUKE 22.46.—MATT. 26.41.—
PROV. 30.7–9.—PS. 121.7.—JER. 15.21.—
1 JOHN 5.18.—REV. 3.10.—2 PET. 2.9.

Don't be discouraged, any of you. Do the work, for I am with you.

I am the vine, and you are the branches. Whoever remains in me, and I in him, will bear much fruit; for you can do nothing without me.—I have the strength to face all conditions by the power that Christ gives me.—Build up your strength in union with the Lord and by means of his mighty power.—The joy that the LORD gives you will make you strong.

Have courage! You are now hearing the same words the prophets spoke.—Give strength to hands that are tired and to knees that tremble with weakness. Tell everyone who is discouraged, "Be strong and don't be afraid!"—The LORD ordered him, "Go … I myself am sending you."

If God is for us, who can be against us?—God in his mercy has given us this work to do, and so we are not discouraged.

Let us not become tired of doing good; for if we do not give up, the time will come when we will reap the harvest.—Thanks be to God who gives us the victory through our Lord Jesus Christ!

HAG. 2.4.—JOHN 15.5.—PHIL. 4.13.—EPH. 6.10.—
NEH. 8.10.—ZECH. 8.9.—ISA. 35.3, 4.—
JUDG. 6.14.—ROM. 8.31.—2 COR. 4.1.—
GAL. 6.9.—1 COR. 15.57.

FEBRUARY 4

The Lord has said that his people are never to return there.

They did not keep thinking about the country they had left; if they had, they would have had the chance to return. Instead, it was a better country they longed for, the heavenly country. [Moses] preferred to suffer with God's people rather than to enjoy sin for a little while. He reckoned that to suffer scorn for the Messiah was worth far more than all the treasures of Egypt.—My righteous people, however, will believe and live; but if any of them turns back, I will not be pleased with him. We are not people who turn back and are lost. Instead, we have faith and are saved.—Anyone who starts to plough and then keeps looking back is of no use to the Kingdom of God.

I will boast only about the cross of our Lord Jesus Christ; for by means of his cross the world is dead to me, and I am dead to the world.—The Lord says, "You must leave them and separate yourselves from them. Have nothing to do with what is unclean, and I will accept you."

God, who began this good work in you, will carry it on until it is finished on the Day of Christ Jesus.

DEUT.17.16.—HEB. 11.15, 16, 25, 26.—
HEB.10.38, 39.—LUKE 9.62.—GAL. 6.14.—
2 COR. 6.17.—PHIL. 1.6.

I have come in order that you might have life — life in all its fullness.

You must not eat the fruit of that tree; if you do, you will die the same day.—She took some of the fruit and ate it. Then she gave some to her husband, and he also ate it.

Sin pays its wage – death; but God's free gift is eternal life in union with Christ Jesus our Lord.—Through the sin of one man death began to rule because of that one man. But how much greater is the result of what was done by the one man, Jesus Christ! All who receive God's abundant grace and are freely put right with him will rule in life through Christ.—Just as death came by means of a man, in the same way the rising from death comes by means of a man. For just as all people die because of their union with Adam, in the same way all will be raised to life because of their union with Christ.—Our Saviour, Christ Jesus … has ended the power of death and through the gospel has revealed immortal life.

God has given us eternal life, and this life has its source in his Son. Whoever has the Son has this life; whoever does not have the Son of God does not have life.—God did not send his Son into the world to be its judge, but to be its saviour.

JOHN 10.10.—GEN. 2.17.—GEN. 3.6.—ROM. 6.23.—
ROM. 5.17.—1 COR. 15.21, 22.—2 TIM. 1.10.—
1 JOHN 5.11, 12.—JOHN 3.17.

*Our Lord poured out his abundant grace on me and gave
me the faith and love which are ours in union with
Christ Jesus.*

You know the grace of our Lord Jesus Christ; rich as he
was, he made himself poor for your sake, in order to make
you rich by means of his poverty.—Where sin increased,
God's grace increased much more.

He did this to demonstrate for all time to come the
extraordinary greatness of his grace in the love he showed
to us in Christ Jesus. For it is by God's grace that you have
been saved through faith. It is not the result of your own
efforts, but God's gift, so that no one can boast about
it.—We know that a person is put right with God only
through faith in Jesus Christ, never by doing what the Law
requires. We, too, have believed in Christ Jesus in order to
be put right with God through our faith in Christ, and not
by doing what the Law requires. For no one is put right with
God by doing what the Law requires.—He saved us. It was
not because of any good deeds that we ourselves had done,
but because of his own mercy that he saved us, through the
Holy Spirit, who gives us new birth and new life by washing
us. God poured out the Holy Spirit abundantly on us
through Jesus Christ our Saviour.

1 TIM. 1.14.—2 COR. 8.9.—ROM. 5.20.—
EPH. 2.7-9.—GAL. 2.16.—TITUS 3.5, 6.

You will have all you want to eat, and you will give thanks to the LORD your God for the fertile land that he has given you.

Make certain that you do not forget the LORD your God.— When one of them saw that he was healed, he came back, praising God in a loud voice. He threw himself to the ground at Jesus' feet and thanked him. The man was a Samaritan. Jesus said, "There were ten men who were healed; where are the other nine? Why is this foreigner the only one who came back to give thanks to God?"

Everything that God has created is good ... everything is to be received with a prayer of thanks, because the word of God and the prayer make it acceptable to God.—Whoever will eat anything does so in honour of the Lord, because he gives thanks to God for the food.—It is the LORD's blessing that makes you wealthy. Hard work can make you no richer.

Praise the LORD, my soul! All my being, praise his holy name! Praise the LORD, my soul, and do not forget how kind he is. He forgives all my sins and heals all my diseases. He keeps me from the grave and blesses me with love and mercy.

DEUT. 8.10.—DEUT. 8.11.—LUKE 17.15–18.—
1 TIM. 4.4, 5.—ROM. 14.6.—PROV. 10.22.—
PS. 103.1–4.

I do not call you servants any longer, because a servant does not know what his master is doing. Instead, I call you friends, because I have told you everything I heard from my Father.

The LORD said to himself, "I will not hide from Abraham what I am going to do."—Jesus answered, "The knowledge about the secrets of the Kingdom of heaven has been given to you, but not to them."—But it was to us that God made known his secret by means of his Spirit. The Spirit searches everything, even the hidden depths of God's purposes.— God's secret wisdom … hidden from mankind, but which he had already chosen for our glory even before the world was made.

Happy are those whom you choose, whom you bring to live in your sanctuary. We shall be satisfied with the good things of your house, the blessings of your sacred Temple.—The LORD is the friend of those who obey him and he affirms his covenant with them.—I gave them the message that you gave me, and they received it; they know that it is true that I came from you, and they believe that you sent me.

You are my friends if you do what I command you.

JOHN 15.15.—GEN. 18.17.—MATT. 13.11.—
1 COR. 2.10.—1 COR. 2.7.—PS. 65.4.—PS. 25.14.—
JOHN 17.8.—JOHN 15.14.

FEBRUARY 9

Now he is enjoying himself here.

Your days of grief will come to an end. I, the LORD, will be your eternal light, more lasting than the sun and moon.— The Sovereign LORD will destroy death for ever! He will wipe away the tears from everyone's eyes and take away the disgrace his people have suffered throughout the world.— These are the people who have come safely through the terrible persecution. They have washed their robes and made them white with the blood of the Lamb. That is why they stand before God's throne and serve him day and night in his temple. He who sits on the throne will protect them with his presence. Never again will they hunger or thirst; neither sun nor any scorching heat will burn them, because the Lamb, who is in the centre of the throne, will be their shepherd, and he will guide them to springs of life-giving water.—He will wipe away all tears from their eyes. There will be no more death, no more grief or crying or pain. The old things have disappeared.

LUKE 16.25.—ISA. 60.20.—ISA. 25.8.—
REV. 7.14-17.—REV. 21.4.

*Your eyes are like a lamp for the body. When your eyes are
sound, your whole body is full of light.*

Whoever does not have the Spirit cannot receive the gifts
that come from God's Spirit. Such a person really does not
understand them; they are nonsense to him, because their
value can be judged only on a spiritual basis.—Open my
eyes, so that I may see the wonderful truths in your law.

I am the light of the world. Whoever follows me will
have the light of life and will never walk in darkness.—All
of us ... reflect the glory of the Lord with uncovered faces;
and that same glory coming from the Lord, who is the Spirit,
transforms us into his likeness in an ever greater degree of
glory.—The God who said, "Out of the darkness the light
shall shine!" is the same God who made his light shine in
our hearts, to bring us the knowledge of God's glory shining
in the face of Christ.

I ... ask the God of our Lord Jesus Christ, the glorious
Father, to give you the Spirit, who will make you wise and
reveal God to you, so that you will know him ... so that you
will know what is the hope to which he has called you, how
rich are the wonderful blessings he promises his people.

LUKE 11.34.—1 COR. 2.14.—PS. 119.18.—
JOHN 8.12.—2 COR. 3.18.—2 COR. 4.6.—
EPH. 1.16–18.

*Then the people who feared the LORD spoke to one another,
and the LORD listened and heard what they said. In his
presence, there was written down in a book a record of those
who feared the LORD and respected him.*

Jesus himself drew near and walked along with them.—
Where two or three come together in my name, I am there
with them.—All my other fellow-workers, whose names are
in God's book of the living.

Christ's message in all its richness must live in your
hearts. Teach and instruct each other with all wisdom. Sing
psalms, hymns, and sacred songs; sing to God with thanksgiving in your hearts.—In order that none of you be deceived by sin and become stubborn, you must help one
another every day, as long as the word "Today" in the
scripture applies to us.

You can be sure that on the Judgement Day everyone
will have to give account of every useless word he has ever
spoken. Your words will be used to judge you – to declare
you either innocent or guilty.—Their sentence is written
down.

MAL. 3.16.—LUKE 24.15.—MATT. 18.20.—
PHIL. 4.3.—COL. 3.16.—HEB. 3.13.—
MATT. 12.36, 37.—ISA. 65.6.

"They will be my people," says the LORD Almighty. "On the day when I act, they will be my very own."

I have made you known to those you gave me out of the world. They belonged to you, and you gave them to me. They have obeyed your word. I pray for them. I do not pray for the world but for those you gave me, for they belong to you. All I have is yours, and all you have is mine; and my glory is shown through them. Father! You have given them to me, and I want them to be with me where I am, so that they may see my glory, the glory you gave me; for you loved me before the world was made.

I will come back and take you to myself, so that you will be where I am.—He comes on that Day to receive glory from all his people and honour from all who believe.—We who are living at that time will be gathered up along with them in the clouds to meet the Lord in the air. And so we will always be with the Lord.—You will be like a beautiful crown for the LORD.

MAL. 3.17.—JOHN 17.6, 9, 10, 24.—JOHN 14.3.—
2 THESS. 1.10.—1 THESS. 4.17.—ISA. 62.3.

FEBRUARY 13

Above the dome there was something that looked like a throne made of sapphire, and sitting on the throne was a figure that looked like a man.

The man Christ Jesus.—He became like man and appeared in human likeness.—Since the children, as he calls them, are people of flesh and blood, Jesus himself became like them and shared their human nature. He did this so that through his death he might destroy the Devil, who has the power over death.

I am the living one! I was dead, but now I am alive for ever and ever.—Christ has been raised from death and will never die again – death will no longer rule over him. Because he died, sin has no power over him; and now he lives his life in fellowship with God.—Suppose that you should see the Son of Man go back up to the place where he was before?—He raised Christ from death and seated him at his right side in the heavenly world.—The full content of divine nature lives in Christ, in his humanity.

Though it was in weakness that he was put to death on the cross, it is by God's power that he lives. In union with him we also are weak; but in our relations with you we shall share God's power in his life.

EZEK. 1.26.—1 TIM. 2.5.—PHIL. 2.7.—HEB. 2.14.
REV. 1.18.—ROM. 6.9, 10.—JOHN 6.62.—
EPH. 1.20.—COL. 2.9.—2 COR. 13.4.

FEBRUARY 14

Let it be so for now. For in this way we shall do all that God requires.

I love to do your will, my God! I keep your teaching in my heart.

Do not think that I have come to do away with the Law of Moses and the teachings of the prophets. I have not come to do away with them, but to make their teachings come true. Remember that as long as heaven and earth last, not the least point nor the smallest detail of the Law will be done away with.—The LORD is a God who is eager to save, so he exalted his laws and teachings.—You will be able to enter the Kingdom of heaven only if you are more faithful than the teachers of the Law and the Pharisees in doing what God requires.

What the Law could not do, because human nature was weak, God did. He condemned sin in human nature by sending his own Son, who came with a nature like man's sinful nature, to do away with sin. God did this so that the righteous demands of the Law might be fully satisfied in us who live according to the Spirit, and not according to human nature.—Christ has brought the Law to an end, so that everyone who believes is put right with God.

MATT. 3.15.—PS. 40.8.—MATT. 5.17, 18.—
ISA. 42.21.—MATT. 5.20.—ROM. 8.3,4.—ROM. 10.4

Can anyone really say that his conscience is clear, that he has got rid of his sin?

The LORD looks down from heaven at mankind to see if there are any who are wise, any who worship him. But they have all gone wrong; they are all equally bad.—Those who obey their human nature cannot please God.

I know that good does not live in me – that is, in my human nature. For even though the desire to do good is in me, I am not able to do it. I don't do the good I want to do; instead, I do the evil that I do not want to do.—All of us have been sinful; even our best actions are filthy through and through.

The whole world is under the power of sin; and so the gift which is promised on the basis of faith in Jesus Christ is given to those who believe.—God was making all mankind his friends through Christ. God did not keep an account of their sins.

If we say that we have no sin, we deceive ourselves, and there is no truth in us. But if we confess our sins to God, he will keep his promise and do what is right: he will forgive us our sins and purify us from all our wrongdoing.

PROV. 20.9.—PS. 14.2, 3.—ROM. 8.8.—
ROM. 7.18, 19.—ISA. 64.6.—GAL. 3.22.—
2 COR. 5.19.—1 JOHN 1.8, 9.

FEBRUARY 16

There is a fragrance about you; the sound of your name recalls it.

Your life must be controlled by love, just as Christ loved us and gave his life for us as a sweet-smelling offering and sacrifice that pleases God.—This stone is of great value for you that believe.—God raised him to the highest place above and gave him the name that is greater than any other name. And so, in honour of the name of Jesus all beings in heaven, on earth, and in the world below will fall on their knees.—The full content of divine nature lives in Christ, in his humanity.

If you love me, you will obey my commandments.— God has poured out his love into our hearts by means of the Holy Spirit, who is God's gift to us.—The sweet smell of the perfume filled the whole house.—They realized then that they had been companions of Jesus.

O LORD, our Lord, your greatness is seen in all the world! Your praise reaches up to the heavens.—Immanuel … God is with us.—He will be called, "Wonderful Counsellor", "Mighty God", "Eternal Father", "Prince of Peace".—The LORD is like a strong tower, where the righteous can go and be safe.

S. OF S. 1.3.—EPH. 5.2.—1 PET. 2.7.—
PHIL. 2.9, 10.—COL. 2.9.—JOHN 14.15.—
ROM. 5.5.—JOHN 12.3.—ACTS 4.13.—
PS. 8.1.—MATT. 1.23.—ISA. 9.6.—PROV. 18.10.

*[He] shall carry [the sacrificed bull] ... outside the camp to
the ritually clean place where the ashes are poured out, and
there he shall burn it on a wood fire.*

So they took charge of Jesus. He went out, carrying his
cross, and came to "The Place of the Skull", as it is called.
(In Hebrew it is called "Golgotha".) There they crucified
him.—The Jewish High Priest brings the blood of the
animals into the Most Holy Place to offer it as a sacrifice
for sins; but the bodies of the animals are burnt outside the
camp. For this reason Jesus also died outside the city, in
order to purify the people from sin with his own blood. Let
us, then, go to him outside the camp and share his shame.—
To share in his sufferings.

Be glad that you are sharing Christ's sufferings, so that
you may be full of joy when his glory is revealed.—This
small and temporary trouble we suffer will bring us a
tremendous and eternal glory, much greater than the
trouble.

LEV. 4.12.—JOHN 19.16–18.—HEB. 13.11–13.—
PHIL. 3.10.—1 PET. 4.13.—2 COR. 4.17.

FEBRUARY 18

You are my place of safety when trouble comes.

There are many who pray: "Give us more blessings, O LORD. Look on us with kindness!"—Every morning I will sing aloud of your constant love. You have been a refuge for me, a shelter in my time of trouble.

I felt secure and said to myself, "I will never be defeated." You were good to me, LORD; you protected me like a mountain fortress. But then you hid yourself from me, and I was afraid. I called to you, LORD; I begged for your help: "What will you gain from my death? What profit from my going to the grave? Are dead people able to praise you? Can they proclaim your unfailing goodness? Hear me, LORD, and be merciful! Help me, LORD!"

"For one brief moment I left you; with deep love I will take you back. I turned away angry for only a moment, but I will show you my love for ever." So says the LORD who saves you.—You will be sad, but your sadness will turn into gladness.—Tears may flow in the night, but joy comes in the morning.

JER. 17.17.—PS. 4.6.—PS. 59.16.—PS. 30.6-10.—
ISA. 54.7, 8.—JOHN 16.20.—PS. 30.5.

It is the LORD who gives wisdom; from him come knowledge and understanding.

Trust in the LORD with all your heart. Never rely on what you think you know.—If any of you lacks wisdom, he should pray to God, who will give it to him; because God gives generously and graciously to all.—What seems to be God's foolishness is wiser than human wisdom, and what seems to be God's weakness is stronger than human strength.—I will give you such words and wisdom that none of your enemies will be able to refute or contradict what you say.—God purposely chose what the world considers nonsense in order to shame the wise. This means that no one can boast in God's presence.

The explanation of your teachings gives light and brings wisdom to the ignorant.—I keep your law in my heart, so that I will not sin against you.

They were all well impressed with him and marvelled at the eloquent words that he spoke.—Nobody has ever talked like this man!—God has brought you into union with Christ Jesus, and God has made Christ to be our wisdom.

PROV. 2.6.—PROV. 3.5.—JAS 1.5.—
1 COR. 1.27, 29.—PS. 119.130.—PS. 119.11.—
LUKE 4.22.—JOHN 7.46.—1 COR. 1.30.

After a life of suffering, he will again have joy; he will know that he did not suffer in vain.

Jesus ... said, "It is finished!" Then he bowed his head and died.—Christ was without sin, but for our sake God made him share our sin in order that in union with him we might share the righteousness of God.

They are the people I made for myself, and they will sing my praises!—God ... kept his secret hidden ... in order that at the present time, by means of the church, the angelic rulers and powers in the heavenly world might learn of his wisdom in all its different forms. God did this according to his eternal purpose, which he achieved through Christ Jesus our Lord.—He did this to demonstrate for all time to come the extraordinary greatness of his grace in the love he showed us in Christ Jesus.

You believed in Christ, and God put his stamp of ownership on you by giving you the Holy Spirit he had promised. The Spirit is the guarantee that we shall receive what God has promised his people, and this assures us that God will give complete freedom to those who are his.

You are the chosen race, the King's priests, the holy nation, God's own people, chosen to proclaim the wonderful acts of God, who called you out of darkness into his own marvellous light.

ISA. 53.11.—JOHN 19.30.—2 COR. 5.21.—
ISA. 43.21.—EPH. 3.9-11.—EPH. 2.7.—
EPH. 1.13, 14.—1 PET. 2.9.

I am the LORD and I make you holy.

I am the LORD your God, and I have set you apart from the other nations. You shall be holy and belong only to me, because I am the LORD and I am holy. I have set you apart from the other nations so that you would belong to me alone.

Those who have been called by God, who live in the love of God the Father.—Dedicate them to yourself by means of the truth; your word is truth.—May the God who gives us peace make you holy in every way and keep your whole being – spirit, soul, and body – free from every fault at the coming of our Lord Jesus Christ.

Jesus … died outside the city, in order to purify the people from sin with his own blood.—Our God and Saviour Jesus Christ … gave himself for us, to rescue us from all wickedness and to make us a pure people who belong to him alone and are eager to do good.—He purifies people from their sins, and both he and those who are made pure all have the same Father. That is why Jesus is not ashamed to call them his brothers.—For their sake I dedicate myself to you, in order that they, too, may be truly dedicated to you.—You … were made a holy people by his Spirit, to obey Jesus Christ and be purified by his blood.

LEV. 20.8.—LEV. 20.24, 26.—JUDE 1.—
JOHN 17.17.—1 THESS. 5.23.—HEB. 13.12.—
TITUS 2.13, 14.—HEB. 2.11.—JOHN 17.19.—
1 PET. 1.2.

Those who have reverence for the LORD will learn from him the path they should follow.

The eyes are like a lamp for the body. If your eyes are sound, your whole body will be full of light.

Your word is a lamp to guide me and a light for my path.—If you wander off the road to the right or the left, you will hear his voice behind you saying, "Here is the road. Follow it."—The LORD says, "I will teach you the way you should go; I will instruct you and advise you. Don't be stupid like a horse or a mule, which must be controlled with a bit and bridle to make it submit." The wicked will have to suffer, but those who trust in the LORD are protected by his constant love. You that are righteous, be glad and rejoice because of what the Lord has done. You that obey him, shout for joy!—With faithfulness and love he leads all who keep his covenant and obey his commands.

LORD, I know that no one is the master of his own destiny; no person has control over his own life.—Teach me your ways, O LORD; make them known to me.

PS. 25.25.—MATT. 6.22.—PS. 119.105.—
ISA. 30.21.—PS. 32.8-11.—PS. 25.10.—
JER. 10.23.—PS. 25.4.

The sprinkled blood that promises much better things than does the blood of Abel.

There is the Lamb of God, who takes away the sin of the world!—The Lamb that was killed.—The blood of bulls and goats can never take away sins. For this reason, when Christ was about to come into the world, he said to God: "You do not want sacrifices and offerings, but you have prepared a body for me." We are all purified from sin by the offering that he made of his own body once and for all.

Then Abel brought the first lamb born to one of his sheep … and gave the best parts of it as an offering. The LORD was pleased with Abel and his offering.—Christ loved us and gave his life for us as a sweet-smelling offering and sacrifice that pleases God.

Let us come near to God with a sincere heart and a sure faith, with hearts that have been purified from a guilty conscience and with bodies washed with clean water.—We have … complete freedom to go into the Most Holy Place by means of the death of Jesus.

HEB. 12.24.—JOHN 1.29.—REV. 13.8.—
HEB. 10.4, 5, 10.—GEN. 4.4.—EPH. 5.2.—
HEB. 10.22.—HEB. 10.19.

FEBRUARY 24

The sovereign LORD says, "I will once again let the Israelites ask me for help."

You do not have what you want because you do not ask God for it.

Ask, and you will receive; seek, and you will find; knock, and the door will be opened to you. For everyone who asks will receive, and anyone who seeks will find, and the door will be opened to him who knocks.—We have courage in God's presence, because we are sure that he hears us if we ask him for anything that is according to his will. He hears us whenever we ask him; and since we know this is true, we know also that he gives us what we ask from him.—If any of you lacks wisdom, he should pray to God, who will give it to him; because God gives generously and graciously to all.—Open your mouth, and I will feed you.—They should always pray and never become discouraged.

The LORD watches over the righteous and listens to their cries. The righteous call to the LORD, and he listens.—You will ask him in my name; and I do not say that I will ask him on your behalf, for the Father himself loves you. He loves you because you love me. Ask and you will receive, so that your happiness may be complete.

**EZEK. 36.37.—JAS 4.2.—MATT. 7.7, 8.—
1 JOHN 5.14, 15.—JAS 1.5.—PS. 81.10.—
LUKE 18.1.—PS. 34.15, 17.—JOHN 16.26, 27, 24.**

Resist the Devil, and he will run away from you.

From east to west everyone will fear him and his great power.—Jesus answered, "Go away, Satan! The scripture says, 'Worship the Lord your God and serve only him!'" Then the Devil left Jesus; and angels came and helped him.

Build up your strength in union with the Lord and by means of his mighty power. Put on all the armour that God gives you, so that you will be able to stand up against the Devil's evil tricks.—Have nothing to do with the worthless things that people do, things that belong to the darkness. Instead, bring them out to the light.—Keep Satan from getting the upper hand of us; for we know what his plans are.—Be alert, be on the watch! Your enemy, the Devil, roams round like a roaring lion, looking for someone to devour. Be firm in your faith and resist him, because you know that your fellow-believers in all the world are going through the same kind of sufferings.

Who will accuse God's chosen people? God himself declared them not guilty!

JAS 4.7.—ISA. 59.19.—MATT. 4.10, 11.—
EPH. 6.10, 11.—EPH. 5.11.—2 COR. 2.11.—
1 PET. 5.8, 9.—ROM. 8.33.

Let us examine our ways and turn back to the LORD.

Examine me and test me, LORD; judge my desires and thoughts.—Sincerity and truth are what you require; fill my mind with your wisdom.—I have considered my conduct, and I promise to follow your instructions. Without delay I hurry to obey your commands.—Everyone should examine himself first, and then eat the bread and drink from the cup.

If we confess our sins to God, he will keep his promise and do what is right: he will forgive us our sins and purify us from all our wrongdoing.—If anyone does sin, we have someone who pleads with the Father on our behalf – Jesus Christ, the righteous one.—We have, then, my brothers, complete freedom to go into the Most Holy Place by means of the death of Jesus. He opened for us a new way, a living way, through the curtain – that is, through his own body. We have a great priest in charge of the house of God. So let us come near to God with a sincere heart and a sure faith, with hearts that have been purified from a guilty conscience and with bodies washed with clean water.

LAM. 3.40.—PS. 26.2.—PS. 51.6.—
PS. 119.59, 60.—1 COR. 11.28.—1 JOHN 1.9.—
1 JOHN 2.1.—HEB. 10.19–22.

Think of yourselves as dead, so far as sin is concerned, but living in fellowship with God through Christ Jesus.

Whoever hears my words and believes in him who sent me has eternal life. He will not be judged, but has already passed from death to life.—So far as the Law is concerned, however, I am dead – killed by the Law itself – in order that I might live for God. I have been put to death with Christ on his cross, so that it is no longer I who live, but it is Christ who lives in me. This life that I live now, I live by faith in the Son of God, who loved me and gave his life for me.

Because I live, you also will live.—I give them eternal life, and they shall never die. No one can snatch them away from me. What my Father has given me is greater than everything, and no one can snatch them away from the Father's care. The Father and I are one.

You have been raised to life with Christ, so set your hearts on the things that are in heaven, where Christ sits on his throne at the right-hand side of God. For you have died, and your life is hidden with Christ in God.

ROM. 6.11.—JOHN 5.24.—GAL. 2.19, 20.—
JOHN 14.19.—JOHN 10.28-30.—COL. 3.1, 3.

God loved the world so much that he gave his only Son, so that everyone who believes in him may not die but have eternal life.

God … through Christ changed us from enemies into his friends and gave us the task of making others his friends also. Our message is that God was making all mankind his friends through Christ. God did not keep an account of their sins, and he has given us the message which tells how he makes them his friends. Here we are, then, speaking for Christ, as though God himself were making his appeal through us. We plead on Christ's behalf: let God change you from enemies into his friends! Christ was without sin, but for our sake God made him share our sin in order that in union with him we might share the righteousness of God.—God is love. And God showed his love for us by sending his only Son into the world, so that we might have life through him. This is what love is: it is not that we have loved God, but that he loved us and sent his Son to be the means by which our sins are forgiven. Dear friends, if this is how God loved us, then we should love one another.

JOHN 3.16.—2 COR. 5.18–21.—1 JOHN 4.8–11.

Never boast about tomorrow. You don't know what will happen between now and then.

When the time came for me to show you favour I heard you; when the day arrived for me to save you, I helped you.—The light will be among you a little longer. Continue on your way while you have the light, so that the darkness will not come upon you; for the one who walks in the dark does not know where he is going. Believe in the light, then, while you have it, so that you will be the people of the light.

Work hard at whatever you do, because there will be no action, no thought, no knowledge, no wisdom in the world of the dead – and that is where you are going.

Lucky man! You have all the good things you need for many years. Take life easy, eat, drink, and enjoy yourself! You fool! This very night you will have to give up your life; then who will get all these things you have kept for yourself? This is how it is with those who pile up riches for themselves but are not rich in God's sight.

The world and everything in it that people desire is passing away; but he who does the will of God lives for ever.

PROV. 27.1.—2 COR. 6.2.—JOHN 12.35, 36.—
ECCLES. 9.10.—LUKE 12.19-21.—1 JOHN 2.17.

The Spirit produces love.

God is love, and whoever lives in love lives in union with God and God lives in union with him.—God has poured out his love into our hearts by means of the Holy Spirit, who is God's gift to us.—This stone is of great value for you that believe.—We love because God first loved us.— We are ruled by the love of Christ, now that we recognize that one man died for everyone, which means that all share in his death. He died for all, so that those who live should no longer live for themselves, but only for him who died and was raised to life for their sake.

You yourselves have been taught by God how you should love one another.—My commandment is this: love one another, just as I love you.—Above everything, love one another earnestly, because love covers over many sins.—Your life must be controlled by love, just as Christ loved us and gave his life for us as a sweet-smelling offering and sacrifice that pleases God.

GAL. 5.22.—1 JOHN 4.16.—ROM. 5.5.—
1 PET. 2.7.—1 JOHN 4.19.—2 COR. 5.14, 15.—
1 THESS. 4.9.—JOHN 15.21.—1 PET. 4.8.—
EPH. 5.2.

God has given me children in the land of my trouble.

Let us give thanks to the God and Father of our Lord Jesus Christ, the merciful Father, the God from whom all help comes! He helps us in all our troubles, so that we are able to help others who have all kinds of troubles, using the same help that we ourselves have received from God. Just as we have a share in Christ's many sufferings, so also through Christ we share in God's great help.

Be glad about this, even though it may now be necessary for you to be sad for a while because of the many kinds of trials you suffer. Their purpose is to prove that your faith is genuine. Even gold ... is tested by fire; and so your faith, which is much more precious than gold, must also be tested, so that it may endure. Then you will receive praise and glory and honour on the Day when Jesus Christ is revealed.— The Lord stayed with me and gave me strength.

Those who suffer because it is God's will for them, should by their good actions trust themselves completely to their Creator, who always keeps his promises.

GEN. 41.52.—2 COR. 1.3-5.—1 PET. 1.6, 7.—
2 TIM. 4.17.—1 PET. 4.19.

Trust in the LORD with all your heart. Never rely on what you think you know. Remember the LORD in everything you do, and he will show you the right way.

Trust in God at all times, my people. Tell him all your troubles, for he is our refuge.

The LORD says, "I will teach you the way you should go; I will instruct you and advise you. Don't be stupid like a horse or a mule, which must be controlled with a bit and bridle to make it submit." The wicked will have to suffer, but those who trust in the LORD are protected by his constant love.—If you wander off the road to the right or the left, you will hear his voice behind you saying, "Here is the road. Follow it."

If you do not go with us, don't make us leave this place. How will anyone know that you are pleased with your people and with me if you do not go with us? Your presence with us will distinguish us from any other people on earth.

PROV. 3.5, 6.—PS. 62.8.—PS. 32.8-10.—
ISA. 30.21.—EXOD. 33.15, 16.

77

Set your hearts on the things that are in heaven, ... not on things here on earth.

Do not love the world or anything that belongs to the world. If you love the world, you do not love the Father.— Do not store up riches for yourselves here on earth, where moths and rust destroy, and robbers break in and steal. Instead, store up riches for yourselves in heaven, where moths and rust cannot destroy, and robbers cannot break in and steal. For your heart will always be where your riches are.

Our life is a matter of faith, not of sight.—For this reason we never become discouraged. Even though our physical being is gradually decaying, yet our spiritual being is renewed day after day. And this small and temporary trouble we suffer will bring us a tremendous and eternal glory, much greater than the trouble. For we fix our attention, not on things that are seen, but on things that are unseen. What can be seen lasts only for a time, but what cannot be seen lasts for ever.—The rich blessings that God keeps for his people. He keeps them for you in heaven, where they cannot decay or spoil or fade away.

COL. 3.1, 2.—1 JOHN 2.15.—MATT. 6.19–21.—
2 COR. 5.7.—2 COR. 4.16–18.—1 PET. 1.4.

Lord, rescue me from all this trouble.

LORD, I look up to you, up to heaven, where you rule. As a servant depends on his master, as a maid depends on her mistress, so we will keep looking to you, LORD our God, until you have mercy on us.—Hear my cry, O God; listen to my prayer! In despair and far from home I call to you! Take me to a safe refuge, for you are my protector, my strong defence against my enemies. Let me live in your sanctuary all my life; let me find safety under your wings.— The poor and the helpless have fled to you and have been safe in times of trouble. You give them shelter from storms.

Christ himself suffered for you and left you an example, so that you would follow in his steps. He committed no sin, and no one ever heard a lie come from his lips. When he was insulted, he did not answer back with an insult; when he suffered, he did not threaten, but placed his hopes in God, the righteous Judge.

ISA. 38.14.—PS. 123.1, 2.—PS. 61.1-4.—
ISA. 25.4.—1 PET. 2.21-23.

He ... guards those who are devoted to him.

The LORD ... always went ahead of you to find a place for you to camp. To show you the way, he went in front of you in a pillar of fire by night and in a pillar of cloud by day.—Like an eagle teaching its young to fly, catching them safely on its spreading wings ... the LORD alone led his people.—The LORD guides a man in the way he should go and protects those who please him. If they fall, they will not stay down, because the LORD will help them up.—The good man suffers many troubles, but the LORD saves him from them all.—The righteous are guided and protected by the LORD, but the evil are on the way to their doom.—We know that in all things God works for good with those who love him, those whom he has called according to his purpose.—We have the LORD our God to help us and to fight our battles.

The LORD your God is with you; his power gives you victory. The LORD will take delight in you, and in his love he will give you new life. He will sing and be joyful over you.

PROV. 2.8.—DEUT. 1.32, 33.—DEUT. 32.11, 12.—
PS. 37.23, 24.—PS. 34.19.—PS. 1.6.—ROM. 8.28.—
2 CHR. 32.8.—ZEPH 3.17.

Your Creator will be like a husband to you — The LORD Almighty is his name.

There is a deep secret truth revealed in this scripture, which I understand as applying to Christ and the church.

No longer will you be called "Forsaken," ... your new name will be, "God is Pleased with Her," ... because the LORD is pleased with you ... As a groom is delighted with his bride, so your God will delight in you.—He has sent me to comfort all who mourn, to give to those who mourn in Zion joy and gladness instead of grief, a song of praise instead of sorrow.

Jerusalem rejoices because of what the LORD has done. She is like a bride dressed for her wedding. God has clothed her with salvation and victory.

I will make you my wife; I will be true and faithful; I will show you constant love and mercy and make you mine for ever.

Who ... can separate us from the love of Christ?

ISA. 54.5.—EPH. 5.32.—ISA. 62.4, 5.—
ISA. 61.2, 3.—ISA. 61.10.—HOS. 2.19.—ROM. 8.35.

MARCH 8

You forgive all my sins.

There is no other God like you, O LORD; you forgive the sins of your people who have survived. You do not stay angry for ever, but you take pleasure in showing us your constant love. You will be merciful to us once again. You will trample our sins underfoot and send them to the bottom of the sea!

"For one brief moment I left you; with deep love I will take you back. I turned away angry for only a moment, but I will show you my love for ever." So says the LORD who saves you.—I will forgive their sins and I will no longer remember their wrongs.

Happy are those whose sins are forgiven, whose wrongs are pardoned. Happy is the man whom the LORD does not accuse of doing wrong and who is free from all deceit.—The blood of Jesus, his Son, purifies us from every sin.

ISA. 38.17.—MIC. 7.18, 19.—ISA. 54.7, 8.—
JER. 31.34.—PS. 32.1, 2.—1 JOHN 1.7.

MARCH 9

God ... generously gives us everything for our enjoyment.

Make certain that you do not forget the LORD your God;
do not fail to obey any of his laws that I am giving you today.
When you have all you want to eat and have built good
houses to live in ... make sure that you do not become
proud and forget the LORD your God ... who gives you the
power to become rich.

If the LORD does not build the house, the work of the
builders is useless; if the LORD does not protect the city, it
is useless for the sentries to stand guard. It is useless to work
so hard for a living, getting up early and going to bed late.
For the LORD provides for those he loves, while they are
asleep.—Your people did not conquer the land with their
swords; they did not win it by their own power; it was by
your power and your strength, by the assurance of your
presence, which showed that you loved them.—There are
many who pray: "Give us more blessings, O LORD. Look
on us with kindness!"

**1 TIM. 6.17.—DEUT. 8.11, 12, 14, 18.—
PS. 127.1, 2.—PS. 44.3.—PS. 4.6.**

The LORD Provides.

God himself will provide one.

Don't think that the LORD is too weak to save you or too deaf to hear your call for help!—The Saviour will come from Zion and remove all wickedness from the descendants of Jacob.

Happy is the man who has the God of Jacob to help him and who depends on the LORD his God.—The LORD watches over those who obey him, those who trust in his constant love. He saves them from death.

With all his abundant wealth through Christ Jesus, my God will supply all your needs.—God has said, "I will never leave you; I will never abandon you." Let us be bold, then, and say, "The Lord is my helper, I will not be afraid. What can anyone do to me?"—The LORD protects and defends me; I trust in him. He gives me help and makes me glad; I praise him with joyful songs.

GEN. 22.14.—GEN. 22.8.—ISA. 59.1.—
ROM. 11.26.—PS. 146.5.—PS. 33.18, 19.—
PHIL. 4.19.—HEB. 13.5, 6.—PS. 28.7.

May the LORD bless you and take care of you.

It is the LORD's blessing that makes you wealthy. Hard work can make you no richer.—You bless those who obey you, LORD; your love protects them like a shield.

He will not let you fall; your protector is always awake. The protector of Israel never dozes or sleeps. The LORD will guard you; he is by your side to proect you. The LORD will protect you from all danger; he will keep you safe. He will protect you as you come and go now and for ever.—I watch over it and water it continually. I guard it night and day so that no one will harm it.

Holy Father! Keep them safe by the power of your name. While I was with them, I kept them safe by the power of your name, the name you gave me. I protected them.

The Lord will rescue me from all evil and take me safely into his heavenly Kingdom. To him be the glory for ever and ever! Amen.

NUM. 6.24.—PROV. 10.22.—PS. 5.12.—
PS. 121.3–5, 7, 8.—ISA. 27.3.—JOHN 17.11, 12.—
2 TIM. 4.18.

May the LORD be kind and gracious to you; may the LORD look on you with favour and give you peace.

No one has ever seen God. The only Son, who is the same as God and is at the Father's side, he has made him known.—He reflects the brightness of God's glory and is the exact likeness of God's own being.—They do not believe, because their minds have been kept in the dark by the evil god of this world. He keeps them from seeing the light shining on them, the light that comes from the Good News about the glory of Christ, who is the exact likeness of God.

Look on your servant with kindness; save me in your constant love. I call to you, LORD; don't let me be disgraced.—You were good to me, LORD; you protected me like a mountain fortress. But then you hid yourself from me, and I was afraid.—How happy are the people who worship you with songs, who live in the light of your kindness!

The LORD gives strength to his people and blesses them with peace.

Courage! It is I. Don't be afraid!

NUM. 6.25, 26.—JOHN 1.18.—HEB. 1.3.—
2 COR. 4.4.—PS. 31.16, 17.—PS. 30.7.—
PS. 89.15.—PS. 29.11.—MATT. 14.27.

There is one God, and there is one who brings God and mankind together, the man Christ Jesus.

Since the children ... are people of flesh and blood, Jesus himself became like them and shared their human nature.

Turn to me now and be saved, people all over the world! I am the only God there is.

We have someone who pleads with the Father on our behalf – Jesus Christ, the righteous one.—In union with Christ Jesus, you who used to be far away have been brought near by the sacrificial death of Christ. Christ himself has brought us peace.—When Christ ... entered once and for all into the Most Holy Place ... he took his own blood and obtained eternal salvation for us. For this reason Christ is the one who arranges a new covenant, so that those who have been called by God may receive the eternal blessings that God has promised.—He is able ... to save those who come to God through him, because he lives for ever to plead with God for them.

1 TIM. 2.5.—HEB. 2.14.—ISA. 45.22.—
1 JOHN 2.1.—EPH. 2.13, 14.—HEB. 9.12, 15.—
HEB. 7.25.

Bring credit to the teaching about God our Saviour in all they do.

Your way of life should be as the gospel of Christ requires.—Happy are you if you are insulted because you are Christ's followers. If any of you suffers, it must not be because he is a murderer or a thief or a criminal or a meddler in other people's affairs.—Be innocent and pure as God's perfect children, who live in a world of corrupt and sinful people. You must shine among them like stars lighting up the sky.—Your light must shine before people, so that they will see the good things you do and praise your Father in heaven.

Never let go of loyalty and faithfulness. Tie them round your neck; write them on your heart. If you do this, both God and man will be pleased with you.—My brothers, fill your minds with those things that are good and that deserve praise: things that are true, noble, right, pure, lovely, and honourable.

TITUS 2.10.—PHIL. 1.27.—31 PET. 4.14, 15.—
PHIL. 2.15.—MATT. 5.16.—PROV. 3.3, 4.—
PHIL. 4.8.

Perfect through suffering.

"The sorrow in my heart is so great that it almost crushes me. Stay here and keep watch with me." He went a little farther on, threw himself face downwards on the ground, and prayed, "My Father, if it is possible, take this cup of suffering from me! Yet not what I want, but what you want."—In great anguish he prayed even more fervently; his sweat was like drops of blood falling to the ground.

The danger of death was all round me; the horrors of the grave closed in on me; I was filled with fear and anxiety.—Insults have broken my heart, and I am in despair. I had hoped for sympathy, but there was none; for comfort, but I found none.—When I look beside me, I see that there is no one to help me, no one to protect me. No one cares for me.

We despised him and rejected him; he endured suffering and pain. No one would even look at him – we ignored him as if he were nothing.

HEB. 2.10.—MATT. 26.38, 39.—LUKE 22.44.—
PS. 116.3.—PS. 69.20.—PS. 142.4.—ISA. 53.3.

MARCH 16

You don't even know what your life tomorrow will be! You are like a puff of smoke, which appears for a moment and then disappears.

My days race by, not one of them good. My life passes like the swiftest boat, as fast as an eagle swooping down on a rabbit.—You carry us away like a flood; we last no longer than a dream. We are like weeds that sprout in the morning, that grow and burst into bloom, then dry up and die in the evening.—We are all born weak and helpless. All lead the same short, troubled life. We grow and wither as quickly as flowers.

The world and everything in it that people desire is passing away; but he who does the will of God lives for ever. They will disappear, but you will remain; they will all wear out like clothes. You will discard them like clothes, and they will vanish. But you are always the same, and your life never ends.—Jesus Christ is the same yesterday, today, and for ever.

JAS 4.14.—JOB 9.25, 26.—PS. 90.5, 6.—
JOB 14.1, 2.—1 JOHN 2.17.—PS. 102.26, 27.—
HEB. 13.8.

*The man shall put his hand on its head, and it will be
accepted as a sacrifice to take away his sins.*

For you know what was paid to set you free from the
worthless manner of life handed down by your ancestors.
It was not something that can be destroyed, such as silver
or gold; it was the costly sacrifice of Christ, who was like a
lamb without defect or flaw.—Christ himself carried our
sins in his body to the cross.

The free gift he gave us in his dear Son!

Come as living stones, and let yourselves be used in
building the spiritual temple, where you will serve as holy
priests to offer spiritual and acceptable sacrifices to God
through Jesus Christ.—So then, my brothers, because of
God's great mercy to us I appeal to you: Offer yourselves
as a living sacrifice to God, dedicated to his service and
pleasing to him.

To him who is able to keep you from falling, and to
bring you faultless and joyful before his glorious presence
– to the only God our Saviour, through Jesus Christ our
Lord, be glory, majesty, might, and authority, from all ages
past, and now, and for ever and ever!

LEV. 1.4.—PET. 1.18, 19.—1 PET. 2.24.—
EPH. 1.6.—1 PET. 2.5.—ROM. 12.1.—JUDE 24, 25.

My eyes grew tired from looking to heaven.

I am worn out, O LORD; have pity on me! Give me strength; I am completely exhausted and my whole being is deeply troubled. How long, O LORD, will you wait to help me? Come and save me, LORD; in your mercy rescue me from death.—I am terrified, and the terrors of death crush me. I am gripped by fear and trembling; I am overcome with horror. I wish I had wings, like a dove. I would fly away and find rest.

You need to be patient.

They still had their eyes fixed on the sky as he went away, when two men dressed in white suddenly stood beside them and said, "Galileans, why are you standing there looking up at the sky? This Jesus, who was taken from you into Heaven, will come back in the same way that you saw him go to heaven."—We ... are citizens of heaven, and we eagerly wait for our Saviour, the Lord Jesus Christ, to come from heaven.—We wait for the blessed Day we hope for, when the glory of our great God and Saviour Jesus Christ will appear.

ISA. 38.14.—PS. 6.2-4.—PS. 55.4-6.—
HEB. 10.36.—ACTS 1.10, 11.—PHIL. 3.20.—
TITUS 2.13.

MARCH 19

God chose his Servant and sent him first to you, to bless you by making every one of you turn away from his wicked ways.

Let us give thanks to the God and Father of our Lord Jesus Christ! Because of his great mercy he gave us new life by raising Jesus Christ from death. This fills us with a living hope.

Our great God and Saviour Jesus Christ ... gave himself for us, to rescue us from all wickedness and to make us a pure people who belong to him alone and are eager to do good.—Be holy in all that you do, just as God who called you is holy. The scripture says, "Be holy because I am holy."

The God and Father of our Lord Jesus Christ ... has blessed us by giving us every spiritual blessing in the heavenly world.—The full content of divine nature lives in Christ, in his humanity, and you have been given full life in union with him.—Out of the fullness of his grace he has blessed us all, giving us one blessing after another.

God ... did not even keep back his own Son, but offered him for us all! He gave us his Son – will he not also freely give us all things?

ACTS 3.26.—1 PET. 1.3.—TITUS 2.13, 14.—
1 PET. 1.15, 16.—EPH. 1.3.—COL. 2.9, 10.—
JOHN 1.16—ROM. 8.32.

*The explanation of your teachings gives light and brings
wisdom to the ignorant.*

The message that we have heard from his Son and announce is this: God is light, and there is no darkness at all
in him.—The God who said, "Out of darkness the light
shall shine!" is the same God who made his light shine in
our hearts, to bring us the knowledge of God's glory shining
in the face of Christ.—The Word … was the same as God.
The Word was the source of life, and his life brought light
to mankind.—If we live in the light – just as he is in the light
– then we have fellowship with one another, and the blood
of Jesus, his Son, purifies us from every sin.

I keep your law in my heart, so that I will not sin against
you.—You have been made clean already by the teaching I
have given you.

You yourselves used to be in the darkness, but since you
have become the Lord's people, you are in the light. So you
must live like people who belong to the light.—You are the
chosen race, the King's priests, the holy nation, God's own
people, chosen to proclaim the wonderful acts of God, who
called you out of darkness into his own marvellous light.

PS. 119.130.—1 JOHN 1.5.—2 COR. 4.6.—
JOHN 1.1, 4.—1 JOHN 1.7.—PS. 119.11.—
JOHN 15.3.—EPH. 5.8.—1 PET. 2.9.

Wake up, and strengthen what you still have before it dies completely.

The end of all things is near. You must be self-controlled and alert, to be able to pray.—Be alert, be on the watch! Your enemy, the Devil, roams round like a roaring lion, looking for someone to devour.—Be on your guard! Make certain that you do not forget, as long as you live, what you have seen with your own eyes.—My righteous people, however, will believe and live; but if any of them turns back, I will not be pleased with him. We are not people who turn back and are lost. Instead, we have faith and are saved.

What I say to you, then, I say to all: Watch!

Do not be afraid—I am with you! I am your God – let nothing terrify you! I will make you strong and help you; I will protect you and save you. I am the LORD your God; I strengthen you.

REV. 3.2.—1 PET. 4.7.—1 PET. 5.8.—DEUT. 4.9.—
HEB. 10.38, 39.—MARK 13.37.—ISA. 41.10, 13.

*Lot looked round and saw that the whole Jordan Valley
... had plenty of water, like the Garden of the LORD ...
before the LORD destroyed the cities of Sodom and
Gomorrah. So Lot chose the whole Jordan Valley for
himself.*

Lot ... that good man.

Do not deceive yourselves; no one makes a fool of God.
A person will reap exactly what he sows.—Remember Lot's
wife!

Do not try to work together as equals with unbelievers,
for it cannot be done. How can right and wrong be partners? How can light and darkness live together? "You must
leave them and separate yourselves from them. Have nothing to do with what is unclean ... says the Lord Almighty."—Have nothing at all to do with such people. You
yourselves used to be in the darkness, but since you have
become the Lord's people, you are in the light. So you must
live like people who belong to the light ... Try to learn what
pleases the Lord. Have nothing to do with the worthless
things that people do, things that belong to the darkness.
Instead, bring them out to the light.

GEN. 13.10, 11.—2 PET. 2.7, 8.—GAL. 6.7.—
LUKE 17.31.—2 COR. 6.14, 17.—
EPH. 5.7, 8, 10, 11.

MARCH 23

Holy, holy, holy, is the LORD God Almighty.

You are enthroned as the Holy One, the one whom Israel praises.—"Do not come any closer. Take off your sandals, because you are standing on holy ground. I am the God of your ancestors, the God of Abraham, Isaac and Jacob." So Moses covered his face, because he was afraid to look at God.—To whom can the holy God be compared? Is there anyone else like him?—I am the LORD your God, the holy God of Israel, who saves you. I alone am the LORD, the only one who can save you.

Be holy in all that you do, just as God who called you is holy. The scripture says, "Be holy because I am holy."—Don't you know that your body is the temple of the Holy Spirit, who lives in you and who was given to you by God? You do not belong to yourselves but to God.—We are the temple of the living God! As God himself has said, "I will make my home with my people and live among them; I will be their God, and they shall be my people."—Do two men start travelling together without arranging to meet?

REV. 4.8.—PS.22.3.—EXOD.3.5, 6.—ISA. 40.25.—
ISA. 43.3, 11.—1 PET. 1.15, 16.—1 COR. 6.19.—
2 COR. 6.16.—AMOS. 3.3.

Abram put his trust in the LORD, and because of this the LORD was pleased with him and accepted him.

His faith did not leave him, and he did not doubt God's promise; his faith filled him with power, and he gave praise to God. He was absolutely sure that God would be able to do what he had promised. That is why Abraham, through faith, "was accepted as righteous by God." The words … were not written for him alone. They were written also for us who are to be accepted as righteous, who believe in him who raised Jesus our Lord from death.

When God promised Abraham and his descendants that the world would belong to him, he did so, not because Abraham obeyed the Law, but because he believed and was accepted as righteous by God.

The person who is put right with God through faith shall live.—Let us hold on firmly to the hope we profess, because we can trust God to keep his promise.—Our God is in heaven; he does whatever he wishes.—There is nothing that God cannot do. How happy you are to believe that the Lord's message to you will come true.

GEN. 15.6.—ROM. 4.20-24.—ROM. 4.13.—
ROM. 1.17.—HEB. 10.23.—PS. 115.3.—
LUKE 1.37, 45.

I will never leave you; I will never abandon you.

Let us be bold, then, and say, "The Lord is my helper, I will not be afraid. What can anyone do to me?"

I will be with you and protect you wherever you go, and I will bring you back to this land. I will not leave you until I have done all that I have promised you.—Be determined and confident. Do not be afraid of them. Your God, the LORD himself, will be with you. He will not fail you or abandon you.

Demas fell in love with this present world and has deserted me. No one stood by me the first time I defended myself; all deserted me. May God not count it against them! But the Lord stayed with me and gave me strength.—My father and mother may abandon me, but the LORD will take care of me.

I will be with you always, to the end of the age.—I am the living one! I was dead, but now I am alive for ever and ever.—When I go, you will not be left all alone; I will come back to you.

HEB. 13.5.—HEB. 13.6.—GEN. 28.15.—
DEUT. 31.6.—2 TIM. 4.10, 16, 17.—PS. 27.10.—
MATT. 28.20.—REV. 1.18.—JOHN 14.18.

The Kingdom of heaven will be like this. Once there was a man who was about to go on a journey; he called his servants and put them in charge of his property. He gave to each one according to his ability.

Surely you know that when you surrender yourselves as slaves to obey someone, you are in fact slaves of the master you obey.

It is one and the same Spirit who does all this; as he wishes, he gives a different gift to each person. The Spirit's presence is shown in some way in each person for the good of all.—Each one, as a good manager of God's different gifts, must use for the good of others the special gift he has received from God.—The one thing required of such a servant is that he be faithful to his master.—Much is required from the person to whom much is given; much more is required from the person to whom much more is given.

Who, then, is capable of such a task?—I have the strength to face all conditions by the power that Christ gives me.

MATT. 25.14, 15.—ROM. 6.16.—1 COR. 12.11, 7.—
1 PET. 4.10.—1 COR. 4.2.—LUKE 12.48.—
2 COR. 2.16.—PHIL. 4.13.

If you do what is right, you are certain to be rewarded.

After a long time the master of those servants came back and settled accounts with them. The servant who had received five thousand coins came in and handed over the other five thousand. "You gave me five thousand coins, sir," he said. "Look! Here are another five thousand that I have earned." "Well done, you good and faithful servant!" said his master. "You have been faithful in managing small amounts, so I will put you in charge of large amounts. Come on in and share my happiness!"

All of us must appear before Christ, to be judged by him. Each one will receive what he deserves, according to everything he has done, good or bad, in his bodily life.

I have done my best in the race, I have run the full distance, and I have kept the faith. Now there is waiting for me the victory prize of being put right with God, which the Lord, the righteous Judge, will give me on that Day.

I am coming soon. Keep safe what you have, so that no one will rob you of your victory prize.

PROV. 11.18.—MATT. 25.19–21.—2 COR. 5.10.—
2 TIM. 4.7, 8.—REV. 3.11.

Be determined and confident!

The LORD is my light and my salvation; I will fear no one. The LORD protects me from all danger; I will never be afraid.—He strengthens those who are weak and tired. Even those who are young grow weak; young men can fall exhausted. But those who trust in the LORD for help find their strength renewed. They will rise on wings like eagles; they will run and not get weary; they will walk and not grow weak.—My mind and my body may grow weak, but God is my strength; he is all I ever need.

If God is for us, who can be against us?—The LORD is with me, I will not be afraid; what can anyone do to me?

By your power we defeat our enemies.—In all these things we have complete victory through him who loved us!

Now begin the work, and may the LORD be with you.

JOSH. 1.18.—PS.27.1.—ISA. 40.29-31.—
PS. 73.26.—ROM. 8.31.—PS. 118.6.—PS. 44.5.—
ROM. 8.37.—1 CHR. 22.16.

Come you that are blessed by my Father! Come and possess the kingdom which has been prepared for you ever since the creation of the world.

Do not be afraid, little flock, for your Father is pleased to give you the Kingdom.—God chose the poor people of this world to be rich in faith and to possess the kingdom which he promised to those who love him.—We will also possess with Christ what God has kept for him; for if we share Christ's suffering, we will also share his glory.

The Father himself ... loves you because you love me.—God is not ashamed for them to call him their God, because he has prepared a city for them.

Whoever wins the victory will receive this from me: I will be his God, and he will be my son.—Now there is waiting for me the victory prize of being put right with God, which the Lord, the righteous Judge, will give me on that Day – and not only to me, but to all those who wait with love for him to appear.—God, who began this good work in you, will carry it on until it is finished on the Day of Christ Jesus.

MATT. 25.34.—LUKE 12.32.—JAS 2.5.—
ROM. 8.17.—JOHN 16.27.—HEB. 11.16.—
REV. 21.7.—2 TIM. 4.8.—PHIL. 1.6.

MARCH 30

Isaac ... went out in the early evening to take a walk in the fields.

May my words and my thoughts be acceptable to you, O LORD, my refuge and my redeemer.

When I look at the sky, which you have made, at the moon and the stars, which you set in their places – what is man, that you think of him; mere man, that you care for him?—How wonderful are the things the LORD does! All who are delighted with them want to understand them.

Happy are those who reject the advice of evil men, who do not follow the example of sinners or join those who have no use for God. Instead, they find joy in obeying the Law of the LORD, and they study it day and night.—Be sure that the book of the Law is always read in your worship. Study it day and night.—My soul will feast and be satisfied, and I will sing glad songs of praise to You. As I lie in bed, I remember you; all night long I think of you.

GEN. 24.62, 63.—PS. 19.14.—PS. 8.3, 4.—
PS. 111.2.—PS. 1.1, 2.—JOSH. 1.8.—PS. 63.5, 6.

104

*With all his abundant wealth through Christ Jesus, my
God will supply all your needs.*

Be concerned above everything else with the Kingdom of
God and with what he requires of you, and he will provide
you with all these other things.—God ... did not even keep
back his own Son, but offered him for us all! He gave us his
Son – will he not also freely give us all things?—Everything
belongs to you: Paul, Apollos, and Peter; this world, life and
death, the present and the future – all these are yours, and
you belong to Christ, and Christ belongs to God.—We
seem to have nothing, yet we really possess everything.

The LORD is my shepherd; I have everything I need.—
The LORD is our protector and glorious king, blessing us
with kindness and honour. He does not refuse any good
thing to those who do what is right.—God ... generously
gives us everything for our enjoyment.—God is able to give
you more than you need, so that you will always have all you
need for yourselves and more than enough for every good
cause.

PHIL. 4.19.—MATT. 6.33.—ROM. 8.32.—
1 COR. 3.21-23.—2 COR. 6.10.—PS. 23.1.—
PS. 84.11.—1 TIM. 6.17.—2 COR. 9.8.

APRIL 1

The Spirit produces ... joy.

Joy which the Holy Spirit gives.—A great and glorious joy which words cannot express.

Although saddened, we are always glad ... I am running over with joy.—We ... boast of our troubles.

Jesus, on whom our faith depends from beginning to end ... because of the joy that was waiting for him ... thought nothing of the disgrace of dying on the cross.—I have told you this so that my joy may be in you and that your joy may be complete.—Just as we have a share in Christ's many sufferings, so also through Christ we share in God's great help.

May you always be joyful in your union with the Lord. I say it again: rejoice!—The joy that the LORD gives you will make you strong.

You will show me the path that leads to life; your presence fills me with joy and brings me pleasure for ever.—The Lamb, who is in the centre of the throne, will be their shepherd, and he will guide them to springs of life-giving water. And God will wipe away every tear from their eyes.

GAL. 5.22.—ROM. 14.17.—1 PET. 1.8.—
2 COR. 6.10; 7.4.—ROM. 5.3.—HEB. 12.2.—
JOHN 15.11.—2 COR. 1.5.—PHIL. 4.4.—
NEH. 8.10.—PS. 16.11.—REV. 7.17.

*If you are going to turn to the LORD with all your hearts,
you must get rid of all the foreign gods and the images of the
goddess Astarte. Dedicate yourselves completely to the LORD
and worship only him.*

My children, keep yourselves safe from false gods!—"You
must leave them and separate yourselves from them. Have
nothing to do with what is unclean, and I will accept you. I
will be your father, and you shall be my sons and daugh-
ters," says the Lord Almighty.—You cannot serve both
God and money.

Do not worship any other god, because I, the LORD,
tolerate no rivals.—Serve him with an undivided heart and
a willing mind. He knows all our thoughts and desires.

Sincerity and truth are what you require; fill my mind
with your wisdom.—Man looks at the outward appearance,
but I look at the heart.—My dear friends, if our conscience
does not condemn us, we have courage in God's presence.

1 SAM. 7.3.—1 JOHN 5.21.—2 COR. 6.17, 18.—
MATT. 6.24.—EXOD. 34.14.—1 CHR. 28.9.—
PS. 51.6.—1 SAM. 16.7.—1 JOHN 3.21.

APRIL 3

Do not forget one thing, my dear friends! There is no difference in the Lord's sight between one day and a thousand years; to him the two are the same. The Lord is not slow to do what he has promised, as some think.

"My thoughts," says the LORD, "are not like yours, and my ways are different from yours. As high as the heavens are above the earth, so high are my ways and thoughts above yours. My word is like the snow and the rain that come down from the sky to water the earth … so also will be the word that I speak – it will not fail to do what I plan for it; it will do everything I send it to do."

God has made all people prisoners of disobedience, so that he might show mercy to them all. How great are God's riches! How deep are his wisdom and knowledge! Who can explain his decisions? Who can understand his ways?

2 PET. 3.8, 9.—ISA. 55.8-11.—ROM. 11.32, 33.

Don't be afraid! I am the first and the last.

You have not come ... to what you can feel, to Mount Sinai with its blazing fire, the darkness and the gloom, the storm ... Instead, you have come to Mount Zion ... to God, who is the judge of all mankind, and to the spirits of good people made perfect. You have come to Jesus, who arranged the new covenant.—Jesus, on whom our faith depends from beginning to end.—Our High Priest is not one who cannot feel sympathy for our weaknesses. We have a High Priest who was tempted in every way that we are, but did not sin. Let us have confidence, then, and approach God's throne, where there is grace. There we will receive mercy and find grace to help us just when we need it.

The LORD, who rules and protects Israel, the LORD Almighty, has this to say: "I am the first, the last, the only God; there is no other god but me."—"Mighty God", "Eternal Father", "Prince of Peace".

LORD, from the very beginning you are God. You are my God, holy and eternal.—The LORD alone is God; God alone is our defence.

REV. 1.17.—HEB. 12.18, 22–24.—HEB. 12.2.—
HEB. 4.15, 16.—ISA. 44.6.—ISA. 9.6.—HAB. 1.12.—
2 SAM. 22.32.

"Let me go; daylight is coming." "I won't, unless you bless me."

If the enemies of my people want my protection, let them make peace with me. Yes, let them make peace with me.

You are a woman of great faith! What you want will be done for you.—Let it happen, then, just as you believe!— When you pray, you must believe and not doubt at all. Whoever doubts is like a wave in the sea that is driven and blown about by the wind. A person like that ... must not think that he will receive anything from the Lord.

As they came near the village to which they were going, Jesus acted as if he were going farther; but they held him back, saying, "Stay with us." ... He disappeared from their sight. They said to each other, "Wasn't it like a fire burning in us when he talked to us on the road and explained the Scriptures to us?"—Tell me your plans, so that I may serve you and continue to please you ... I will go with you, and I will give you victory.

GEN. 32.26.—ISA. 27.5.—MATT. 15.28.—
MATT. 9.29.—JAS 1.6, 7.—
LUKE 24.28, 29, 31, 32.—EXOD. 33.13, 14.

He lives for ever to plead with God for them.

Who ... will condemn them? Not Christ Jesus, who died ... and is ... pleading with him for us.—Christ did not go into a man-made Holy Place, which was a copy of the real one. He went into heaven itself, where he now appears on our behalf in the presence of God.

If anyone does sin, we have someone who pleads with the Father on our behalf – Jesus Christ, the righteous one.—There is one who brings God and mankind together, the man Christ Jesus.

We have a great High Priest who has gone into the very presence of God – Jesus, the Son of God. Our High Priest is not one who cannot feel sympathy for our weaknesses. On the contrary, we have a High Priest who was tempted in every way that we are, but did not sin. Let us have confidence, then, and approach God's throne, where there is grace. There we will receive mercy and find grace to help us just when we need it.—It is through Christ that all of us ... are able to come in the one Spirit into the presence of the Father.

HEB. 7.25.—ROM. 8.34.—HEB. 9.24.—
1 JOHN 2.1.—1 TIM. 2.5.—HEB. 4.14–16.—
EPH. 2.18.

Although saddened, we are always glad; we seem poor, but we make many people rich; we seem to have nothing, yet we really possess everything.

We boast of the hope we have of sharing God's glory! We also boast of our troubles.—In all our troubles I am still full of courage; I am running over with joy.—You believe in him ... so you rejoice with a great and glorious joy which words cannot express.

They have been severely tested by the troubles they went through; but their joy was so great that they were extremely generous in their giving, even though they are very poor.—I am less than the least of all God's people; yet God gave me this privilege of taking to the Gentiles the Good News about the infinite riches of Christ, and of making all people see how God's secret plan is to be put into effect. God, who is the Creator of all things, kept his secret hidden through all the past ages.

God chose the poor people of this world to be rich in faith and to possess the kingdom which he promised to those who love him.—God is able to give you more than you need, so that you will always have all you need for yourselves and more than enough for every good cause.

2 COR. 6.10.—ROM. 5.2, 3.—2 COR. 7.4.—
1 PET. 1.8.—2 COR. 8.2.—EPH. 3.8, 9.—JAS 2.5.—
2 COR. 9.8.

APRIL 8

In union with Christ you have become rich in all things.

When we were still helpless, Christ died for the wicked at the time that God chose.—God ... did not even keep back his own Son ... will he not also freely give us all things?

The full content of divine nature lives in Christ, in his humanity, and you have been given full life in union with him. He is supreme over every spiritual ruler and authority.

Remain united to me, and I will remain united to you. A branch cannot bear fruit by itself; it can do so only if it remains in the vine. In the same way you cannot bear fruit unless you remain in me. I am the vine, and you are the branches. Whoever remains in me, and I in him, will bear much fruit; for you can do nothing without me.—Even though the desire to do good is in me, I am not able to do it.—Each one of us has received a special gift in proportion to what Christ has given.

If you remain in me and my words remain in you, then you will ask for anything you wish, and you shall have it.—Christ's message in all its richness must live in your hearts.

1 COR. 1.5.—ROM. 5.6.—ROM. 8.32.—
COL. 2.9, 10.—JOHN 15.4, 5.—ROM. 7.18.—
EPH. 4.7.—JOHN 15.7.—COL. 3.16.

Do not be afraid – I will save you.

Do not be afraid – you will not be disgraced again; you will not be humiliated. You will forget your unfaithfulness as a young wife, and your desperate loneliness as a widow. Your Creator will be like a husband to you – the LORD Almighty is his name. The holy God of Israel will save you.—I have swept your sins away like a cloud. Come back to me; I am the one who saves you.—It was the costly sacrifice of Christ, who was like a lamb without defect or flaw.

The one who will rescue them is strong – his name is the LORD Almighty. He himself will take up their cause.— What my Father has given me is greater than everything, and no one can snatch them away from the Father's care.

May God our Father and the Lord Jesus Christ give you grace and peace. In order to set us free from this present evil age, Christ gave himself for our sins, in obedience to the will of our God and Father. To God be the glory for ever and ever! Amen.

ISA. 43.1.—ISA. 54.4, 5.—ISA. 44.22.—
1 PET. 1.19.—JER. 50.34.—JOHN 10.29.—
GAL. 1.3–5.

I am dark but beautiful.

I have been evil from the day I was born; from the time I was conceived, I have been sinful.—"You became famous in every nation for your perfect beauty, because I was the one who made you so lovely." This is what the Sovereign LORD says.

Lord! I am a sinful man!—How beautiful you are, my love!

I am ashamed of all I have said and repent in dust and ashes.—How beautiful you are, my love; how perfect you are!

When I want to do what is good, what is evil is the only choice I have.—Courage, my son! Your sins are forgiven.

I know that good does not live in me—that is, in my human nature.—You have been given full life in union with him.—A mature individual in union with Christ.

You have been purified from sin; you have been dedicated to God; you have been put right with God by the Lord Jesus Christ and by the Spirit of our God.—You are … chosen to proclaim the wonderful acts of God, who called you out of darkness into his own marvellous light.

S. OF S. 1.5.—PS. 51.5.—EZEK. 16.14.—
LUKE 5.8.—S. OF S. 4.1.—JOB 42.6.—
S. OF S. 4.7.—ROM. 7.21.—MATT. 9.2.—
ROM. 7.18.—COL. 2.19.—COL. 1.28.—
1COR. 6.11.—1 PET. 2.9.

*The more you talk, the more likely you are to sin. If you are
wise, you will keep quiet.*

My dear brothers! Everyone must be quick to listen, but
slow to speak and slow to become angry.—It is better to be
patient than powerful. It is better to win control over
yourself than over whole cities.—If a person never makes
a mistake in what he says, he is perfect and is also able to
control his whole being.—Your words will be used to judge
you – to declare you either innocent or guilty.—LORD, place
a guard at my mouth, a sentry at the door of my lips.

Christ himself suffered for you and left you an example,
so that you would follow in his steps. He committed no sin,
and no one ever heard a lie come from his lips. When he
was insulted, he did not answer back with an insult; when
he suffered, he did not threaten, but placed his hopes in
God, the righteous Judge.—Think of what he went
through; how he put up with so much hatred from sinners!
So do not let yourselves become discouraged and give up.

They have never been known to tell lies; they are
faultless.

PROV. 10.19.—JAS 1.19.—PROV. 16.32.—
JAS 3.2.—MATT. 12.37.—PS. 141.3.—
1 PET. 2.21–23.—HEB. 12.3.—REV. 14.5.

What the Law could not do, because human nature was weak, God did. He condemned sin in human nature by sending his own Son, who came with a nature like man's sinful nature, to do away with sin.

The Jewish Law is not a full and faithful model of the real things; it is only a faint outline of the good things to come. The same sacrifices are offered for ever, year after year. If the people worshipping God had really been purified from their sins ... all sacrifices would stop.—Everyone who believes in him is set free from all the sins from which the Law of Moses could not set you free.

Since the children ... are people of flesh and blood, Jesus himself became like them and shared their human nature. He did this so that through his death he might destroy the Devil, who has the power over death, and in this way set free those who were slaves all their lives because of their fear of death. For it is clear that it is not the angels that he helps. Instead, as the scripture says, "He helps the descendants of Abraham." This means that he had to become like his brothers in every way.

ROM. 8.3.—HEB. 10.1, 2.—ACTS 13.39.—
HEB. 2.14–17.

APRIL 13

Honour the LORD by making him an offering from the best of all that your land produces.

Remember that the person who sows few seeds will have a small crop; the one who sows many seeds will have a large crop.—Every Sunday each of you must put aside some money, in proportion to what he has earned, and save it up.

God is not unfair. He will not forget the work you did or the love you showed for him in the help you gave and are still giving to your fellow-Christians.

My brothers, because of God's great mercy to us I appeal to you: Offer yourselves as a living sacrifice to God, dedicated to his service and pleasing to him. This is the true worship that you should offer.—We are ruled by the love of Christ, now that we recognize that one man died for everyone, which means that all share in his death. He died for all, so that those who live should no longer live for themselves, but only for him who died and was raised to life for their sake.—Whatever you do, whether you eat or drink, do it all for God's glory.

PROV. 3.9.—2 COR. 9.6.—1 COR. 16.2.—
HEB. 6.10.—ROM. 12.1.—2 COR. 5.14, 15.—
1 COR. 10.31.

*My soul will feast and be satisfied, and I will sing glad songs
of praise to you. As I lie in bed, I remember you; all night
long I think of you.*

O God, how difficult I find your thoughts; how many of
them there are! If I counted them, they would be more than
the grains of sand. When I awake, I am still with you.—How
sweet is the taste of your instructions – sweeter even than
honey!—Your love is better than wine.

What else have I in heaven but you? Since I have you,
what else could I want on earth?

Like an apple tree among the trees of the forest, so is
my dearest compared with other men. I love to sit in its
shadow, and its fruit is sweet to my taste. He brought me
to his banqueting hall and raised the banner of love over
me.—He is majestic, like the Lebanon Mountains with their
towering cedars. His mouth is sweet to kiss; everything
about him enchants me. This is what my lover is like,
women of Jerusalem.

PS. 63.5, 6.—PS. 139.17, 18.—PS. 119.103.—
S. OF S. 1.2.—PS. 73.25.—S. OF S. 2.3, 4.—
S. OF S. 5.15, 16.

APRIL 15

*The one who will rescue them is strong — his name is the
LORD Almighty.*

I know how terrible your sins are and how many crimes you
have committed.—I have given help to a famous soldier.—
The LORD, the one who saves you and sets you free.—Powerful to save.—Able to keep you from falling.—Where sin
increased, God's grace increased much more.

Whoever believes in the Son is not judged; but whoever
does not believe has already been judged, because he has
not believed in God's only Son.—He is able, now and
always, to save those who come to God through him.

Am I too weak to save them?

Who, then, can separate us from the love of Christ? I
am certain that nothing can separate us from his love:
neither death nor life, neither angels nor other heavenly
rulers or powers, neither the present nor the future, neither
the world above nor the world below – there is nothing in
all creation that will ever be able to separate us from the
love of God which is ours through Christ Jesus our Lord.

JER. 50.34.—AMOS 5.12.—PS. 89.19.—
ISA. 49.26.—ISA. 63.1.—JUDE 24.—
ROM. 5.20.—JOHN 3.18.—HEB. 7.25.—
ISA. 50.2.—ROM. 8.35, 38, 39.

I was afraid and thought that he had driven me out of his presence. But he heard my cry, when I called to him for help.

I am sinking in deep mud, and there is no solid ground; I am out in deep water, and the waves are about to drown me.—Water began to close over me, and I thought death was near. From the bottom of the pit, O LORD, I cried out to you, and when I begged you to listen to my cry, you heard. You answered me and told me not to be afraid.

Will the Lord always reject us? Will he never again be pleased with us? Has he stopped loving us? Does his promise no longer stand? Has God forgotten to be merciful? Has anger taken the place of his compassion? Then I said, "What hurts me most is this – that God is no longer powerful." I will remember your great deeds, LORD; I will recall the wonders you did in the past.—I know that I will live to see the LORD's goodness in this present life.

PS. 31.22.—PS. 69.2.—LAM. 3.54-57.—
PS. 77.7-11.—PS. 27.13.

Giving thanks is the sacrifice that honours me.

Christ's message in all its richness must live in your hearts. Teach and instruct each other with all wisdom. Sing psalms, hymns, and sacred songs; sing to God with thanksgiving in your hearts. Everything you do or say, then, should be done in the name of the Lord Jesus, as you give thanks through him to God the Father.—He bought you for a price. So use your bodies for God's glory.

You are ... the King's priests ... chosen to proclaim the wonderful acts of God, who called you out of darkness into his own marvellous light.—Come as living stones, and let yourselves be used in building the spiritual temple, where you will serve as holy priests to offer spiritual and acceptable sacrifices to God through Jesus Christ.—Let us ... always offer praise to God as our sacrifice through Jesus, which is the offering presented by lips that confess him as Lord.

I will praise him for what he has done; may all who are oppressed listen and be glad! Proclaim with me the LORD's greatness; let us praise his name together!

PS. 50.23.—COL. 3.16, 17.—1 COR. 6.20.—
1 PET. 2.9.—1 PET. 2.5.—HEB. 13.15.—
PS. 34.2, 3.

I will send them a prophet like you from among their own people.

I [Moses] stood between you and the LORD at that time to tell you what he said, because you were afraid.—There is one God, and there is one who brings God and mankind together, the man Christ Jesus.

Moses was a humble man, more humble than anyone else on earth.—Take my yoke and put it on you, and learn from me, because I am gentle and humble in spirit; and you will find rest.—The attitude you should have is the one that Christ Jesus had: he always had the nature of God, but he did not think that by force he should try to become equal with God. Instead of this, of his own free will he gave up all he had, and took the nature of a servant. He became like man and appeared in human likeness.

Moses was faithful in God's house as a servant, and he spoke of the things that God would say in the future. But Christ is faithful as the Son in charge of God's house. We are his house if we keep up our courage and our confidence in what we hope for.

DEUT. 18.18.—DEUT. 5.5.—1 TIM. 2.5.—
NUM. 12.3.—MATT. 11.29.—PHIL. 2.5-7.—
HEB. 3.5, 6.

I am telling you the truth: I am the gate for the sheep.

The curtain hanging in the Temple was torn in two from top to bottom.—Christ died for sins once and for all, a good man on behalf of sinners, in order to lead you to God.—The way into the Most Holy Place has not yet been opened as long as the outer Tent still stands.

I am the gate. Whoever comes in by me will be saved; he will come in and go out and find pasture.

No one goes to the Father except by me.—Through Christ ... all of us ... are able to come in the one Spirit into the presence of the Father. So then, you ... are not foreigners or strangers any longer; you are now fellow-citizens with God's people and members of the family of God.—We have ... complete freedom to go into the Most Holy Place by means of the death of Jesus. He opened for us a new way, a living way, through the curtain – that is, through his own body.—We have peace with God through our Lord Jesus Christ. He has brought us by faith into this experience of God's grace, in which we now live. And so we boast of the hope we have of sharing God's glory!

JOHN 10.7.—MATT. 27.51.—1 PET. 3.18.—
HEB. 9.8.—JOHN 10.9.—JOHN 14.6.—
EPH. 2.18, 19.—HEB. 10.19, 20.—ROM. 5.1.

APRIL 20

Do not keep for yourselves anything that was condemned to destruction.

The Lord says, "You must leave them and separate yourselves from them. Have nothing to do with what is unclean."—I appeal to you, my friends, as strangers and refugees in this world! Do not give in to bodily passions, which are always at war against the soul.—Hate their very clothes, stained by their sinful lusts.

My dear friends, we are now God's children, but it is not yet clear what we shall become. But we know that when Christ appears, we shall be like him, because we shall see him as he really is. Everyone who has this hope in Christ keeps himself pure, just as Christ is pure.—God has revealed his grace for the salvation of all mankind. That grace instructs us to give up ungodly living and worldly passions, and to live self-controlled, upright, and godly lives in this world, as we wait for the blessed Day we hope for, when the glory of our great God and Saviour Jesus Christ will appear. He gave himself for us, to rescue us from all wickedness and to make us a pure people who belong to him alone and are eager to do good.

DEUT. 13.17.—2 COR. 6.17.—1 PET. 2.11.—
JUDE 23.—1 JOHN 3.2, 3.—TITUS 2.11–14.

APRIL 21

Stand firm in your life in the Lord.

I follow faithfully the road he chooses, and never wander to either side.

The LORD loves what is right and does not abandon his faithful people. He protects them for ever.—The LORD will protect you from all danger; he will keep you safe.

My righteous people ... will believe and live; but if any of them turns back, I will not be pleased with him. We are not people who turn back and are lost. Instead, we have faith and are saved.—If they had belonged to our fellowship, they would have stayed with us. But they left so that it might be clear that none of them really belonged to us.

If you obey my teaching, you are really my disciples.—Whoever holds out to the end will be saved.—Be alert, stand firm in the faith, be brave, be strong.—Keep safe what you have, so that no one will rob you of your victory prize.—Those who win the victory will be clothed like this in white, and I will not remove their names from the book of the living.

PHIL. 4.1.—JOB 23.11.—PS. 37.28.—
PS. 121.7.—HEB. 10.38, 39.—1 JOHN 2.19.—
JOHN 8.31.—MATT. 24.13.—1 COR. 16.13.—
REV. 3.11.—REV. 3.5.

APRIL 22

*If he is offering one of his cattle as a burnt offering, he must
bring a bull without any defects. He must present it … so
that the LORD will accept him. The man shall put his hand
on its head, and it will be accepted as a sacrifice to take
away his sins.*

Where is the lamb for the sacrifice? God himself will
provide one.—There is the Lamb of God, who takes away
the sins of the world!—We are all purified from sin by the
offering that he made of his own body once and for
all.—To give his life to redeem many people.

No one takes my life away from me. I give it up of my
own free will. I have the right to give it up, and I have the
right to take it back.—I will love them with all my heart.—
The Son of God, who loved me and gave his life for me.

Christ was without sin, but for our sake God made him
share our sin in order that in union with him we might share
the righteousness of God.—The free gift he gave us in his
dear Son!

LEV. 1.3, 4.—GEN. 22.7, 8.—JOHN 1.29.—
HEB. 10.10.—MATT. 20.28.—JOHN 10.18.—
HOS. 14.4.—GAL. 2.20.—2 COR. 5.21.—EPH. 1.6.

The LORD protected me.

We were not helped at all by our pagan worship on the hilltops. Help for Israel comes only from the LORD our God.—The LORD is my protector; he is my strong fortress. My God is my protection, and with him I am safe. He protects me like a shield; he defends me and keeps me safe.—Let everyone who lives in Zion shout and sing! Israel's holy God is great, and he lives among his people.

His angel guards those who honour the LORD and rescues them from danger. The righteous call to the LORD, and he listens; he rescues them from all their troubles.— God has always been your defence; his eternal arms are your support.—Let us be bold, then, and say, "The Lord is my helper, I will not be afraid. What can anyone do to me?"— The LORD alone is God; God alone is our defence. He is the God who makes me strong, who makes my pathway safe.

By God's grace I am what I am.

PS. 18.18.—JER. 3.23.—PS. 18.2.—ISA. 12.6.—
PS. 34.7, 17.—DEUT. 33.27.—HEB. 13.6.—
PS. 18.31, 32.—1 COR. 15.10.

The LORD blessed Sarah, as he had promised.

Trust in God at all times, my people. Tell him all your troubles, for he is our refuge.—David was now in great trouble … but the LORD his God gave him courage.—God will certainly take care of you and lead you out of this land to the land he solemnly promised to Abraham, Isaac, and Jacob.—"I have seen the cruel suffering of my people in Egypt. I have heard their groans, and I have come down to set them free." He led the people out of Egypt, performing miracles and wonders in Egypt and at the Red Sea and for forty years in the desert.—The LORD kept every one of the promises that he had made to the people of Israel.

We can trust God to keep his promise.—Whatever he promises, he does; he speaks, and it is done.—Heaven and earth will pass away, but my words will never pass away.— Grass withers and flowers fade, but the word of our God endures for ever.

GEN. 21.1.—PS. 62.8.—1 SAM. 30.6.—
GEN. 50.24.—ACTS 7.34, 36.—JOSH. 21.45.—
HEB. 10.23.—NUM. 23.19.—MATT. 24.35.—
ISA. 40.8.

You will name him Jesus – because he will save his people from their sins.

You know that Christ appeared in order to take away sins.—That we might die to sin and live for righteousness.—He is able, now and always, to save those who come to God through him, because he lives for ever to plead with God for them.

Because of our sins he was wounded, beaten because of the evil we did. We are healed by the punishment he suffered, made whole by the blows he received. The LORD made the punishment fall on him, the punishment all of us deserved.—The Messiah must suffer ... and in his name the message about repentance and the forgiveness of sins must be preached to all nations.—He has appeared once and for all, to remove sin through the sacrifice of himself.

God raised him to his right-hand side as Leader and Saviour, to give the people of Israel the opportunity to repent.—It is through Jesus that the message about forgiveness of sins is preached to you; and that everyone who believes in him is set free from all the sins from which the Law of Moses could not set you free.—Your sins are forgiven for the sake of Christ.

MATT. 1.21.—1 JOHN 3.5.—1 PET. 2.24.—
HEB. 7.25.—ISA. 53.5, 6.—LUKE 24.46, 47.—
HEB. 9.26.—ACTS 5.31.—ACTS 13.38, 39.—
1 JOHN 2.12.

APRIL 26

His left hand is under my head, and his right hand
caresses me.

His eternal arms are your support.—When [Peter] noticed
the strong wind, he was afraid and started to sink down in
the water. "Save me, Lord!" he cried. At once Jesus reached
out and grabbed hold of him and said, "How little faith you
have! Why did you doubt?"—The LORD guides a man in
the way he should go and protects those who please him.
If they fall, they will not stay down, because the LORD will
help them up.

This is the tribe the LORD loves and protects; he guards
them all the day long, and he dwells in their midst.—Leave
all your worries with him, because he cares for you.—Anyone who strikes you strikes what is most precious to me.

They shall never die. No one can snatch them away
from me. What my Father has given me is greater than
everything.

S. OF S. 2.6.—DEUT. 33.27.—MATT. 14.30, 31.—
PS. 37.23, 24.—DEUT. 33.12.—1 PET. 5.7.—
ZECH. 2.8.—JOHN 10.28, 29.

My brothers ... there is not much time left.

We are all born weak and helpless. All lead the same short, troubled life. We grow and wither as quickly as flowers; we disappear like shadows.—The world and everything in it that people desire is passing away; but he who does the will of God lives for ever.—As all people die because of their union with Adam, in the same way all will be raised to life because of their union with Christ. Death is destroyed, victory is complete!—If we live, it is for the Lord that we live, and if we die, it is for the Lord that we die. So whether we live or die, we belong to the Lord.—What is life? To me, it is Christ. Death, then, will bring more.

Do not lose your courage ... because it brings with it a great reward. You need to be patient, in order to do the will of God and receive what he promises. For, as the scripture says, "Just a little while longer, and he who is coming will come; he will not delay."—The night is nearly over, day is almost here. Let us stop doing the things that belong to the dark, and let us take up weapons for fighting in the light.— The end of all things is near. You must be self-controlled and alert, to be able to pray.

1 COR. 7.29.—JOB 14.1,2.—1 JOHN 2.17—
1 COR. 15.22, 54.—ROM. 14.8.—PHIL. 1.21.—
HEB. 10.35–37.—ROM. 13.12.—1 PET. 4.7.

There is the Lamb of God!

The blood of bulls and goats can never take away sins. For this reason, when Christ was about to come into the world, he said to God: "You do not want sacrifices and offerings, but you have prepared a body for me. You are not pleased with animals burnt whole on the altar or with sacrifices to take away sins. Then I said, 'Here I am, to do your will, O God, just as it is written of me in the book of the Law.'"—He was treated harshly, but endured it humbly; he never said a word. Like a lamb about to be slaughtered, like a sheep about to be sheared, he never said a word.

You know what was paid to set you free ... It was not something that can be destroyed, such as silver or gold; it was the costly sacrifice of Christ, who was like a lamb without defect or flaw ... revealed in these last days for your sake. Through him you believe in God ... and so your faith and hope are fixed on God.

The Lamb who was killed is worthy to receive power, wealth, wisdom, and strength, honour, glory, and praise!

JOHN 1.29.—HEB. 10.4-7.—ISA. 53.7.—
1 PET. 1.18-21.—REV. 5.12.

Remember the great things he has done for you.

Remember how the LORD your God led you on this long journey through the desert these past forty years, sending hardships to test you, so that he might know what you intended to do and whether you would obey his commands. Remember that the LORD your God corrects and punishes you just as a father disciplines his children.

I know that your judgements are righteous, LORD, and that you punished me because you are faithful. My punishment was good for me, because it made me learn your commands. Before you punished me, I used to go wrong, but now I obey your word.—He has punished me severely, but he has not let me die.—He does not punish us as we deserve or repay us according to our sins and wrongs. As high as the sky is above the earth, so great is his love for those who honour him. He knows what we are made of; he remembers that we are dust.

1 SAM. 12.24.—DEUT. 8.2, 5.—
PS. 119.75, 71, 67.—PS. 118.18.—
PS. 103.10, 11, 14.

Whoever obeys his word is the one whose love for God has really been made perfect.

God has raised from death our Lord Jesus, who is the Great Shepherd of the sheep as the result of his sacrificial death, by which the eternal covenant is sealed. May the God of peace provide you with every good thing you need in order to do his will, and may he, through Jesus Christ, do in us what pleases him. And to Christ be the glory for ever and ever! Amen.

If we obey God's commands, then we are sure that we know him.—Whoever loves me will obey my teaching. My Father will love him, and my Father and I will come to him and live with him.—Everyone who lives in union with Christ does not continue to sin; but whoever continues to sin has never seen him or known him. Let no one deceive you, my children! Whoever does what is right is righteous, just as Christ is righteous.—Love is made perfect in us in order that we may have courage on Judgement Day; and we will have it because our life in this world is the same as Christ's.

1 JOHN 2.5.—HEB. 13.20, 21.—1 JOHN 2.3.—
JOHN 14.23.—1 JOHN 3.6, 7.—1 JOHN 4.17.

MAY 1

The Spirit produces ... peace.

To be controlled by the Spirit results in life and peace.

God has called you to live in peace.—Peace is what I leave with you; it is my own peace that I give you. I do not give it as the world does. Do not be worried and upset; do not be afraid.—May God, the source of hope, fill you with all joy and peace by means of your faith in him, so that your hope will continue to grow by the power of the Holy Spirit.

I know whom I have trusted, and I am sure that he is able to keep safe until that Day what he has entrusted to me.—You, LORD, give perfect peace to those who keep their purpose firm and put their trust in you.

Because everyone will do what is right, there will be peace and security for ever. God's people will be free from worries, and their homes peaceful and safe.—Whoever listens to me will have security. He will be safe, with no reason to be afraid.

Those who love your law have perfect security.

GAL. 5.22.—ROM. 8.6.—1 COR. 7.15.—
JOHN 14.27.—ROM. 15.13.—2 TIM. 1.12.—
ISA. 26.3.—ISA. 32.17, 18.—PROV. 1.33.—
PS. 119.165.

MAY 2

The LORD is here! He is in this place, and I didn't know it!

Where two or three come together in my name, I am there with them.—I will be with you always, to the end of the age.—I will go with you, and I will give you victory.

Where could I go to escape from you? Where could I get away from your presence? If I went up to heaven, you would be there; if I lay down in the world of the dead, you would be there.—I am a God who is everywhere and not in one place only. No one can hide where I cannot see him. Do you not know that I am everywhere in heaven and on earth?

Not even all heaven is large enough to hold you, so how can this Temple that I have built be large enough?—I am the high and holy God, who lives for ever. I live in a high and holy place, but I also live with people who are humble and repentant, so that I can restore their confidence and hope.

GEN. 28.16.—MATT. 18.20.—MATT. 28.20.—
EXOD. 33.14.—PS. 139.7, 8.—JER. 23.23, 24.—
1 KGS 8.27.—ISA. 57.15.

MAY 3

You must be perfect – just as your Father in heaven is perfect!

I am the Almighty God. Obey me and always do what is right.—You shall be holy and belong only to me, because I am the LORD and I am holy. I have set you apart from the other nations so that you would belong to me alone.

He bought you for a price. So use your bodies for God's glory.

You have been given full life in union with him. He is supreme over every spiritual ruler and authority.—He gave himself for us, to rescue us from all wickedness.—Do your best to be pure and faultless in God's sight and to be at peace with him.

Happy are those whose lives are faultless, who live according to the law of the LORD.—Whoever looks closely into the perfect law that sets people free, who keeps on paying attention to it and does not simply listen and then forget it, but puts it into practice – that person will be blessed by God in what he does.—Examine me, O God, and know my mind; test me, and discover my thoughts. Find out if there is any evil in me and guide me in the everlasting way.

MATT. 5.48.—GEN. 17.1.—LEV. 20.26.—
1 COR. 6.20.—COL. 2.10.—TITUS 2.14.—
2 PET. 3.14.—PS. 119.1.—JAS 1.25.—
PS. 139.23, 24.

MAY 4

Don't think that the LORD is too weak to save you or too deaf to hear your call for help!

You answered me when I called to you; with your strength you strengthened me.—While I was praying, Gabriel, whom I had seen in the earlier vision, came flying down to where I was. It was the time for the evening sacrifice to be offered.

Don't hide yourself from me! Don't be angry with me; don't turn your servant away. You have been my help; don't leave me, don't abandon me, O God, my saviour.—O LORD, don't stay away from me! Come quickly to my rescue!

Sovereign LORD, you made the earth and the sky by your great power and might; nothing is too difficult for you.—From such terrible dangers of death he saved us, and will save us; and we have placed our hope in him that he will save us again.—Will God not judge in favour of his own people who cry to him day and night for help? Will he be slow to help them? I tell you, he will judge in their favour and do it quickly.

ISA. 59.1.—PS. 138.3.—DAN. 9.21.—PS. 27.9.—
PS. 22.19.—JER. 32.17.—2 COR. 1.10.—
LUKE 18.7, 8.

*Do not start worrying: where will my food come from? Or
my drink? Or my clothes? Your Father in heaven knows
that you need all these things.*

Honour the LORD, all his people; those who obey him have
all they need. Even lions go hungry for lack of food, but
those who obey the LORD lack nothing good.—He does
not refuse any good thing to those who do what is right.
LORD Almighty, how happy are those who trust in you!

I would like you to be free from worry.—Don't worry
about anything, but in all your prayers ask God for what
you need, always asking him with a thankful heart.

For only a penny you can buy two sparrows, yet not one
sparrow falls to the ground without your Father's consent.
As for you, even the hairs of your head have all been
counted. So do not be afraid; you are worth much more
than many sparrows!—Why are you frightened? Have you
still no faith?—Have faith in God.

MATT. 6.31, 32.—PS. 34.9, 10.—PS. 84.11, 12.—
1 COR. 7.32.—PHIL. 4.6.—MATT. 10.29-31.—
MARK 4.40.—MARK 11.22.

MAY 6

Love and faithfulness will meet; righteousness and peace will embrace.

The LORD, the God who saves his people.

The LORD is a God who is eager to save, so he exalted his laws and teachings, and he wanted his people to honour them.

God was making all mankind his friends through Christ. God did not keep an account of their sins.—God offered him, so that by his sacrificial death he should become the means by which people's sins are forgiven through their faith in him. God did this in order to demonstrate that he is righteous. In the past he was patient and overlooked people's sins; but in the present time he deals with their sins, in order to demonstrate his righteousness. In this way God shows that he himself is righteous and that he puts right everyone who believes in Jesus.—Because of our sins he was wounded, beaten because of the evil we did. We are healed by the punishment he suffered, made whole by the blows he received.—Who will accuse God's chosen people? God himself declares them not guilty!—The person who depends on his faith, not on his deeds, and who believes in the God who declares the guilty to be innocent, it is his faith that God takes into account in order to put him right with himself.

PS. 85.10.—ISA. 45.21.—ISA. 42.21.—
2 COR. 5.19.—ROM. 3.25, 26.—ISA. 53.5.—
ROM. 8.33.—ROM. 4.5.

You are going to hear the noise of battles close by and the news of battles far away; but do not be troubled.

God is our shelter and strength, always ready to help in times of trouble. So we will not be afraid, even if the earth is shaken and mountains fall into the ocean depths; even if the seas roar and rage, and the hills are shaken by the violence.—Go into your houses, my people, and shut the door behind you. Hide yourselves for a little while until God's anger is over. The LORD is coming from his heavenly dwelling-place to punish the people of the earth for their sins.—In the shadow of your wings I find protection until the raging storms are over.—Your life is hidden with Christ in God.

He is not afraid of receiving bad news; his faith is strong, and he trusts in the LORD.

I have told you this so that you will have peace by being united to me. The world will make you suffer. But be brave! I have defeated the world!

MATT. 24.6.—PS. 46.1-3.—ISA. 26.20, 21.—
PS. 57.1.—COL. 3.3.—PS. 112.7.—JOHN 16.33.

The LORD says, "It was my will that he should suffer."

"Now my heart is troubled – and what shall I say? Shall I say, 'Father, do not let this hour come upon Me?' But that is why I came – so that I might go through this hour of suffering. Father, bring glory to your name!" Then a voice spoke from heaven, "I have brought glory to it, and I will do so again."—"Father," he said, "if you will, take this cup of suffering away from me. Not my will, however, but your will be done." An angel from heaven appeared to him and strengthened him.

He was humbled and walked the path of obedience all the way to death – his death on the cross.—The Father loves me because I am willing to give up my life, in order that I may receive it back again.—I have come down from heaven to do not my own will but the will of him who sent me.—Do you think that I will not drink the cup of suffering which my Father has given me?

He who sent me is with me; he has not left me alone, because I always do what pleases him.—My own dear Son, with whom I am pleased.—The one I have chosen, with whom I am pleased.

ISA. 53.10.—JOHN 12.27, 28.—LUKE 22.42, 43.—
PHIL. 2.8.—JOHN 10.17.—JOHN 6.38.—
JOHN 18.11.—JOHN 8.29.—MATT. 3.17.—
ISA. 42.1.

MAY 9

To have faith is to be sure of the things we hope for, to be certain of the things we cannot see.

If our hope in Christ is good for this life only and no more, then we deserve more pity than anyone else in all the world.

What no one ever saw or heard, what no one ever thought could happen, is the very thing God prepared for those who love him. It was to us that God made known his secret by means of his Spirit.—You believed in Christ, and God put his stamp of ownership on you by giving you the Holy Spirit he had promised. The Spirit is the guarantee that we shall receive what God has promised his people.

Jesus said to [Thomas], "Do you believe because you see me? How happy are those who believe without seeing me!"—You love him, although you have not seen him, and you believe in him, although you do not now see him. So you rejoice with a great and glorious joy which words cannot express, because you are receiving the salvation of your souls, which is the purpose of your faith in him.

Our life is a matter of faith, not of sight.—Do not lose your courage … because it brings with it a great reward.

HEB. 11.1.—1 COR. 15.19.—1 COR. 2.9, 10.—
EPH. 1.13, 14.—JOHN 20.29.—1 PET. 1.8, 9.—
2 COR. 5.7.—HEB. 10.35.

*The Son of God appeared for this very reason, to destroy
what the Devil had done.*

We are not fighting against human beings but against the
wicked spiritual forces in the heavenly world, the rulers,
authorities, and cosmic powers of this dark age.—Since the
children, as he calls them, are people of flesh and blood,
Jesus himself became like them and shared their human
nature. He did this so that through his death he might
destroy the Devil.—Christ freed himself from the power of
the spiritual rulers and authorities; he made a public spectacle of them by leading them as captives in his victory
procession.—Then I heard a loud voice in heaven saying,
"Now God's salvation has come! Now God has shown his
power as King! Now his Messiah has shown his authority!
For the one who stood before our God and accused our
brothers day and night has been thrown out of heaven. Our
brothers won the victory over him by the blood of the
Lamb and by the truth which they proclaimed; and they
were willing to give up their lives and die."

Thanks be to God who gives us the victory through our
Lord Jesus Christ!

**1 JOHN 3.8.—EPH. 6.12.—HEB. 2.14.—COL. 2.15.—
REV. 12.10, 11.—1 COR. 15.57.**

MAY 11

Come back to your right senses and stop your sinful ways.

All of you are people who belong to the light, who belong to the day. So then, we should not be sleeping like the others; we should be awake and sober.

The time has come for you to wake up from your sleep. For the moment when we will be saved is closer now than it was when we first believed. The night is nearly over, day is almost here. Let us stop doing the things that belong to the dark, and let us take up weapons for fighting in the light.—Put on God's armour now! Then when the evil day comes, you will be able to resist the enemy's attacks; and after fighting to the end, you will still hold your ground.—Give up all the evil you have been doing, and get yourselves new minds and hearts.—Get rid of every filthy habit and all wicked conduct. Submit to God and accept the word that he plants in your hearts, which is able to save you.—My children, remain in union with him, so that when he appears we may be full of courage and need not hide in shame from him on the Day he comes. You know that Christ is righteous; you should know, then, that everyone who does what is right is God's child.

1 COR. 15.34.—1 THESS. 5.5, 6.—
ROM. 13.11, 12.—EPH. 6.13.—EZEK. 18.31.—
JAS 1.21.—1 JOHN 2.28, 29.

Dear friends, let us love one another, because love comes from God. Whoever loves is a child of God and knows God.

God has poured out his love into our hearts by means of the Holy Spirit, who is God's gift to us.—The Spirit that God has given you does not make you slaves and cause you to be afraid; instead, the Spirit makes you God's children, and by the Spirit's power we cry out to God, "Father! my Father!" God's Spirit joins himself to our spirits to declare that we are God's children.—Whoever believes in the Son of God has this testimony in his own heart. The testimony is this: God has given us eternal life, and this life has its source in his Son.

God showed his love for us by sending his only Son … so that we might have life through him.—By the sacrificial death of Christ we are set free, that is, our sins are forgiven.—He did this to demonstrate for all time to come the extraordinary greatness of his grace in the love he showed us in Christ Jesus.

Dear friends, if this is how God loved us, then we should love one another.

1 JOHN 4.7.—ROM. 5.5.—ROM. 8.15, 16.—
1 JOHN 5.10, 11.—1 JOHN 4.9.—EPH. 1.7.—
EPH. 2.7.—1 JOHN 4.11.

Lift up their hands in prayer without anger or argument.

People will worship the Father as he really is, offering him the true worship that he wants. God is Spirit, and only by the power of his Spirit can people worship him as he really is.—When you pray, I will answer you. When you call to me, I will respond.—When you stand and pray, forgive anything you may have against anyone.

No one can please God without faith, for whoever comes to God must have faith that God exists and rewards those who seek him.—When you pray, you must believe and not doubt at all. Whoever doubts is like a wave in the sea that is driven and blown about by the wind. A person like that ... must not think that he will receive anything from the Lord.

If I had ignored my sins, the Lord would not have listened to me.—I am writing this to you, my children, so that you will not sin; but if anyone does sin, we have someone who pleads with the Father on our behalf – Jesus Christ, the righteous one.

1 TIM. 2.8.—JOHN 4.23, 24.—ISA. 58.9.—
MARK 11.25.—HEB. 11.6.—JAS 1.6-8.—
PS. 66.18.—1 JOHN 2.1.

To share in his sufferings.

A pupil should be satisfied to become like his teacher, and a slave like his master.

We despised him and rejected him; he endured suffering and pain. No one would even look at him – we ignored him as if he were nothing.—I chose you from this world, and you do not belong to it; that is why the world hates you.

I had hoped for sympathy, but there was none.—No one stood by me the first time I defended myself; all deserted me.

Foxes have holes, and birds have nests, but the Son of Man has nowhere to lie down and rest.—There is no permanent city for us here on earth; we are looking for the city which is to come.

Let us run with determination the race that lies before us. Let us keep our eyes fixed on Jesus, on whom our faith depends from beginning to end. He did not give up because of the cross! On the contrary, because of the joy that was waiting for him, he thought nothing of the disgrace of dying on the cross, and he is now seated at the right-hand side of God's throne.

PHIL. 3.10.—MATT. 10.25.—ISA. 53.3.—
JOHN 15.19.—PS. 69.20.—2 TIM. 4.16.—
MATT. 8.20.—HEB. 13.14.—HEB. 12.1, 2.

*He will wipe away all tears from their eyes. There will be no
more death, no more grief or crying or pain. The old things
have disappeared.*

The Sovereign LORD will destroy death for ever! He will
wipe away the tears from everyone's eyes and take away the
disgrace his people have suffered throughout the world.
The LORD himself has spoken!—No longer will the sun be
your light by day or the moon be your light by night: I, the
LORD, will be your eternal light … your days of grief will
come to an end.—No one who lives in our land will ever
again complain of being ill, and all sins will be forgiven.—
There will be no weeping there, no calling for help.—For
ever free from sorrow and grief.

The last enemy to be defeated will be death. Then the
scripture will come true: "Death is destroyed; victory is
complete!"—What cannot be seen lasts for ever.

REV. 21.4.—ISA. 25.8.—ISA. 60.19, 20.—
ISA. 33.24.—ISA. 65.19.—ISA. 35.10.—
1 COR. 15.26, 54.—2 COR. 4.18.

A servant of Christ Jesus.

You call me Teacher and Lord, and it is right that you do so, because that is what I am.—Whoever wants to serve me must follow me, so that my servant will be with me where I am. And my Father will honour anyone who serves me.—Take my yoke and put it on you, and learn from me, because I am gentle and humble in spirit; and you will find rest. For the yoke I will give you is easy, and the load I will put on you is light.

All those things that I might count as profit I now reckon as loss for Christ's sake.—Now you have been set free from sin and are the slaves of God. Your gain is a life fully dedicated to him, and the result is eternal life.

I do not call you servants any longer, because a servant does not know what his master is doing. Instead, I call you friends, because I have told you everything I have heard from my Father.—You are no longer a slave but a son.

Stand, then, as free people, and do not allow yourselves to become slaves again. My brothers, you were called to be free. But do not let this freedom become an excuse for letting your physical desires control you.

ROM. 1.1.—JOHN 13.13.—JOHN 12.26.—
MATT. 11.29, 30.—PHIL. 3.7.—ROM. 6.22.—
JOHN 15.15.—GAL. 4.7.—GAL. 5.1, 13.

I am the LORD your God. Obey my laws and my commands.

Be holy in all that you do, just as God who called you is holy.—Whoever says that he remains in union with God should live just as Jesus Christ did. You know that Christ is righteous; you should know, then, that everyone who does what is right is God's child.—Whether or not a man is circumcised means nothing; what matters is to obey God's commandments.—Whoever breaks one commandment is guilty of breaking them all.

There is nothing in us that allows us to claim that we are capable of doing this work. The capacity we have comes from God.—Teach me, LORD, the meaning of your laws.

Keep on working with fear and trembling to complete your salvation, because God is always at work in you to make you willing and able to obey his own purpose.—May the God of peace provide you with every good thing you need in order to do his will, and may he, through Jesus Christ, do in us what pleases him.

EZEK. 20.19.—1 PET. 1.15.—1 JOHN 2.6, 29.—
1 COR. 7.19.—JAS 2.10.—2 COR. 3.5.—
PS. 119.33.—PHIL. 2.12, 13.—HEB. 13.20, 21.

*Just as the Father is himself the source of life, in the same
way he has made his Son to be the source of life.*

Our Saviour, Christ Jesus ... has ended the power of death
and through the gospel has revealed immortal life.—I am
the resurrection and the life.—Because I live, you also will
live.—We are all partners with Christ.—They ... received
their share of the Holy Spirit.—You ... may come to share
the divine nature.—The first man, Adam, was created a
living being; but the last Adam is the life-giving Spirit. Listen
to this secret truth: we shall not all die, but when the last
trumpet sounds, we shall all be changed in an instant, as
quickly as the blinking of an eye. For when the trumpet
sounds, the dead will be raised, never to die again, and we
shall all be changed.

Holy, holy, holy, is the Lord God Almighty, who was,
who is, and who is to come ... who lives for ever and
ever.—God, the blessed and only Ruler, the King of kings
and the Lord of lords. He alone is immortal.—To the
eternal King ... be honour and glory for ever and ever!
Amen.

JOHN 5.26.—2 TIM. 1.10.—JOHN 11.25.—
JOHN 14.19.—HEB. 3.14.—HEB. 6.4.—2 PET. 1.4.—
1 COR. 15.45, 51, 52.—REV. 4.8, 9.—
1 TIM. 6.15, 16.—1 TIM. 1.17.

Wash away all my evil and make me clean from my sin!

I will purify them from the sins that they have committed against me, and I will forgive their sins and their rebellion.— I will sprinkle clean water on you and make you clean from all your idols and everything else that has defiled you.

No one can enter the Kingdom of God unless he is born of water and the Spirit.—The blood of goats and bulls and the ashes of a burnt calf are sprinkled on the people who are ritually unclean, and this purifies them by taking away their ritual impurity. Since this is true, how much more is accomplished by the blood of Christ! Through the eternal Spirit he offered himself as a perfect sacrifice to God. His blood will purify our consciences from useless rituals, so that we may serve the living God.

He saved them, as he had promised, in order to show his great power.—To you alone, O LORD, to you alone, and not to us, must glory be given because of your constant love and faithfulness.

PS. 51.2.—JER. 33.8.—EZEK. 36.25.—JOHN 3.5.—
HEB. 9.13, 14.—PS. 106.8—PS. 115.1.

Watch yourself.

Every athlete in training submits to strict discipline, in order to be crowned with a wreath that will not last; but we do it for one that will last for ever. That is why I run straight for the finishing-line; that is why I am like a boxer who does not waste his punches. I harden my body with blows and bring it under complete control, to keep myself from being disqualified after having called others to the contest.—Put on all the armour that God gives you, so that you will be able to stand up against the Devil's evil tricks. For we are not fighting against human beings but against the wicked spiritual forces in the heavenly world, the rulers, authorities, and cosmic powers of this dark age.

Those who belong to Christ Jesus have put to death their human nature with all its passions and desires. The Spirit has given us life; he must also control our lives.— Those who are led by God's Spirit are God's sons.—Practise these things and devote yourself to them, in order that your progress may be seen by all.

1 TIM. 4.16.—1 COR. 9.25–27.—EPH. 6.11, 12.—
GAL. 5.24, 25.—ROM. 8.14.—1 TIM. 4.15.

MAY 21

Build up your strength in union with the LORD and by means of his mighty power.

My Grace is all you need, for my power is greatest when you are weak. I am most happy, then, to be proud of my weaknesses, in order to feel the protection of Christ's power over me. I am content with weaknesses, insults, hardships, persecutions, and difficulties for Christ's sake. For when I am weak, then I am strong.—I will praise your power, Sovereign LORD; I will proclaim your goodness, yours alone.—I have complete confidence in the gospel; it is God's power to save all who believe.

I have the strength to face all conditions by the power that Christ gives me.—I toil and struggle, using the mighty strength which Christ supplies and which is at work in me.—We who have this spiritual treasure are like common clay pots, in order to show that the supreme power belongs to God, not to us.

The joy that the LORD gives you will make you strong.—May you be made strong with all the strength which comes from his glorious power, so that you may be able to endure everything with patience. And with joy give thanks to the Father.

EPH. 6.10.—2 COR. 12.9, 10—PS. 71.16.—
ROM. 1.16.—PHIL. 4.13.—COL. 1.29.—
2 COR. 4.7.—NEH. 8.10.—COL. 1.11.

Peace is what I leave with you; it is my own peace that I give you. I do not give it as the world does.

The world and everything in it that people desire is passing away.—Every living man is no more than a puff of wind, no more than a shadow. All he does is for nothing; he gathers wealth, but doesn't know who will get it.—What did you gain from doing the things that you are now ashamed of? The result of those things is death!

Martha, Martha! You are worried and troubled over so many things, but just one is needed. Mary has chosen the right thing, and it will not be taken away from her.—I would like you to be free from worry.

I have told you this so that you will have peace by being united to me. The world will make you suffer. But be brave! I have defeated the world!—May the LORD himself, who is our source of peace, give you peace at all times and in every way.—May the LORD bless you and take care of you; may the LORD be kind and gracious to you; may the LORD look on you with favour and give you peace.

JOHN 14.17.—1 JOHN 2.17.—PS. 39.5, 6.—
ROM. 6.21.—LUKE 10.41, 42.—1 COR. 7.32.—
JOHN 16.33.—2 THESS. 3.16.—NUM. 6.24–26.

Put [the two stones] on the shoulder-straps of the ephod to represent the twelve tribes of Israel. In this way Aaron will carry their names on his shoulders, so that I, the LORD, will always remember my people.

Jesus lives on for ever, and his work as priest does not pass on to someone else. And so he is able, now and always, to save those who come to God through him, because he lives for ever to plead with God for them.—Him who is able to keep you from falling, and to bring you faultless and joyful before his glorious presence.

Let us ... hold firmly to the faith we profess. For we have a great High Priest who has gone into the very presence of God – Jesus, the Son of God. Our High Priest is not one who cannot feel sympathy for our weaknesses. On the contrary, we have a High Priest who was tempted in every way that we are, but did not sin. Let us have confidence, then, and approach God's throne, where there is grace.

This is the tribe the LORD loves and protects; he guards them all the day long, and he dwells in their midst.

EXOD. 28.12.—HEB. 7.24, 25.—JUDE 24.—
HEB. 4.14–16.—DEUT. 33.12.

158

*Do not make God's Holy Spirit sad; for the Spirit is God's
mark of ownership on you, a guarantee that the Day will
come when God will set you free.*

The love that the Spirit gives.—The Helper, the Holy
Spirit.—He saved them from all their suffering. It was not
an angel, but the LORD himself who saved them. In his love
and compassion he rescued them. He had always taken care
of them in the past, but they rebelled against him and made
his holy spirit sad. So the LORD became their enemy and
fought against them.

We are sure that we live in union with God and that he
lives in union with us, because he has given us his Spirit.—
You believed in Christ, and God put his stamps of ownership on you by giving you the Holy Spirit he had promised.
The Spirit is the guarantee that we shall receive what God
has promised his people, and this assures us that God will
give complete freedom to those who are his.—What I say
is this: let the Spirit direct your lives, and you will not satisfy
the desires of the human nature. For what our human
nature wants is opposed to what the Spirit wants, and what
the Spirit wants is opposed to what our human nature
wants. These two are enemies, and this means that you
cannot do what you want to do.

The Spirit … comes to help us, weak as we are.

EPH. 4.30.—ROM. 15.30.—JOHN 14.26.—
ISA. 63.9, 10.—1 JOHN 4.13.—EPH. 1.13, 14.—
GAL. 5.16, 17.—ROM. 8.26.

How wonderful are the good things you keep for those who honour you!

No one has ever seen or heard of a God like you, who does such deeds for those who put their hope in him.—What no one ever saw or heard, what no one ever thought could happen, is the very thing God prepared for those who love him. But it was to us that God made known his secret by means of his Spirit.—You will show me the path that leads to life; your presence fills me with joy and brings me pleasure for ever.

How precious, O God, is your constant love! We find protection under the shadow of your wings. We feast on the abundant food you provide; you let us drink from the river of your goodness.

Spiritual exercise is valuable in every way, because it promises life both for the present and for the future.

PS. 31.19.—ISA. 64.4.—1 COR. 2.9, 10.—
PS. 16.11.—PS. 36.7, 8.—1 TIM. 4.8.

MAY 26

Our Lord Jesus, who is the Great Shepherd of the sheep.

I am the good shepherd. I know my sheep. My sheep listen to my voice; I know them, and they follow me. I give them eternal life, and they shall never die. No one can snatch them away from me.

The LORD is my shepherd; I have everything I need. He lets me rest in fields of green grass and leads me to quiet pools of fresh water. He gives me new strength. He guides me in the right paths, as he has promised.

All of us were like sheep that were lost, each of us going his own way. But the LORD made the punishment fall on him, the punishment all of us deserved.—I am the good shepherd, who is willing to die for the sheep.—I will look for those that are lost, bring back those that wander off, bandage those that are hurt, and heal those that are sick.— You were like sheep that had lost their way, but now you have been brought back to follow the Shepherd and Keeper of your souls.

HEB. 13.20.—JOHN 10.14, 27, 28.—PS. 23.1–3.—
ISA. 53.6.—JOHN 10.11.—EZEK. 34.16.—
1 PET. 2.25.

The LORD is good; he protects his people in times of trouble; he takes care of those who turn to him.

Give thanks to the LORD Almighty, because he is good and his love is eternal.—God is our shelter and strength, always ready to help in times of trouble.—You are my defender and protector. You are my God; in you I trust.—Israel, how happy you are! There is no one like you, a nation saved by the LORD. The LORD himself is your shield and your sword.—This God – how perfect are his deeds, how dependable his words! He is like a shield for all who seek his protection. The LORD alone is God; God alone is our defence.

The person who loves God is known by him.—The solid foundation that God has laid cannot be shaken; and on it are written these words: "The Lord knows those who are his" and "Whoever says that he belongs to the Lord must turn away from wrongdoing."—The righteous are guided and protected by the LORD, but the evil are on the way to their doom.—I know you very well and I am pleased with you.

NAHUM 1.7.—JER.33.11.—PS. 46.1.—PS. 91.2.—
DEUT. 33.29.—2 SAM. 22.31, 32.—1 COR. 8.3.—
2 TIM. 2.19.—PS. 1.6.—EXOD. 33.17.

MAY 28

We eagerly wait for our Saviour.

For God has revealed his grace for the salvation of all mankind. That grace instructs us to give up ungodly living and worldly passions, and to live self-controlled, upright and godly lives in this world, as we wait for the blessed Day we hope for, when the glory of our great God and Saviour Jesus Christ will appear. He gave himself for us, to rescue us from all wickedness and to make us a pure people who belong to him alone and are eager to do good.—We wait for what God has promised: new heavens and a new earth, where righteousness will be at home. And so, my friends, as you wait for that Day, do your best to be pure and faultless in God's sight and to be at peace with him.

Christ ... was offered in sacrifice once to take away the sins of many. He will appear a second time, not to deal with sin, but to save those who are waiting for him.—When it happens, everyone will say, "He is our God! We have put our trust in him, and he has rescued us. He is the LORD! We have put our trust in him, and now we are happy and joyful because he has saved us."

PHIL. 3.20.—TITUS 2.11–14.—2 PET. 3.13, 14.—
HEB. 9.28.—ISA. 25.9.

163

MAY 29

*The life of every living thing is in the blood, and that is why
the LORD has commanded that all blood be poured out on
the altar to take away the people's sins. Blood, which is life,
takes away sins.*

There is the Lamb of God, who takes away the sin of the
world!—The blood of the Lamb.—The costly sacrifice of
Christ, who was like a lamb without defect or flaw.—Sins
are forgiven only if blood is poured out.—The blood of
Jesus, his Son, purifies us from every sin.

When Christ ... entered ... the Most Holy Place, he ...
took his own blood and obtained eternal salvation for
us.—We have, then, my brothers, complete freedom to go
into the Most Holy Place by means of the death of Jesus.
He opened for us a new way, a living way, through the
curtain – that is, through his own body. So let us come near
to God with a sincere heart and a sure faith.

He bought you for a price. So use your bodies for God's
glory.

LEV. 17.11.—JOHN 1.29.—REV. 7.14.—
1 PET. 1.19.—HEB. 9.22.—1 JOHN 1.7.—
HEB. 9.12.—HEB. 10.19, 20, 22.—1 COR. 6.20.

Let us ... do our best to receive that rest.

Go in through the narrow gate, because the gate to hell is wide and the road that leads to it is easy, and there are many who travel it. But the gate to life is narrow and the way that leads to it is hard, and there are few people who find it.—The Kingdom of heaven has suffered violent attacks, and violent men try to seize it.—Do not work for food that goes bad; instead, work for the food that lasts for eternal life. This is the food which the son of Man will give you.—Try even harder to make God's call and his choice of you a permanent experience. In this way you will be given the full right to enter the eternal Kingdom of our Lord and Saviour Jesus Christ.—Run ... in such a way as to win the prize. Every athlete in training submits to strict discipline, in order to be crowned with a wreath that will not last; but we do it for one that will last for ever.

Whoever receives that rest which God promised will rest from his own work, just as God rested from his.—I, the LORD, will be your eternal light; the light of my glory will shine on you.

HEB. 4.11.—MATT. 7.13, 14.—MATT. 11.12.—
JOHN 6.27.—2 PET. 1.10, 11.—1 COR. 9.24, 25.—
HEB. 4.10.—ISA. 60.19.

You have struggled with God and with men, and you have won; so your name will be Israel.

He fought against God – he fought against an angel and won. He wept and asked for a blessing.—His faith did not leave him, and he did not doubt God's promise; his faith filled him with power, and he gave praise to God.

Have faith in God. I assure you that whoever tells this hill to get up and throw itself in the sea and does not doubt in his heart, but believes that what he says will happen, it will be done for him. For this reason I tell you: when you pray and ask for something, believe that you have received it, and you will be given whatever you ask for.—Everything is possible for the person who has faith.—How happy you are to believe that the Lord's message to you will come true!

Lord, make our faith greater.

GEN. 32.28.—HOS. 12.3, 4.—ROM. 4.20.—
MARK 11.22–24.—MARK 9.23.—LUKE 1.45.—
LUKE 17.5.

The Spirit produces patience, kindness.

I, the LORD, am a God who is full of compassion and pity, who is not easily angered and who shows great love and faithfulness.

Live a life that measures up to the standard God set when he called you. Be always humble, gentle, and patient. show your love by being tolerant with one another.—Be kind and tender-hearted to one another, and forgive one another, as God has forgiven you through Christ.—The wisdom from above is pure first of all; it is also peaceful, gentle, and friendly; it is full of compassion and produces a harvest of good deeds; it is free from prejudice and hypocrisy.—Love is patient and kind.

Let us not become tired of doing good; for if we do not give up, the time will come when we will reap the harvest.—Be patient, then, my brothers, until the Lord comes. See how patient a farmer is as he waits for his land to produce precious crops. He waits patiently for the autumn and spring rains. You also must be patient. Keep your hopes high, for the day of the Lord's coming is near.

GAL. 5.22.—EXOD. 34.6.—EPH. 4.1, 2.—
EPH. 4.32.—JAS 3.17.—1 COR. 13.4.—GAL. 6.9.—
JAS 5.7, 8.

*You are to eat it quickly, for you are to be dressed for travel.
It is the Passover Festival to honour me, the LORD.*

Get up and go; there is no safety here any more.—There is
no permanent city for us here on earth; we are looking for
the city which is to come.—There still remains for God's
people a rest.

Be ready for whatever comes, dressed for action and
with your lamps lit, like servants who are waiting for their
master to come back from a wedding feast. When he comes
and knocks, they will open the door for him at once. How
happy are those servants whose master finds them awake
and ready when he returns!—Have your minds ready for
action. Keep alert and set your hope completely on the
blessing which will be given you when Jesus Christ is
revealed.—The one thing I do … is to forget what is behind
me. I run straight towards the goal in order to win the prize,
which is God's call through Christ Jesus to the life above.

EXOD. 12.11.—MIC. 2.10.—HEB. 13.14.—
HEB. 4.9.—LUKE 12.35-37.—1 PET. 1.13.—
PHIL. 3.13-15.

The Son of Man will come at an hour when you are not expecting him. Be on your guard, then, because you do not know the day or the hour.

Don't let yourselves become occupied with too much feasting and drinking and with the worries of this life, or that Day may suddenly catch you like a trap. For it will come upon all people everywhere on earth. Be on the alert and pray always that you will have the strength to go safely through all those things that will happen and to stand before the Son of Man.

The Day of the Lord will come as a thief comes at night. When people say, "Everything is quiet and safe," then suddenly destruction will hit them! It will come as suddenly as the pains that come upon a woman in labour, and people will not escape. But you, brothers, are not in the darkness, and the Day should not take you by surprise like a thief. All of you are people who belong to the light, who belong to the day. We do not belong to the night or to the darkness. So then, we should not be sleeping like the others; we should be awake and sober.

MATT. 24.44, 25.13.—LUKE 21.34–36.—
1 THESS. 5.2–6.

The new Temple will be more splendid than the old one, and there I will give my people prosperity and peace.

The Temple that my son Solomon is to build must be splendid and world-famous.—The dazzling light of the LORD's presence filled the Temple.

"Tear down this Temple, and in three days I will build it again." The temple Jesus was speaking about was his body.—Because of the far brighter glory now the glory that was so bright in the past is gone.—The Word became a human being and, full of grace and truth, lived among us. We saw his glory, the glory which he received as the Father's only Son.—In these last days [God] has spoken to us through his Son. He is the one through whom God created the universe, the one whom God has chosen to possess all things at the end.

Glory to God in the highest heaven, and peace on earth to those with whom he is pleased!—Prince of Peace.—Christ himself has brought us peace.—God's peace, which is far beyond human understanding, will keep your hearts and minds safe in union with Christ Jesus.

HAG. 2.9.—1 CHR. 22.5.—2 CHR. 7.1.—
JOHN 2.19, 21.—2 COR. 3.10.—JOHN 1.14.—
HEB. 1.1, 2.—LUKE 2.14.—ISA. 9.6.—
EPH. 2.14.—PHIL. 4.7.

When you have done all you have been told to do, say, "We are ordinary servants; we have only done our duty."

What ... can we boast about? Nothing! And what is the reason for this? Is it that we obey the Law? No, but that we believe.—Who made you superior to others? Didn't God give you everything you have? Well, then, how can you boast, as if what you have were not a gift?—It is by God's grace that you have been saved through faith. It is not the result of your own efforts, but God's gift, so that no one can boast about it. God has made us what we are, and in our union with Christ Jesus he has created us for a life of good deeds, which he has already prepared for us to do.

By God's grace I am what I am, and the grace that he gave me was not without effect. On the contrary, I have worked harder than any of the other apostles, although it was not really my own doing, but God's grace working with me.—All things were created by him, and all things exist through him and for him.—We have only given back what is yours already.

Don't put me, your servant, on trial; no one is innocent in your sight.

LUKE 17.10.—ROM. 3.27.—1 COR. 4.7.—
EPH. 2.8-10.—1 COR. 15.10.—ROM. 11.36.—
1 CHR. 29.14.—PS. 143.2.

In his love he will give you new life.

The LORD did not love you and choose you because you outnumbered other peoples; you were the smallest nation on earth. But the LORD loved you.—We love because God first loved us.—You were far away from God … But now, by means of the physical death of his Son, God has made you his friends, in order to bring you, holy, pure and faultless, into his presence.

This is what love is: it is not that we have loved God, but that he loved us and sent his Son to be the means by which our sins are forgiven.—God has shown us how much he loves us – it was while we were still sinners that Christ died for us!

Then a voice said from heaven, "This is my own dear Son, with whom I am pleased."—The Father loves me because I am willing to give up my life, in order that I may receive it back again.—His Son … reflects the brightness of God's glory and is the exact likeness of God's own being, sustaining the universe with his powerful word. After achieving forgiveness for the sins of mankind, he sat down in heaven at the right-hand side of God, the Supreme Power.

ZEPH. 3.17.—DEUT. 7.7, 8.—1 JOHN 4.19.—
COL. 1.21, 22.—1 JOHN 4.10.—ROM. 5.8.—
MATT. 3.17.—JOHN 10.17.—HEB. 1.2, 3.

They should always pray and never become discouraged.

Suppose one of you should go to a friend's house at midnight and say to him, "Friend, let me borrow three loaves of bread. A friend of mine who is on a journey has just come to my house, and I haven't got any food for him!" And suppose your friends should answer from inside, "Don't bother me! The door is already locked, and my children and I are in bed. I can't get up and give you anything." Well, what then? I tell you that even if he will not get up and give you the bread because you are his friend, yet he will get up and give you everything you need because you are not ashamed to keep on asking.—Pray on every occasion, as the Spirit leads. For this reason keep alert and never give up; pray always for all God's people.

Let me go ... I won't, unless you bless me. You have struggled with God and with men, and you have won.—Be persistent in prayer, and keep alert as you pray, giving thanks to God.

Jesus went up a hill to pray and spent the whole night there praying to God.

LUKE 18.1.—LUKE 11.5–8.—EPH. 6.18.—
GEN. 32.26, 28.—COL. 4.2.—LUKE 6.12.

The LORD ... made him successful in everything he did.

Happy are those who obey the LORD, who live by his commands. Your work will provide for your needs; you will be happy and prosperous.—Trust in the LORD and do good; live in the land and be safe. Seek your happiness in the LORD, and he will give you your heart's desire.—Don't be afraid or discouraged, for I, the LORD your God, am with you wherever you go.

Be concerned above everything else with the Kingdom of God and with what he requires of you, and he will provide you with all these other things.

As long as ... he served the LORD faithfully, ... God blessed him.—Make certain that you do not forget the LORD your God; do not fail to obey any of his laws that I am giving you today. You must never think that you have made yourselves wealthy by your own power and strength.

The LORD your God has been with you and given you peace on all sides.

GEN. 39.3.—PS. 128.1, 2.—PS. 37.3, 4.—
JOSH. 1.9.—MATT. 6.33.—2 CHR. 26.5.—
DEUT. 8.11, 17.—1 CHR. 22.18.

JUNE 9

Nobody has ever talked like this man!

You are the most handsome of men; you are an eloquent speaker. God has always blessed you.—The Sovereign LORD has taught me what to say, so that I can strengthen the weary.—His mouth is sweet to kiss; everything about him enchants me. This is what my lover is like.

They were all well impressed with him and marvelled at the eloquent words that he spoke.—He wasn't like the teachers of the Law; instead, he taught with authority.

Christ's message in all its richness must live in your hearts.—Accept … the word of God as the sword which the Spirit gives you.—The word of God is alive and active, sharper than any double-edged sword.—The weapons we use in our fight are not the world's weapons but God's powerful weapons, which we use to destroy strongholds. We destroy false arguments; we pull down every proud obstacle that is raised against the knowledge of God; we take every thought captive and make it obey Christ.

JOHN 7.46.—PS. 45.2.—ISA. 50.4.—S. OF S. 5.16.—
LUKE 4.22.—MATT. 7.29.—COL. 3.16.—
EPH. 6.17.—HEB. 4.12.—2 COR. 10.4, 5.

*The younger son ... went to a country far away, where he
wasted his money in reckless living.*

Some of you were like that. But you have been purified from
sin; you have been dedicated to God; you have been put
right with God by the Lord Jesus Christ and by the Spirit
of our God.—All of us ... lived according to our natural
desires, doing whatever suited the wishes of our own bodies
and minds. In our natural condition we, like everyone else,
were destined to suffer God's anger. But God's mercy is so
abundant, and his love for us is so great, that while we were
spiritually dead in our disobedience he brought us to life
with Christ. It is by God's grace that you have been saved.
In our union with Christ Jesus he raised us up with him to
rule with him in the heavenly world.

This is what love is: it is not that we have loved God,
but that he loved us and sent his Son to be the means by
which our sins are forgiven.

God has shown us how much he loves us – it was while
we were still sinners that Christ died for us! We were God's
enemies, but he made us his friends through the death of
his Son. Now that we are God's friends, how much more
will we be saved by Christ's life!

LUKE 15.13.—1 COR. 6.11.—EPH. 2.3-6.—
1 JOHN 4.10.—ROM. 5.8, 10.

He got up and started back to his father. He was still a long way from home when his father saw him; his heart was filled with pity, and he ran, threw his arms around his son, and kissed him.

The LORD is merciful and loving, slow to become angry and full of constant love. He does not keep on rebuking; he is not angry for ever. He does not punish us as we deserve or repay us according to our sins and wrongs. As high as the sky is above the earth, so great is his love for those who honour him. As far as the east is from the west, so far does he remove our sins from us. As a father is kind to his children, so the LORD is kind to those who honour him.

The Spirit makes you God's children, and by the Spirit's power we cry out to God, "Father! my Father!" God's Spirit joins himself to our spirits to declare that we are God's children.—You who used to be far away have been brought near by the sacrificial death of Christ. You … are not foreigners or strangers any longer; you are now fellow-citizens with God's people and members of the family of God.

LUKE 15.20.—PS. 103.8–13.—ROM. 8.15, 16.—
EPH. 2.13, 19.

JUNE 12

*Everything that will not burn ... is to be purified by
passing it through fire.*

The LORD your God is using him to test you, to see if you
love the LORD with all your heart.—He will come to judge
like one who refines and purifies silver. As a metal-worker
refines silver and gold, so the LORD's messenger will purify
the priests, so that they will bring to the LORD the right
kind of offerings.—The quality of each person's work will be
seen when the Day of Christ exposes it. For on that Day
fire will reveal everyone's work; the fire will test it and show
its real quality.

I will take action against you. I will purify you just as
metal is refined, and will remove all your impurity.—I will
refine my people like metal and put them to the test.

You have put us to the test, God; as silver is purified by
fire, so you have tested us ... we went through fire and
flood, but now you have brought us to a place of safety.

When you pass through fire, you will not be burnt; the
hard trials that come will not hurt you.

NUM. 31.23.—DEUT. 13.3.—MAL. 3.3.—
1 COR. 3.13.—ISA. 1.25.—JER. 9.7.—
PS. 66.10, 12.—ISA. 43.2.

Remain united to me, and I will remain united to you.

I have been put to death with Christ on his cross, so that it is no longer I who live, but it is Christ who lives in me. This life that I live now, I live by faith in the Son of God, who loved me and gave his life for me.

I know that good does not live in me – that is, in my human nature. For even though the desire to do good is in me, I am not able to do it. What an unhappy man I am! Who will rescue me from this body that is taking me to death? Thanks be to God, who does this through our Lord Jesus Christ!—If Christ lives in you, the Spirit is life for you because you have been put right with God, even though your bodies are going to die because of sin.—You must … continue faithful on a firm and sure foundation, and must not allow yourselves to be shaken from the hope you gained when you heard the gospel.

My children, remain in union with him, so that when he appears we may be full of courage and need not hide in shame from him on the Day he comes.—Whoever says that he remains in union with God should live just as Jesus Christ did.

JOHN 15.4.—GAL. 2.19, 20.—ROM. 7.18, 24, 25.—
ROM. 8.10.—COL. 1.23.—1 JOHN 2.28.—
1 JOHN 2.6.

JUNE 14

Just as we have a share in Christ's many sufferings, so also through Christ we share in God's great help.

To share in his sufferings.—Be glad that you are sharing Christ's sufferings, so that you may be full of joy when his glory is revealed.—If we have died with him, we shall also live with him.—Since we are his children, we will possess the blessings he keeps for his people, and we will also possess with Christ what God has kept for him; for if we share Christ's suffering, we will also share his glory.

To those who were to receive what he promised, God wanted to make it very clear that he would never change his purpose; so he added his vow to the promise. There are these two things, then, that cannot change and about which God cannot lie. So we who have found safety with him are greatly encouraged to hold firmly to the hope placed before us.—May our Lord Jesus Christ himself and God our Father, who loved us and in his grace gave us unfailing courage and a firm hope, encourage you and strengthen you to always do and say what is good.

2 COR. 1.5.—PHIL. 3.10.—1 PET. 4.13.—
2 TIM. 2.11.—ROM. 8.17.—HEB. 6.17, 18.—
2 THESS. 2.16, 17.

There are some things that the LORD our God has kept secret; but he has revealed his Law, and we and our descendants are to obey it for ever.

LORD, I have given up my pride and turned away from my arrogance. I am not concerned with great matters or with subjects too difficult for me. Instead, I am content and at peace. As a child lies quietly in its mother's arms, so my heart is quiet within me.

The LORD is the friend of those who obey him and he affirms his covenant with them.—There is a God in heaven, who reveals mysteries.—These are only hints of his power, only the whispers that we have heard.

I do not call you servants any longer, because a servant does not know what his master is doing. Instead, I call you friends, because I have told you everything I have heard from my Father.—If you love me, you will obey my commandments. I will ask the Father, and he will give you another Helper, who will stay with you for ever. He is the Spirit who reveals the truth about God.

DEUT. 29.29.—PS. 131.1, 2.—PS. 25.14.—
DAN. 2.28.—JOB 26.14.—JOHN 15.15.—
JOHN 14.15–17.

Be careful how you live. Don't live like ignorant people, but like wise people. Make good use of every opportunity you have, because these are evil days.

Make sure you obey the law that Moses commanded you: love the LORD your God, do his will, obey his commandments, be faithful to him, and serve him with all your heart and soul.—Be wise in the way you act towards those who are not believers, making good use of every opportunity you have. Your speech should always be pleasant and interesting, and you should know how to give the right answer to everyone.—Avoid every kind of evil.

The bridegroom was late in coming, so the girls began to nod and fall asleep. It was already midnight when the cry rang out, "Here is the bridegroom! Come and meet him!" Be on your guard, then, because you do not know the day or the hour.

My brothers, try even harder to make God's call and his choice of you a permanent experience; if you do so, you will never abandon your faith.—How happy are those servants whose master finds them awake and ready when he returns!

EPH. 5.15, 16.—JOSH. 22.5.—COL. 4.5, 6.—
1 THESS. 5.22.—MATT. 25.5, 6, 13.—
2 PET. 1.10.—LUKE 12.37.

*In all your prayers ask God for what you need, always
asking him with a thankful heart.*

I love the LORD, because he hears me; he listens to my
prayers. He listens to me every time I call to him.

When you pray, do not use a lot of meaningless words,
as the pagans do, who think that their gods will hear them
because their prayers are long.—The Spirit also comes to
help us, weak as we are. For we do not know how we ought
to pray; the Spirit himself pleads with God for us in groans
that words cannot express.

I want the men to pray, men who are dedicated to God
and can lift up their hands in prayer without anger or
argument.—Pray on every occasion, as the Spirit leads. For
this reason keep alert and never give up; pray always for all
God's people.

Whenever two of you on earth agree about anything
you pray for, it will be done for you by my Father in heaven.

PHIL. 4.6.—PS. 116.1, 2.—MATT. 6.7.—
ROM. 8.26.—1 TIM. 2.8.—EPH. 6.18.—MATT. 18.19.

Put the two stone tablets inside the box and put the lid on
top of it. I will meet you there.

The way into the Most Holy Place has not yet been
opened.—Jesus again gave a loud cry and breathed his last.
Then the curtain hanging in the Temple was torn in two
from top to bottom.

We have, my brothers, complete freedom to go into the
Most Holy Place by means of the death of Jesus. He opened
for us a new way, a living way, through the curtain – that is,
through his own body. Let us come near to God with a
sincere heart and a sure faith, with hearts that have been
purified from a guilty conscience and with bodies washed
with clean water.—Let us have confidence, then, and approach God's throne, where there is grace. There we will
receive mercy and find grace to help us just when we need
it.

Christ Jesus ... sets them free. God offered him, so that
by his sacrificial death he should become the means by
which people's sins are forgiven through their faith in
him.—It is through Christ that all of us ... are able to come
in the one Spirit into the presence of the Father.

EXOD. 25.21, 22.—HEB. 9.8.—
MATT. 27.50, 51.—HEB. 10.19, 20, 22.—
HEB. 4.16.—ROM. 3.24, 25.—EPH. 2.18.

Try to live a holy life, because no one will see the LORD without it.

No one can see the Kingdom of God unless he is born again.—Nothing that is impure will enter the city.—How perfect you are!

Be holy, because I, the LORD your God, am holy.—Be obedient to God, and do not allow your lives to be shaped by those desires you had when you were still ignorant. Instead, be holy in all that you do, just as God who called you is holy. The scripture says, "Be holy because I am holy." You call him Father, when you pray to God, who judges all people by the same standard, according to what each one has done; so then, spend the rest of your lives here on earth in reverence for him.—Get rid of your old self, which made you live as you used to – the old self that was being destroyed by its deceitful desires. Your hearts and minds must be made completely new, and you must put on the new self, which is created in God's likeness and reveals itself in the true life that is upright and holy.—Even before the world was made, God had already chosen us to be his through our union with Christ, so that we would be holy and without fault before him.

HEB. 12.14.—JOHN 3.3.—REV. 21.27.—
S. OF S. 4.7.—LEV. 19.2.—1 PET. 1.14–17.—
EPH. 4.22–24.—EPH. 1.4.

JUNE 20

Take this baby and nurse him for me, and I will pay you.

Go and work in the vineyard, and I will pay you a fair wage.—I assure you that anyone who gives you a drink of water because you belong to me will certainly receive his reward.—Be generous, and you will be prosperous. Help others, and you will be helped.—God is not unfair. He will not forget the work you did or the love you showed for him in the help you gave and are still giving to your fellow-Christians.

God will reward each one according to the work he has done.

"When, Lord, did we ever see you hungry and feed you, or thirsty and give you a drink? When did we ever see you a stranger and welcome you in our homes, or naked and clothe you?" The King will reply, "I tell you, whenever you did this for one of the least important of these brothers of mine, you did it for me! Come, you that are blessed by my Father! Come and possess the kingdom which has been prepared for you ever since the creation of the world."

EXOD. 2.9.—MATT. 20.4.—MARK 9.41.—
PROV. 11.25.—HEB. 6.10.—1 COR. 3.8.—
MATT. 25.37, 38, 40, 34.

*Christ himself suffered for you and left you an example, so
that you would follow in his steps.*

Even the Son of Man did not come to be served; he came
to serve.—If one of you wants to be first, he must be the
slave of all.

Jesus of Nazareth ... went everywhere, doing good.—
Help to carry one another's burdens, and in this way you
will obey the law of Christ.

The gentleness and kindness of Christ.—Be humble
towards one another, always considering others better than
yourselves.

Forgive them, Father! They don't know what they are
doing.—Be kind and tender-hearted to one another, and
forgive one another, as God has forgiven you through
Christ.

Whoever says that he remains in union with God
should live just as Jesus Christ did.—Let us keep our eyes
fixed on Jesus, on whom our faith depends from beginning
to end. He did not give up because of the cross! On the
contrary, because of the joy that was waiting for him, he
thought nothing of the disgrace of dying on the cross, and
he is now seated at the right-hand side of God's throne.

1 PET. 2.21.—MARK 10.45.—MARK 10.44.—
ACTS 10.38.—GAL. 6.2.—2 COR. 10.1.—
PHIL. 2.3.—LUKE 23.34.—EPH. 4.32.—
1 JOHN 2.6.—HEB. 12.2.

JUNE 22

You have died, and your life is hidden with Christ in God.

We have died to sin—how then can we go on living in it?—I have been put to death with Christ on his cross, so that it is no longer I who live, but it is Christ who lives in me. This life that I live now, I live by faith in the Son of God, who loved me and gave his life for me.—He died for all, so that those who live should no longer live for themselves, but only for him who died and was raised to life for their sake.—When anyone is joined to Christ, he is a new being; the old is gone, the new has come.

We live in union with the true God – in union with his Son Jesus Christ.—I pray that they may all be one. Father! May they be in us, just as you are in me and I am in you.—All of you are Christ's body, and each one is part of it.—Because I live, you also will live.

To those who win the victory I will give some of the hidden manna. I will also give each of them a white stone on which is written a new name that no one knows except the one who receives it.

COL. 3.3.—ROM. 6.2.—GAL. 2.19, 20.—
2 COR. 5.15.—2 COR. 5.17.—1 JOHN 5.20.—
JOHN 17.21.—1 COR. 12.27.—JOHN 14.19.—
REV. 2.17.

I will ask the Father, and he will give you another Helper,
who will stay with you for ever.

It is better for you that I go away, because if I do not go,
the Helper will not come to you.

God's Spirit joins himself to our spirits to declare that
we are God's children.—The Spirit that God has given you
does not make you slaves and cause you to be afraid;
instead, the Spirit makes you God's children, and by the
Spirit's power we cry out to God, "Father! my Father!"—
The Spirit also comes to help us, weak as we are. For we do
not know how we ought to pray; the Spirit himself pleads
with God for us in groans that words cannot express.

May God, the source of hope, fill you with all joy and
peace by means of your faith in him, so that your hope will
continue to grow by the power of the Holy Spirit.—Hope
does not disappoint us, for God has poured out his love
into our hearts by means of the Holy Spirit, who is God's
gift to us.

We are sure that we live in union with God and that he
lives in union with us, because he has given us his Spirit.

JOHN 14.16, 17.—JOHN 16.7.—ROM 8.16.—
ROM. 8.15.—ROM 8.26.—ROM. 15.13.—
ROM. 5.5.—1 JOHN 4.13.

The LORD's Covenant Box always went ahead of them to find a place for them to camp.

I am always in your care.—He chose for us the land where we live.—Lead me to do your will; make your way plain for me to follow.

Give yourself to the LORD; trust in him, and he will help you.—Remember the LORD in everything you do, and he will show you the right way.—If you wander off the road to the right or the left, you will hear his voice behind you saying, "Here is the road. Follow it."

The LORD is my shepherd; I have everything I need. He lets me rest in fields of green grass and leads me to quiet pools of fresh water.—As a father is kind to his children, so the LORD is kind to those who honour him. He knows what we are made of; he remembers that we are dust.—Your Father in heaven knows that you need all these things.—Leave all your worries with him, because he cares for you.

NUM. 10.33.—PS. 31.15.—PS. 47.4.—PS.5.8.—
PS. 37.5.—PROV. 3.6.—ISA. 30.21.—PS. 23.1, 2.—
PS. 103.13, 14.—MATT. 6.32.—1 PET. 5.7.

JUNE 25

*When Christ appears, we shall be like him, because we
shall see him as he really is.*

Some ... did receive him and believed in him; so he gave
them the right to become God's children.—In this way he
has given us the very great and precious gifts he promised,
so that by means of these gifts you may escape from the
destructive lust that is in the world, and may come to share
the divine nature.

No one has ever seen or heard of a God like you, who
does such deeds for those who put their hope in him.

What we see now is like a dim image in a mirror; then
we shall see face to face. What I know now is only partial;
then it will be complete – as complete as God's knowledge
of me.—Christ ... will change our weak mortal bodies and
make them like his own glorious body, using that power by
which he is able to bring all things under his rule.—I will
see you, because I have done no wrong; and when I awake,
your presence will fill me with joy.

1 JOHN 3.2.—JOHN 1.12.—2 PET. 1.4.—
ISA. 64.4.—1 COR. 13.12.—PHIL. 3.20, 21.—
PS. 17.15.

"Bless me, God ... be with me and keep me from anything evil that might cause me pain." And God gave him what he prayed for.

It is the LORD's blessing that makes you wealthy.—If God decided to do nothing at all, no one could criticize him. If he hid his face, men would be helpless.

Victory comes from the LORD – may he bless his people.—How wonderful are the good things you keep for those who honour you! Everyone knows how good you are, how securely you protect those who trust you.—I do not ask you to take them out of the world, but I do ask you to keep them safe from the Evil One.

Ask, and you will receive; seek, and you will find; knock, and the door will be opened to you. For everyone who asks will receive, and anyone who seeks will find, and the door will be opened to him who knocks.—The LORD will save his people; those who go to him for protection will be spared.

1 CHR. 4.10.—PROV. 10.22.—JOB 34.29.—
PS. 3.8.—PS. 31.19.—JOHN 17.15.—
MATT. 7.7, 8.—PS. 34.22.

Who can stand against it?

Who will be able to endure the day when he comes? Who will be able to survive when he appears? He will be like strong soap, like a fire that refines metal.

I looked, and there was an enormous crowd – no one could count all the people! They were from every race, tribe, nation, and language, and they stood in front of the throne and of the Lamb, dressed in white robes and holding palm branches in their hands. These are the people who have come safely through the terrible persecution. They have washed their robes and made them white with the blood of the Lamb. Never again will they hunger or thirst; neither sun nor any scorching heat will burn them, because the Lamb, who is in the centre of the throne, will be their shepherd, and he will guide them to springs of life-giving water. And God will wipe away every tear from their eyes.

There is no condemnation now for those who live in union with Christ Jesus.—Stand, then, as free people, and do not allow yourselves to become slaves again.

REV. 6.17.—MAL. 3.2.—REV. 7.9, 14, 16, 17.—
ROM. 8.1.—GAL. 5.1.

JUNE 28

I know there is someone in heaven who will come at last to my defence.

We were God's enemies, but he made us his friends through the death of his Son. Now that we are God's friends, how much more will we be saved by Christ's life!—But Jesus lives on for ever, and his work as priest does not pass on to someone else. And so he is able, now and always, to save those who come to God through him, because he lives for ever to plead with God for them.

Because I live, you also will live.—If our hope in Christ is good for this life only and no more, then we deserve more pity than anyone else in all the world. But the truth is that Christ has been raised from death, as the guarantee that those who sleep in death will also be raised.

The LORD says to his people, "I will come to Jerusalem to defend you and to save all of you that turn from your sins."—For by the sacrificial death of Christ we are set free, that is, our sins are forgiven. How great is the grace of God!—For you know what was paid to set you free from the worthless manner of life handed down by your ancestors. It was not something that can be destroyed, such as silver or gold; it was the costly sacrifice of Christ, who was like a lamb without defect or flaw.

JOB 19.25.—ROM. 5.10.—HEB. 7.24, 25.—
JOHN 14.19.—1 COR. 15.19, 20.—ISA. 59.20.—
EPH. 1.7.—1 PET. 1.18, 19.

194

His commands are not too hard for us.

For what my Father wants is that all who see the Son and believe in him should have eternal life.—We receive from him whatever we ask, because we obey his commands and do what pleases him.

The yoke I will give you is easy, and the load I will put on you is light.—If you love me, you will obey my commandments. Whoever accepts my commandments and obeys them is the one who loves me. My Father will love whoever loves me; I too will love him and reveal myself to him.

Happy is the man who becomes wise – who gains understanding. Wisdom can make your life pleasant and lead you safely through it.—Those who love your law have perfect security, and there is nothing that can make them fall.—My inner being delights in the law of God.

What he commands is that we believe in his Son Jesus Christ and love one another, just as Christ commanded us.—If you love someone, you will never do him wrong; to love, then, is to obey the whole Law.

1 JOHN 5.3.—JOHN 6.40.—1 JOHN 3.22.—
MATT. 11.30.—JOHN 14.15, 21.—PROV. 3.13, 17.—
PS. 119.165.—ROM. 7.22.—1 JOHN 3.23.—
ROM. 13.10.

I rebuke and punish all whom I love.

My son, pay attention when the Lord corrects you, and do not be discouraged when he rebukes you. Because the Lord corrects everyone he loves, and punishes everyone he accepts as a son.—As a father corrects a son of whom he is proud.—God bandages the wounds he makes; his hand hurts you, and his hand heals.—Humble yourselves, then, under God's mighty hand, so that he will lift you up in his own good time.—I have tested you in the fire of suffering.

He takes no pleasure in causing us grief or pain.—He does not punish us as we deserve or repay us according to our sins and wrongs. As high as the sky is above the earth, so great is his love for those who honour him. As far as the east is from the west, so far does he remove our sins from us. As a father is kind to his children, so the LORD is kind to those who honour him. He knows what we are made of; he remembers that we are dust.

REV. 3.19.—HEB. 12.5, 6.—PROV. 3.12.—
JOB 5.18.—1 PET. 5.6.—ISA. 48.10.—
LAM. 3.33.—PS. 103.10-14.

JULY 1

The Spirit produces goodness.

Since you are God's dear children, you must try to be like him.—Love your enemies and pray for those who persecute you, so that you may become the sons of your Father in heaven. For he makes his sun to shine on bad and good people alike, and gives rain to those who do good and to those who do evil.—Be merciful just as your Father is merciful.

It is the light that brings a rich harvest of every kind of goodness, righteousness, and truth.

When the kindness and love of God our Saviour was revealed, he saved us. It was not because of any good deeds that we ourselves had done, but because of his own mercy that he saved us, through the Holy Spirit, who gives us new birth and new life by washing us. God poured out the Holy Spirit abundantly on us through Jesus Christ our Saviour.— He is good to everyone and has compassion on all he made.—God, who did not even keep back his own Son, but offered him for us all! He gave us his Son – will he not also freely give us all things?

GAL. 5.22.—EPH. 5.1.—MATT. 5.44, 45.—
LUKE 6.36.—EPH. 5.9.—TITUS 3.4–6.—
PS. 145.9.—ROM. 8.32.

*These are the Passover regulations: no foreigner shall eat the
Passover meal.*

The priests who serve in the Jewish place of worship have
no right to eat any of the sacrifice on our altar.—No one
can see the Kingdom of God unless he is born again.—At
that time you were apart from Christ. You were foreigners
and did not belong to God's chosen people. You had no
part in the covenants, which were based on God's promises
to his people. But now, in union with Christ Jesus, you who
used to be far away have been brought near by the sacrificial
death of Christ.

For Christ himself has brought us peace by making Jews
and Gentiles one people. With his own body he broke down
the wall ... that kept them enemies. He abolished the Jewish
Law ... in order to create out of the two races one new
people in union with himself, in this way making peace.

So then, you Gentiles are not foreigners or strangers
any longer; you are now fellow-citizens with God's people
and members of the family of God.

If anyone hears my voice and opens the door, I will
come into his house and eat with him, and he will eat with
me.

EXOD. 12.43.—HEB. 13.10.—JOHN 3.3.—
EPH. 2.12, 13.—EPH. 2.14, 15.—
EPH. 2.19.—REV. 3.20.

Since we are his children, we will possess the blessings he keeps for his people, and we will also possess with Christ what God has kept for him.

If you belong to Christ, then you are the descendants of Abraham and will receive what God has promised.

See how much the Father has loved us! His love is so great that we are called God's children.—You are no longer a slave but a son. And since you are his son, God will give you all that he has for his sons.—God had already decided that through Jesus Christ he would make us his sons – this was his pleasure and purpose.

Father! I want them to be with me where I am, so that they may see my glory, the glory you gave me.

To those who win the victory, who continue to the end to do what I want ... I will give them authority over the nations.—To those who win the victory I will give the right to sit beside me on my throne, just as I have been victorious and now sit by my Father on his throne.

ROM. 8.17.—GAL. 3.29.—1 JOHN 3.1.—GAL. 4.7.—
EPH. 1.5.—JOHN 17.24.—REV. 2.26.—REV. 3.21.

Sitting next to Jesus.

I will comfort you … as a mother comforts her child.—
Some people brought children to Jesus for him to place his
hands on them. He took the children in his arms, placed his
hands on each of them, and blessed them.—Jesus called his
disciples to him and said, "I feel sorry for these people,
because they have been with me for three days and now
have nothing to eat. I don't want to send them away without
feeding them, for they might faint on their way home."—
Our High Priest is not one who cannot feel sympathy for
our weaknesses.—In his love and compassion he rescued
them.

When I go, you will not be left alone; I will come back
to you.—Can a woman forget her own baby and not love
the child she bore? Even if a mother should forget her child,
I will never forget you.

The Lamb, who is in the centre of the throne, will be
their shepherd, and he will guide them to springs of life-giving water. And God will wipe away every tear from their
eyes.

JOHN 13.23.—ISA. 66.13.—MARK 10.13, 16.—
MATT. 15.32.—HEB. 4.15.—ISA. 63.9.—
JOHN 14.18.—ISA. 49.15.—REV. 7.17.

We ourselves know and believe the love which God has for us.

God's mercy is so abundant, and his love for us is so great, that while we were spiritually dead in our disobedience he brought us to life with Christ. It is by God's grace that you have been saved. In our union with Christ Jesus he raised us up with him to rule with him in the heavenly world. He did this to demonstrate for all time to come the extraordinary greatness of his grace in the love he showed us in Christ Jesus.

God loved the world so much that he gave his only Son, so that everyone who believes in him may not die but have eternal life.—God, who did not even keep back his own Son, but offered him for us all ... will he not also freely give us all things?—He is good to everyone and has compassion on all he made.

We love because God first loved us.—How happy you are to believe that the Lord's message to you will come true!

1 JOHN 4.16.—EPH. 2.4–7.—JOHN 3.16.—
ROM. 8.32.—PS. 145.9.—1 JOHN 4.19.—
LUKE 1.45.

Your speech should always be pleasant and interesting.

An idea well-expressed is like a design of gold, set in silver. A warning given by an experienced person to someone willing to listen is more valuable than gold rings or jewellery made of the finest gold.—Do not use harmful words, but only helpful words, the kind that build up and provide what is needed, so that what you say will do good to those who hear you.—A good person brings good things out of his treasure of good things; a bad person brings bad things out of his treasure of bad things. Your words will be used to judge you.—Wisely spoken words can heal.

The people who feared the LORD spoke to one another, and the LORD listened and heard what they said. In his presence, there was written down in a book a record of those who feared the LORD and respected him.

If instead of talking nonsense you proclaim a worth-while message, you will be my prophet again.—You are so rich in all you have: in faith, speech, and knowledge, in your eagerness to help ... so we want you to be generous also in this service of love.

COL. 4.6.—PROV. 25.11, 12.—EPH. 4.29.—
MATT. 12.35, 37.—PROV. 12.18.—MAL. 3.16.—
JER. 15.19.—2 COR. 8.7.

JULY 7

Then the Spirit led Jesus into the desert to be tempted by the Devil.

In his life on earth Jesus made his prayers and requests with loud cries and tears to God, who could save him from death. Because he was humble and devoted, God heard him. But even though he was God's Son, he learnt through his sufferings to be obedient. When he was made perfect, he became the source of eternal salvation for all those who obey him.—Our High Priest is not one who cannot feel sympathy for our weakness. [He] was tempted in every way that we are, but did not sin.

Every test that you have experienced is the kind that normally comes to people. But God keeps his promise, and he will not allow you to be tested beyond your power to remain firm; at the time you are put to the test, he will give you the strength to endure it, and so provide you with a way out.—My grace is all you need, for my power is greatest when you are weak.

MATT. 4.1.—HEB. 5.7–9.—HEB. 4.15.—
1 COR. 10.13.—2 COR. 12.9.

203

If we confess our sins to God, he will keep his promise. He will forgive us our sins and purify us from all our wrongdoing.

I recognize my faults; I am always conscious of my sins. I have sinned against you – only against you – and done what you consider evil.

He got up and started back to his father. He was still a long way from home when his father saw him; his heart was filled with pity, and he ran, threw his arms round his son, and kissed him.—I have swept your sins away like a cloud. Come back to me; I am the one who saves you.—Your sins are forgiven for the sake of Christ.—God has forgiven you through Christ.—God shows that he himself is righteous and that he puts right everyone who believes in Jesus.

I will sprinkle clean water on you and make you clean.— You will walk with me, clothed in white, because you are worthy to do so.

Jesus Christ is the one who came with the water of his baptism and the blood of his death. He came not only with the water, but with both the water and the blood.

1 JOHN 1.9.—PS. 51.3, 4.—LUKE 15.20.—
ISA. 44.22.—1 JOHN 2.12.—EPH. 4.32.—
ROM. 3.26.—EZEK. 36.25.—REV. 3.4.—1 JOHN 5.6.

I have taken away your sin and will give you new clothes to wear.

Happy are those whose sins are forgiven, whose wrongs are pardoned.—All of us have been sinful; even our best actions are filthy through and through.—I know that good does not live in me – that is, in my human nature. For even though the desire to do good is in me, I am not able to do it.

You were baptized into union with Christ, and now you are clothed ... with the life of Christ.—You have taken off the old self with its habits and have put on the new self. This is the new being which God, its Creator, is constantly renewing in his own image.—I no longer have a righteousness of my own ... gained by obeying the Law. I now have the righteousness that is given through faith in Christ.

Bring the best robe and put it on him.—The linen is the good deeds of God's people.—Jerusalem rejoices because of what the LORD has done. She is like a bride dressed for her wedding. God has clothed her with salvation and victory.

ZECH. 3.4.—PS. 32.1.—ISA. 64.6.—ROM. 7.18.—
GAL. 3.27.—COL. 3.9, 10.—PHIL. 3.9.—
LUKE 15.22.—REV. 19.8.—ISA. 61.10.

JULY 10

No pupil is greater than his teacher.

You call me Teacher and Lord, and it is right that you do so, because that is what I am.

A pupil should be satisfied to become like his teacher, and a slave like his master.—If they persecuted me, they will persecute you too; if they obeyed my teaching, they will obey yours too.—I gave them your message, and the world hated them, because they do not belong to the world, just as I do not belong to the world.

Think of what he went through; how he put up with so much hatred from sinners! So do not let yourselves become discouraged and give up. For in your struggle against sin you have not yet had to resist to the point of being killed.

Let us run with determination the race that lies before us. Let us keep our eyes fixed on Jesus, on whom our faith depends from beginning to end. He did not give up because of the cross! On the contrary, because of the joy that was waiting for him, he thought nothing of the disgrace of dying on the cross, and he is now seated at the right-hand side of God's throne.—Since Christ suffered physically, you too must strengthen yourselves with the same way of thinking that he had.

MATT. 10.24.—JOHN 13.13.—MATT. 10.25.—
JOHN 15.20.—JOHN 17.14.—HEB. 12.3, 4.—
HEB. 12.1, 2.—1 PET. 4.1.

I will be with you to protect you and keep you safe.

Can you take away a soldier's loot? Can you rescue the prisoners of a tyrant? The LORD replies. "That is just what is going to happen. The soldier's prisoners will be taken away, and the tyrant's loot will be seized. I will fight against whoever fights you. Then all mankind will know that I am the LORD, the one who saves you and sets you free. They will know that I am Israel's powerful God." —Do not be afraid – I am with you! I am your God – let nothing terrify you! I will make you strong and help you; I will protect you and save you.

Our High Priest is not one who cannot feel sympathy for our weaknesses ... we have a High Priest who was tempted in every way that we are, but did not sin.—Now he can help those who are tempted, because he himself was tempted and suffered.—The LORD guides a man in the way he should go and protects those who please him. If they fall, they will not stay down, because the LORD will help them up.

JER. 15.20.—ISA. 49.24-26.—ISA. 41.10.—
HEB. 4.15.—HEB. 2.18.—PS. 37.23, 24.

JULY 12

I will go with you, and I will give you victory.

Be determined and confident. Do not be afraid of them. Your God, the LORD himself, will be with you. He will not fail you or abandon you. The LORD himself will lead you and be with you. He will not fail you or abandon you, so do not lose courage or be afraid.—Remember that I have commanded you to be determined and confident! Don't be afraid or discouraged, for I, the LORD your God, am with you wherever you go.—Remember the LORD in everything you do, and he will show you the right way.

God has said, "I will never leave you; I will never abandon you." Let us be bold, then, and say, "The Lord is my helper, I will not be afraid. What can anyone do to me?"—The capacity we have comes from God.

Do not bring us to hard testing.—LORD, I know that no one is the master of his own destiny; no person has control over his own life.—I am always in your care.

EXOD. 33.14.—DEUT. 31.6, 8.—JOSH. 1.9.—
PROV. 3.6.—HEB. 13.5, 6.—2 COR. 3.5.—
MATT. 6.13.—JER. 10.23.—PS. 31.15.

I belong to my lover, and he desires me.

I know whom I have trusted, and I am sure that he is able to keep safe until that Day what he has entrusted to me.—I am certain that nothing can separate us from his love: neither death nor life, neither angels nor other heavenly rulers or powers, neither the present nor the future, neither the world above nor the world below – there is nothing in all creation that will ever be able to separate us from the love of God which is ours through Christ Jesus our Lord.—I protected [those you have given me] and not one of them was lost.

The LORD takes pleasure in his people.—Pleased with the human race.—His love for us is so great.—The greatest love a person can have for his friends is to give his life for them.

He bought you for a price. So use your body for God's glory.—If we live, it is for the Lord that we live, and if we die, it is for the Lord that we die. So whether we live or die, we belong to the Lord.

S. OF S. 7.10.—2 TIM. 1.12.—ROM. 8.38, 39.—
JOHN 17.12.—PS. 149.4.—PRO¹ . 8.31.—
EPH. 2.4.—JOHN 15.13.—1 COR. 6.20.—
ROM. 14.8.

The mouth speaks what the heart is full of.

Christ's message in all its richness must live in your hearts.

Be careful how you think; your life is shaped by your thoughts.—What you say can preserve life or destroy it.—A good man's words are wise, and he is always fair. He keeps the law of his God in his heart and never departs from it.—Do not use harmful words, but only helpful words, the kind that build up and provide what is needed, so that what you say will do good to those who hear you.

We cannot stop speaking of what we ourselves have seen and heard.—I kept on believing, even when I said, "I am completely crushed."

If anyone declares publicly that he belongs to me, I will do the same for him before my Father in heaven.—It is by our faith that we are put right with God; it is by our confession that we are saved.

MATT. 12.34.—COL. 3.16.—PROV. 4.23.—
PROV. 18.21.—PS. 37.30, 31.—EPH. 4.29.—
ACTS 4.20.—PS. 116.10.—MATT. 10.32.—
ROM. 10.10.

May your will be done on earth as it is in heaven.

Praise the LORD, you strong and mighty angels, who obey his commands, who listen to what he says. Praise the LORD, all you heavenly powers, you servants of his, who do his will!

I have come down from heaven not to do my own will but the will of him who sent me.—How I love to do you will, my God! I keep your teaching in my heart.—My Father, if this cup of suffering cannot be taken away unless I drink it, your will be done.

Not everyone who calls me "Lord, Lord" will enter the Kingdom of heaven, but only those who do what my Father in heaven wants them to do.—It is not by hearing the Law that people are put right with God, but by doing what the Law commands.—Now that you know this truth, how happy you will be if you put it into practice!—The person who does not do the good he knows he should do is guilty of sin.

Do not conform yourselves to the standards of this world, but let God transform you inwardly by a complete change of your mind.

MATT. 6.10.—PS. 103.20, 21.—JOHN 6.38.—
PS. 40.8.—MATT. 26.42.—MATT. 7.21.—
ROM. 2.13.—JOHN 13.17.—JAS 4.17.—ROM 12.2.

JULY 16

You will be … a people dedicated to me alone, and you will serve me as priests.

You were killed, and by your sacrificial death you bought for God people from every tribe, language, nation, and race. You have made them a kingdom of priests to serve our God.—You are the chosen race, the King's priests, the holy nation, God's own people, chosen to proclaim the wonderful acts of God, who called you out of darkness into his own marvellous light.

You will be known as the priests of the LORD, the servants of our God.—Priests of God and of Christ.

My Christian brothers, who also have been called by God! Think of Jesus, whom God sent to be the High Priest of the faith we profess.—Let us, then, always offer praise to God as our sacrifice through Jesus, which is the offering presented by lips that confess him as Lord.

God has made us what we are, and in our union with Christ Jesus he has created us for a life of good deeds, which he has already prepared for us to do.—God's temple is holy, and you yourselves are his temple.

EXOD. 19.5, 6.—REV. 5.9, 10.—1 PET. 2.9.—
ISA. 61.6.—REV. 20.6.—HEB. 3.1.—HEB. 13.15.—
EPH. 2.10.—1 COR. 3.17.

*You are a loving and merciful God, always patient, always
kind, and always ready to change your mind and not punish.*

Now LORD, I pray, show us your power and do what you
promised when you said, "I, the LORD, am not easily angered, and I show great love and faithfulness and forgive
sin and rebellion. Yet I will not fail to punish children and
grandchildren to the third and fourth generation for the sins
of their parents."

Do not punish us for the sins of our ancestors. Have
mercy on us now; we have lost all hope. Help us, O God,
and save us; rescue us and forgive our sins for the sake of
your own honour.—Even though our sins accuse us, help
us, LORD, as you have promised. We have turned away from
you many times; we have sinned against you.—We have
sinned against you, LORD; we confess our own sins and the
sins of our ancestors.

If you kept a record of our sins, who could escape being
condemned? But you forgive us, so that we should stand in
awe of you.

JONAH 4.2.—NUM. 14.17, 18.—PS. 79.8, 9.—
JER. 14.7.—JER. 14.20.—PS. 130.3, 4.

JULY 18

He calls his own sheep by name, and he leads them out.

The solid foundation that God has laid cannot be shaken; and on it are written these words: "The Lord knows those who are his" and "Whoever says that he belongs to the Lord must turn away from wrongdoing."—When Judgement Day comes, many will say to me, "Lord, Lord! In your name we spoke God's message, by your name we drove out many demons and performed many miracles!" Then I will say to them, "I never knew you. Get away from me, you wicked people!"—The righteous are guided and protected by the LORD, but the evil are on the way to their doom.

I can never forget you! I have written your name on the palms of my hands. —Close your heart to every love but mine; hold no one in your arms but me.—The LORD is good; he protects his people in times of trouble; he takes care of those who turn to him.

I am going to prepare a place for you. And after I go and prepare a place for you, I will come back and take you to myself, so that you will be where I am.

JOHN 10.3.—2 TIM. 2.19.—MATT. 7.22, 23.—
PS. 1.6.—ISA. 49.16.—S. OF S. 8.6.—
NAHUM 1.7.—JOHN 14.2, 3.

JULY 19

The great things the Mighty God has done for me. His name is holy.

Lord, who among the gods is like you? Who is like you, wonderful in holiness? Who can work miracles and mighty acts like yours?—There is no god like you, O Lord, not one has done what you have done.—Who will not stand in awe of you, Lord? Who will refuse to declare your greatness? You alone are holy.—May your holy name be honoured.

Let us praise the Lord, the God of Israel! He has come to the help of his people and has set them free.

Who is this coming from the city of Bozrah in Edom? Who is this so splendidly dressed in red, marching along in power and strength? It is the Lord, powerful to save, coming to announce his victory.—I have given the throne to one I chose from the people.

To him who by means of his power working in us is able to do so much more than we can ever ask for, or even think of: to God be the glory.

LUKE 1.49.—EXOD.15.11.—PS. 86.8.—
REV. 15.4.—MATT. 6.9.—LUKE 1.68.—ISA. 63.1.—
PS. 89.19.—EPH. 3.20, 21.

215

JULY 20

Just as I do not belong to the world, they do not belong to the world.

We despised him and rejected him; he endured suffering and pain.—Be glad that you are sharing Christ's sufferings, so that you may be full of joy when his glory is revealed.

Jesus ... is the High Priest that meets our needs. He is holy; he has no fault or sin in him; he has been set apart from sinners.—So that you may be innocent and pure as God's perfect children, who live in a world of corrupt and sinful people.

Jesus of Nazareth ... went everywhere, doing good and healing all who were under the power of the Devil, for God was with him.—As often as we have the chance, we should do good to everyone, and especially to those who belong to our family in the faith.

This was the real light – the light that comes into the world and shines on all mankind.—You are like light for the whole world. A city built on a hill cannot be hidden. In the same way your light must shine before people, so that they will see the good things you do and praise your Father in heaven.

JOHN 17.16.—ISA. 53.3.—1 PET. 4.13.—
HEB. 7.26.—PHIL. 2.15.—ACTS 10.38.—
GAL. 6.10.—JOHN 1.9.—MATT. 5.14, 16.

JULY 21

Is there any value in being circumcised?

Much, indeed, in every way!—Keep your covenant with me, your LORD, and dedicate yourselves to me.—At last, when your descendants are humbled and they have paid the penalty for their sin and rebellion, I will remember my covenant with Jacob and with Isaac and with Abraham.

Christ's life of service was on behalf of the Jews, to show that God is faithful, to make his promises to their ancestors come true.—In union with Christ you were circumcised, not with the circumcision that is made by men, but with the circumcision made by Christ.—You were at one time spiritually dead because of your sins and because you were Gentiles without the Law. But God has now brought you to life with Christ. God forgave us all our sins.

Get rid of your old self, which made you live as you used to – the old self that was being destroyed by its deceitful desires. Your hearts and minds must be made completely new, and you must put on the new self, which is created in God's likeness and reveals itself in the true life that is upright and holy.

ROM. 3.1.—ROM. 3.2.—JER. 4.4.—
LEV. 26.41, 42.—ROM. 15.8.—COL. 2.11.—
COL. 2.13.—EPH. 4.22-24.

*Because he died, sin has no power over him; and now he
lives his life in fellowship with God.*

He … shared the fate of evil men.—Christ also was offered
in sacrifice once to take away the sins of many.—Christ
Himself carried our sins in His body to the cross, so that
we might die to sin and live to righteousness.—With one
sacrifice, then, he has made perfect for ever those who are
purified from sin.

Jesus lives on for ever, and his work as priest does not
pass on to someone else. And so he is able, now and always,
to save those who come to God through him, because he
lives for ever to plead with God for them.—It was while we
were still sinners that Christ died for us! By his sacrificial
death we are now put right with God; how much more,
then, will we be saved by him from God's anger!

Since Christ suffered physically, you too must
strengthen yourselves with the same way of thinking that
he had; because whoever suffers physically is no longer
involved with sin. From now on, then, you must live the
rest of your earthly lives controlled by God's will and not
by human desires.

ROM. 6.10.—ISA. 53.12.—HEB. 9.28.—
1 PET. 2.24.—HEB. 10.14.—HEB. 7.24, 25.—
ROM. 5.8, 9.—1 PET 4.1, 2.

Then the end will come.

No one knows, however, when that day or hour will come
– neither the angels in heaven, nor the Son; only the Father
knows. Be on watch, be alert, for you do not know when
the time will come. What I say to you, then, I say to all.
Watch!—The Lord is not slow to do what he has promised,
as some think. Instead, he is patient with you, because he
does not want anyone to be destroyed, but wants all to turn
away from their sins.—The day of the Lord's coming is
near. The Judge is near, ready to appear.—Yes indeed! I am
coming soon!

Since all these things will be destroyed in this way, what
kind of people should you be? Your lives would be holy and
dedicated to God.

The end of all things is near. You must be self-controlled and alert, to be able to pray.—Be ready for whatever
comes, dressed for action and with your lamps lit, like
servants who are waiting for their master to come back
from a wedding feast. When he comes and knocks, they will
open the door for him at once.

COR. 15.24.—MARK 13.32, 33, 37.—2 PET. 3.9.—
JAS 5.8, 9.—REV. 22.20.—2 PET. 3.11.—
1 PET. 4.7.—LUKE 12.35, 36.

Be patient in your troubles.

He is the LORD; he will do whatever seems best to him.—
Though I am innocent, all I can do is beg for mercy from
God my judge.—The LORD gave, and now he has taken
away. May his name be praised!—When God sends us
something good, we welcome it. How can we complain
when he sends us trouble?

Jesus wept.—He endured suffering and pain. But he
endured the suffering that should have been ours, the pain
that we should have borne.

The Lord corrects everyone he loves, and punishes
everyone he accepts as a son. When we are punished, it
seems to us at the time something to make us sad, not glad.
Later, however, those who have been disciplined by such
punishment reap the peaceful reward of a righteous life.—
May you be made strong with all the strength which comes
from his glorious power, so that you may be able to endure
everything with patience.—The world will make you suffer.
But be brave! I have defeated the world!

ROM. 12.12.—1 SAM. 3.18.—JOB 9.15.—
JOB 1.21.—JOB 2.10.—JOHN 11.35.—
ISA. 53.3, 4.—HEB.12.6, 11.—COL. 1.11.—
JOHN 16.33.

We know that we have left death and come over into life.

Whoever hears my words and believes in him who sent me has eternal life. He will not be judged, but has already passed from death to life.—Whoever has the Son has this life; whoever does not have the Son of God does not have life.

It is God himself who makes us, together with you, sure of our life in union with Christ; it is God himself who has set us apart, who has placed his mark of ownership upon us, and who has given us the Holy Spirit in our hearts as the guarantee of all that he has in store for us.—This, then, is how we will know that we belong to the truth; this is how we will be confident in God's presence. My dear friends, if our conscience does not condemn us, we have courage in God's presence.—We know that we belong to God even though the whole world is under the rule of the Evil One.

You were spiritually dead because of your disobedience and sins. He brought us to life with Christ.—He rescued us from the power of darkness and brought us safe into the kingdom of his dear Son.

1 JOHN 3.14.—JOHN 5.24.—1 JOHN 5.12.—
2 COR. 1.21, 22.—1 JOHN 3.19, 21.—
1 JOHN 5.19.—EPH. 2.1, 5.—COL. 1.13.

*It was faith that made Abraham obey when God called him
to go out to a country which God had promised to give him.*

He chose for us the land where we live.—He protected
them and cared for them, as he would protect himself. Like
an eagle teaching its young to fly, catching them safely on
its spreading wings, the LORD kept Israel from falling. The
LORD alone led his people without the help of a foreign god.

I am the LORD your God, the one who wants to teach
you for your own good and direct you in the way you should
go.—He is the greatest teacher of all.

Our life is a matter of faith, not of sight.—There is no
permanent city for us here on earth; we are looking for the
city which is to come.—I appeal to you, my friends, as
strangers and refugees in this world! Do not give in to bodily
passions, which are always at war against the soul.—Get up
and go; there is no safety here any more.

HEB. 11.8.—PS. 47.4.—DEUT. 32.10-12.—
ISA. 48.17.—JOB 36.22.—2 COR. 5.7.—
HEB. 13.14.—1 PET. 2.11.—MIC. 2.10.

Christ, who is the exact likeness of God.

The glory of the LORD will be revealed, and all mankind will see it.—No one has ever seen God. The only Son, who is the same as God and is at the Father's side, he has made him known. The Word became a human being and, full of grace and truth, lived among us. We saw his glory, the glory which he received as the Father's only Son.—Whoever has seen me has seen the Father.—He reflects the brightness of God's glory and is the exact likeness of God's own being.—He appeared in human form.

By whom we are set free, that is, our sins are forgiven. Christ is the visible likeness of the invisible God. He is the first-born Son, superior to all created things.—Those whom God had already chosen he also set apart to become like his Son, so that the Son would be the first among many brothers.

Just as we wear the likeness of the man made of earth, so we will wear the likeness of the Man from heaven.

2 COR. 4.4.—ISA. 40.5.—JOHN 1.18, 14.—
JOHN 14.9.—HEB. 1.3.—1 TIM. 3.16.—
COL. 1.14, 15.—ROM. 8.29.—1 COR. 15.49.

Your life must be controlled by love.

Now I give you a new commandment: love one another. As I have loved you, so you must love one another.— Above everything, love one another earnestly, because love covers over many sins.—Love overlooks all offences.

When you stand and pray, forgive anything you may have against anyone, so that your Father in heaven will forgive the wrongs you have done.—Love your enemies and do good to them; lend and expect nothing back.— Don't be glad when your enemy meets disaster, and don't rejoice when he stumbles.—Do not pay back evil with evil or cursing with cursing; instead, pay back with a blessing, because a blessing is what God promised to give you when he called you.—Do everything possible on your part to live in peace with everybody.—Be kind and tender-hearted to one another, and forgive one another, as God has forgiven you through Christ.

My children, our love should not be just words and talk; it must be true love, which shows itself in action.

EPH. 5.2.—JOHN 13.34.—1 PET.4.8.—
PROV. 10.12.—MARK 11.25.—LUKE 6.35.—
PROV. 24.17.—1 PET. 3.9.—ROM. 12.18.—
EPH. 4.32.—JOHN 3.18.

Why don't you tear the sky apart and come down?

Come to me, my lover, like a gazelle, like a young stag on the mountains where spices grow.—We ... groan within ourselves, as we wait for God to make us his sons and set our whole being free.—O LORD, tear the sky apart and come down; touch the mountains, and they will pour out smoke.

This Jesus, who was taken from you into heaven, will come back in the same way that you saw him go to heaven. He will appear a second time, not to deal with sin, but to save those who are waiting for him.—When it happens, everyone will say, "He is our God! We have put our trust in him, and he has rescued us. He is the LORD! We have put our trust in him, and now we are happy and joyful because he has saved us."

He who gives his testimony to all this says, "Yes indeed! I am coming soon!" So be it. Come, Lord Jesus!—The blessed Day we hope for, when the glory of our great God and Saviour Jesus Christ will appear.—We ... are citizens of heaven.

ISA. 64.1.—S. OF S. 8.14.—ROM. 8.23.—
PS. 144.5.—ACTS 1.11.—HEB. 9.28.—ISA. 25.9.—
REV. 22.20.—TITUS 2.13.—PHIL. 3.20.

Set your hearts on the things that are in heaven, where Christ sits on his throne at the right-hand side of God.

Get wisdom and insight!—The wisdom from above.—The depths of the oceans and seas say that wisdom is not found there.—By our baptism ... we were buried with him and shared his death, in order that, just as Christ was raised from death by the glorious power of the Father, so also we might live a new life. For since we have become one with him in dying as he did, in the same way we shall be one with him by being raised to life as he was.

Let us rid ourselves of everything that gets in the way, and of the sin which holds on to us so tightly, and let us run with determination the race that lies before us.—God ... brought us to life with Christ. In our union with Christ Jesus he raised us up with him to rule with him in the heavenly world.

Those who say such things make it clear that they are looking for a country of their own.—Turn to the LORD, all you humble people of the land, who obey his commands. Do what is right, and humble yourselves before the LORD.

COL. 3.1.—PROV. 4.5.—JAS 3.17.—JOB 28.14.—
ROM. 6.4, 5.—HEB. 12.1.—EPH. 2.4-6.—
HEB. 11.14.—ZEPH. 2.3.

JULY 31

*Take your part in suffering, as a loyal soldier of
Christ Jesus.*

I made him a leader and commander of nations, and
through him I showed them my power.—It was only right
that God, who creates and preserves all things, should make
Jesus perfect through suffering, in order to bring many sons
to share his glory.—We must pass through many troubles
to enter the Kingdom of God.

We are not fighting against human beings but against
the wicked spiritual forces in the heavenly world, the rulers,
authorities, and cosmic powers of this dark age. So put on
God's armour now!—We do not fight from worldly
motives. The weapons we use in our fight are not the
world's weapons but God's powerful weapons, which we
use to destroy strongholds.

The God of all grace, who calls you to share his eternal
glory in union with Christ, will himself perfect you and give
you firmness, strength, and a sure foundation.

2 TIM. 2.3.—ISA. 55.4.—HEB. 2.10.—ACTS 14.22.—
EPH. 6.12, 13.—2 COR. 10.3, 4.—1 PET.5.10.

AUGUST 1

The Spirit produces ... faithfulness.

It is God's grace that you have been saved through faith. It is not the result of your own efforts, but God's gift.—No one can please God without faith.—Whoever believes in the Son is not judged; but whoever does not believe has already been judged, because he has not believed in God's only Son.—I do have faith, but not enough. Help me to have more!

Whoever obeys his word is the one whose love for God has really been made perfect. This is how we can be sure that we are in union with God.—Faith that works through love.—Faith without actions is useless.

Our life is a matter of faith, not of sight.—I have been put to death with Christ on his cross, so that it is no longer I who live, but it is Christ who lives in me. This life that I live now, I live by faith in the Son of God, who loved me and gave his life for me.—You love him, although you do not now see him. So you rejoice with a great and glorious joy which words cannot express, because you are receiving the salvation of your souls, which is the purpose of your faith in him.

GAL. 5.22.—EPH. 2.8.—HEB. 11.6.—JOHN 3.18.—
MARK 9.24.—1 JOHN 2.5.—GAL. 5.6.—JAS 2.20.—
2 COR. 5.7.—GAL. 2.19, 20.—1 PET. 1.8, 9.

August 2

The Lamb that was killed.

You may choose ... a sheep ... but it must be ... without any defects. On the evening ... the whole community of Israel will kill the animals. The people are to take some of the blood and put it on the door-posts and above the doors of the houses in which the animals are to be eaten. When I see the blood, I will pass over you.—The sprinkled blood.—Christ, our Passover lamb, has been sacrificed.—In accordance with his own plan God had already decided that Jesus would be handed over to you.—He saved us and called us ... because of his own purpose and grace. He gave us this grace by means of Christ Jesus before the beginning of time.

By the sacrificial death of Christ we are set free, that is, our sins are forgiven.

Since Christ suffered physically, you too must strengthen yourselves with the same way of thinking that he had; because whoever suffers physically is no longer involved with sin. From now on, then, you must live the rest of your earthly lives controlled by God's will and not by human desires.

REV. 13.8.—EXOD. 12.5—7, 13.—HEB. 12.24.—
1 COR. 5.7.—ACTS 2.23.—2 TIM. 1.9.—
EPH. 1.7.—1 PET. 4.1, 2.

AUGUST 3

He shows mercy to those who honour him.

How wonderful are the good things you keep for those who
honour you! Everyone knows how good you are, how
securely you protect those who trust you. You hide them in
the safety of your presence from the plots of men; in a safe
shelter you hide them from the insults of their enemies.

You call him Father, when you pray to God, who judges
all people by the same standard, according to what each one
has done; so then, spend the rest of your lives here on earth
in reverence for him.—He is near to those who call to him,
who call to him with sincerity. He supplies the needs of
those who honour him; he hears their cries and saves them.

You repented and humbled yourself before me, tearing
your clothes and weeping ... I have heard your prayer.—I
am pleased with those who are humble and repentant, who
fear me and obey me.—The LORD is near to those who are
discouraged; he saves those who have lost all hope.

LUKE 1.50.—PS. 31.19, 20.—1 PET. 1.17.—
PS. 145.18, 19.—2 KGS 22.19.—ISA. 66.2.—
PS. 34.18.

AUGUST 4

"It is finished!" Then he bowed his head and died.

Jesus, on whom our faith depends from beginning to end.—I have shown your glory on earth; I have finished the work you gave me to do.—We are all purified from sin by the offering that he made of his own body once and for all. Every Jewish priest performs his services every day and offers the same sacrifices many times; but these sacrifices can never take away sins. Christ, however, offered one sacrifice for sins, an offering that is effective for ever, and then he sat down at the right-hand side of God. There he now waits until God puts his enemies as a footstool under his feet. With one sacrifice, then, he has made perfect for ever those who are purified from sin.—He cancelled the unfavourable record of our debts with its binding rules and did away with it completely by nailing it to the cross.

I am willing to give up my life, in order that I may receive it back again. No one takes my life away from me. I give it up of my own free will. I have the right to give it up, and I have the right to take it back.—The greatest love a person can have for his friends is to give his life for them.

JOHN 19.30.—HEB. 12.2.—JOHN 17.4.—
HEB. 10.10–14.—COL. 2.14.—
JOHN 10.17, 18.—JOHN 15.13.

Live a new life.

At one time you surrendered yourselves entirely as slaves to impurity and wickedness for wicked purposes. In the same way you must now surrender yourselves entirely as slaves of righteousness for holy purposes.—My brothers, because of God's great mercy to us I appeal to you: Offer yourselves as a living sacrifice to God, dedicated to his service and pleasing to him. This is the true worship that you should offer. Do not conform yourselves to the standards of this world, but let God transform you inwardly by a complete change of your mind.

When anyone is joined to Christ, he is a new being; the old is gone, the new has come.—It does not matter at all whether or not one is circumcised; what does matter is being a new creature. As for those who follow this rule in their lives, may peace and mercy be with them.—In the Lord's name, then, I warn you: do not continue to live like the heathen, whose thoughts are worthless. That was not what you learnt about Christ! You certainly heard about him, and as his followers you were taught the truth that is in Jesus. Put on the new self, which is created in God's likeness and reveals itself in the true life that is upright and holy.

ROM. 6.4.—ROM. 6.19.—ROM. 12.1, 2.—
2 COR. 5.17.—GAL. 6.15, 16.—
EPH. 4.17, 20, 21, 24.

AUGUST 6

The LORD corrects those he loves.

I, and I alone, am God; no other god is real. I kill and I give life, I wound and I heal, and no one can oppose what I do.—[The LORD says] ... "I alone know the plans I have for you, plans to bring you prosperity and not disaster, plans to bring about the future you hope for."—"My thoughts," says the LORD, "are not like yours, and my ways are different from yours."

I am going to take her into the desert again; there I will win her back with words of love.—The LORD your God corrects and punishes you just as a father disciplines his children.—When you are punished, it seems to us at the time something to make us sad, not glad. Later, however, those who have been disciplined by such punishment reap the peaceful reward of a righteous life.—Humble yourselves, then, under God's mighty hand, so that he will lift you up in his own good time.

I know that your judgements are righteous, LORD, and that you punished me because you are faithful.

PROV. 3.12.—DEUT. 32.39.—JER. 29.11.—
ISA. 55.8.—HOS. 2.14.—DEUT. 8.5.—
HEB. 12.11.—1 PET. 5.6.—PS. 119.75.

233

The Helper, the Holy Spirit, whom the Father will send in my name.

If only you knew what God gives and who it is that is asking you for a drink, you would ask him, and he would give you life-giving water.—Bad as you are, you know how to give good things to your children. How much more, then, will the Father in heaven give the Holy Spirit to those who ask him!—I am telling you the truth: the Father will give you whatever you ask him for in my name. Until now you have not asked for anything in my name; ask and you will receive, so that your happiness may be complete.

When ... the Spirit comes, who reveals the truth about God, he will lead you into all the truth. He will not speak on his authority, but he will speak of what he hears, and will tell you of things to come. He will give me glory, because he will take what I say and tell it to you.

They rebelled against him and made his holy spirit sad. So the LORD became their enemy and fought against them.

JOHN 14.26.—JOHN 4.10.—LUKE 11.13.—
JOHN 16.23, 24.—JOHN 16.13, 14.—ISA. 63.10.

234

*The road the righteous travel is like the sunrise, getting
brighter and brighter until daylight has come.*

I do not claim that I have already succeeded or have already
become perfect. I keep striving to win the prize for which
Christ Jesus has already won me to himself.—Let us try to
know the LORD.

Then God's people will shine like the sun in their
Father's Kingdom.—All of us ... reflect the glory of the
Lord with uncovered faces; and that same glory, coming
from the Lord, who is the Spirit, transforms us into his
likeness in an ever greater degree of glory.—When what is
perfect comes, then what is partial will disappear. What we
see now is like a dim image in a mirror; then we shall see
face to face. What I know now is only partial; then it will be
complete – as complete as God's knowledge of me.

My dear friends, we are now God's children, but it is
not yet clear what we shall become. But we know that when
Christ appears, we shall be like him, because we shall see
him as he really is. Everyone who has this hope in Christ
keeps himself pure, just as Christ is pure.

PROV. 4.18.—PHIL. 3.12.—HOS. 6.3.—
MATT. 13.43.—2 COR. 3.18.—
1 COR. 13.10, 12.—1 JOHN 3.2, 3.

How beautiful you are, my love; how pefect you are!

Your head is already covered with wounds, and your heart and mind are sick. From head to foot there is not a healthy spot on your body. You are covered with bruises and sores and open wounds. Your wounds have not been cleaned or bandaged. No ointment has been put on them.—All of us have been sinful; even our best actions are filthy through and through.—I know that good does not live in me – that is, in my human nature.

You have been purified from sin; you have been dedicated to God; you have been put right with God by the Lord Jesus Christ and by the Spirit of our God.—The princess is in the palace – how beautiful she is!—"You became famous in every nation for your perfect beauty, because I was the one who made you so lovely." This is what the Sovereign LORD says.

LORD our God, may your blessings be with us.

They have washed their robes and made them white with the blood of the Lamb.—The church ... in all its beauty – pure and faultless, without spot or wrinkle or any other imperfection.—You have been given full life in union with him.

S. OF S. 4.7.—ISA. 1.5, 6.—ISA. 64.6.—
ROM. 7.18.—1 COR. 6.11.—PS. 45.13.—
EZEK. 16.14.—PS. 90.17.—REV. 7.14.—
EPH. 5.27.—COL. 2.10.

I do not ask you to take them out of the world, but I do ask you to keep them safe from the Evil One.

Innocent and pure as God's perfect children, who live in a world of corrupt and sinful people. You must shine among them like stars lighting up the sky.—You are like salt for all mankind. You are like light for the whole world. Your light must shine before people, so that they will see the good things you do and praise your Father in heaven.

I kept you from sinning against me.

The Lord is faithful, and he will strengthen you and keep you safe from the Evil One.—I acted differently, because I honoured God.—In order to set us free from this present evil age, Christ gave himself for our sins, in obedience to the will of our God and Father.—To him who is able to keep you from falling, and to bring you faultless and joyful before his glorious presence – to the only God our Saviour, through Jesus Christ our Lord, be glory, majesty, might, and authority, from all ages past, and now, and for ever and ever! Amen.

JOHN 17.15.—PHIL. 2.15.—MATT. 5.13, 14, 16.—
GEN. 20.6.—2 THESS. 3.3.—NEH. 5.15.—
GAL. 1.4.—JUDE 24, 25.

So that through his death he might destroy the Devil, who has the power over death.

Our Saviour, Christ Jesus … has ended the power of death and through the gospel has revealed immortal life.—The Sovereign LORD will destroy death for ever! He will wipe away the tears from everyone's eyes and take away the disgrace his people have suffered throughout the world. The LORD himself has spoken! —What will die must be changed into what cannot die. So when this takes place, and the mortal has been changed into the immortal, then the scripture will come true: "Death is destroyed; victory is complete!" "Where, Death, is your victory? Where, Death, is your power to hurt?" Death gets its power to hurt from sin, and sin gets its power from the Law. But thanks be to God who gives us the victory through our Lord Jesus Christ!

The Spirit that God has given us does not make us timid; instead, his Spirit fills us with power, love, and self-control.—Even if I go through the deepest darkness, I will not be afraid, LORD, for you are with me. Your shepherd's rod and staff protect me.

HEB. 2.14.—2 TIM. 1.10.—ISA. 25.8.—
1 COR. 15.53–57.—2 TIM. 1.7.—PS. 23.4.

The LORD ... will not reject us for ever. He may bring us sorrow, but his love for us is sure and strong.

My people, do not be afraid ... I will come to you and save you. I will not destroy you. When I punish you, I will be fair.—"For one brief moment I left you; with deep love I will take you back. I turned away angry for only a moment, but I will show you my love for ever." So says the LORD who saves you. "The mountains and hills may crumble, but my love for you will never end; I will keep for ever my promise of peace." So says the LORD who loves you.—O Jerusalem, you suffering, helpless city, with no one to comfort you, I will rebuilt your foundations with precious stones.

We have sinned against the LORD, so now we must endure his anger for a while. But in the end he will defend us and right the wrongs that have been done to us. He will bring us out to the light; we will live to see him save us.

LAM. 3.31, 32.—JER. 46.27, 28.—
ISA. 54.7, 8, 10.—ISA. 54.11.—MIC. 7.9.

AUGUST 13

He has prepared a city for them.

After I go and prepare a place for you, I will come back and take you to myself, so that you will be where I am.—Rich blessings that God keeps for his people. He keeps them for you in heaven, where they cannot decay or spoil or fade away.—There is no permanent city for us here on earth; we are looking for the city which is to come.

This Jesus, who was taken from you into heaven, will come back in the same way that you saw him go to heaven.—Be patient, then, my brothers, until the Lord comes. See how patient a farmer is as he waits for his land to produce precious crops. He waits patiently for the autumn and spring rains. You also must be patient. Keep your hopes high, for the day of the Lord's coming is near.—Just a little while longer, and he who is coming will come; he will not delay.

We who are living at that time will be gathered up along with them in the clouds to meet the Lord in the air. And so we will always be with the Lord. So then, encourage one another with these words.

HEB. 11.16.—JOHN 14.3.—1 PET. 1.4.—
HEB. 13.14.—ACTS 1.11.—JAS 5.7, 8.—
HEB. 10.37.—1 THESS. 4.17, 18.

AUGUST 14

The joy that the LORD gives you will make you strong.

Sing, heavens! Shout for joy, earth! Let the mountains burst into song! The LORD will comfort his people; he will have pity on his suffering people.—God is my saviour; I will trust him and not be afraid. The LORD gives me power and strength; he is my saviour.—The LORD protects and defends me; I trust in Him. He gives me help and makes me glad; I praise him with joyful songs.—Jerusalem rejoices because of what the LORD has done. She is like a bride dressed for her wedding. God has clothed her with salvation and victory.

In union with Christ Jesus, then, I can be proud of my service for God.—We rejoice because of what God has done through our Lord Jesus Christ, who has now made us God's friends.—I will still be joyful and glad, because the LORD God is my saviour

NEH. 8.10.—ISA. 49.13.—ISA. 12.2.—PS. 28.7.—
ISA. 61.10.—ROM. 15.17.—ROM. 5.11.—HAB. 3.18.

May the God of peace provide you with every good thing you need in order to do his will.

Strive for perfection; listen to my appeals; agree with one another; live in peace. And the God of love and peace will be with you.

It is by God's grace that you have been saved through faith. It is not the result of your own efforts, but God's gift, so that no one can boast about it.—Every good gift and every perfect present comes from heaven; it comes down from God, the Creator of the heavenly lights, who does not change or cause darkness by turning.

Keep on working with fear and trembling to complete your salvation, because God is always at work in you to make you willing and able to obey his own purpose.—Let God transform you inwardly by a complete change of your mind. Then you will be able to know the will of God – what is good and is pleasing to him and is perfect.—Your lives will be filled with the truly good qualities which only Jesus Christ can produce, for the glory and praise of God.

There is nothing in us that allows us to claim that we are capable of doing this work. The capacity we have comes from God.

HEB. 13.20, 21.—2 COR. 13.11.—EPH. 2.8, 9.—
JAS 1.17.—PHIL. 2.12, 13.—ROM. 12.2.—
PHIL. 1.11.—2 COR. 3.5.

AUGUST 16

The Temple that my son ... is to build must be splendid.

Come as living stones, and let yourselves be used in building the spiritual temple.—Surely you know that you are God's temple and that God's Spirit lives in you! So if anyone destroys God's temple, God will destroy him. For God's temple is holy, and you yourselves are his temple.—Don't you know that your body is the temple of the Holy Spirit, who lives in you and who was given to you by God? You do not belong to yourselves but to God; he bought you for a price. So use your bodies for God's glory.—How can God's temple come to terms with pagan idols? For we are the temple of the living God! As God himself has said, "I will make my home with my people and live among them; I will be their God, and they shall be my people."

You ... are built upon the foundation laid by the apostles and prophets, the cornerstone being Christ Jesus himself. He is the one who holds the whole building together and makes it grow into a sacred temple dedicated to the Lord. In union with him you too are being built together with all the others into a place where God lives through his Spirit.

1 CHR. 22.5.—1 PET. 2.5.—1 COR. 3.16, 17.—
1 COR. 6.19, 20.—2 COR. 6.16.—EPH. 2.20-22.

Pray for one another, so that you will be healed.

Abraham spoke again: "Please forgive my boldness in continuing to speak to you, Lord. I am only a man and have no right to say anything. But perhaps there will be only forty-five innocent people instead of fifty. Will you destroy the whole city because there are five too few?" The LORD answered, "I will not destroy the city if I find forty-five innocent people."

Forgive them, Father! They don't know what they are doing.—Pray for those who persecute you.

I pray for them. I do not pray for the world but for those you gave me, for they belong to you. I pray not only for them, but also for those who believe in me because of their message.—Help to carry one another's burdens, and in this way you will obey the law of Christ.

The prayer of a good person has a powerful effect. Elijah was the same kind of person as we are. He prayed earnestly that there would be no rain, and no rain fell on the land for three and a half years.

JAS 5.16.—GEN. 18.27, 28.—LUKE 23.34.—
MATT. 5.44.—JOHN 17.9, 20.—GAL. 6.2.—
JAS 5.16, 17.

There is no god in heaven or on earth who can do the mighty things that you have done!

No one in heaven is like you, LORD; none of the heavenly beings is your equal. LORD God Almighty, none is as mighty as you; in all things you are faithful, O LORD.—There is no god like you, O Lord, not one has done what you have done.—It was your will and purpose to do this; you have done all these great things in order to teach me. How great you are, Sovereign LORD! There is none like you; we have always known that you alone are God.

What no one ever saw or heard, what no one ever thought could happen, is the very thing God prepared for those who love him. But it was to us that God made known his secret by means of his Spirit.—There are some things that the LORD our God has kept secret; but he has revealed his Law, and we and our descendants are to obey it for ever.

DEUT. 3.24.—PS. 89.6, 8.—PS. 86.8.—
2 SAM. 7.21, 22.—1 COR. 2.9, 10.—DEUT. 29.29.

245

Be holy in all that you do, just as God who called you is holy.

You know that ... we encouraged you, we comforted you, and we kept urging you to live the kind of life that pleases God, who calls you to share in his own Kingdom and glory.—You are ... chosen to proclaim the wonderful acts of God, who called you out of darkness into his own marvellous light.

You yourselves used to be in the darkness, but since you have become the Lord's people, you are in the light. So you must live like people who belong to the light, for it is the light that brings a rich harvest of every kind of goodness, righteousness, and truth. Try to learn what pleases the Lord. Have nothing to do with the worthless things that people do, things that belong to the darkness. Instead, bring them out to the light.—Your lives will be filled with the truly good qualities which only Jesus Christ can produce, for the glory and praise of God.

Your light must shine before people, so that they will see the good things you do and praise your Father in heaven.—Whatever you do, whether you eat or drink, do it all for God's glory.

1 PET. 1.15.—1 THESS. 2.11, 12.—1 PET. 2.9.—
EPH. 5.8-11.—PHIL. 1.11.—MATT. 5.16.—
1 COR. 10.31.

AUGUST 20

God is not like men, who lie; he is not a human who changes his mind.

God, the Creator of the heavenly lights, who does not change or cause darkness by turning.—Jesus Christ is the same yesterday, today, and for ever.

His faithfulness will protect and defend you.

To those who were to receive what he promised, God wanted to make it very clear that he would never change his purpose; so he added his vow to the promise. There are these two things, then, that cannot change and about which God cannot lie. So we who have found safety with him are greatly encouraged to hold firmly to the hope placed before us.

God is the only God and … he is faithful. He will keep his covenant and show his constant love to a thousand generations of those who love him and obey his commands.—With faithfulness and love he leads all who keep his covenant and obey his commands.—Happy is the man who has the God of Jacob to help him and who depends on the LORD his God … he always keeps his promises.

NUM. 23.19.—JAS 1.17.—HEB. 13.8.—
PS. 91.4.—HEB. 6.17, 18.—DEUT. 7.9.—
PS. 25.10.—PS. 146.5, 6.

You are all I want, O LORD.

Everything belongs to you ... and you belong to Christ, and Christ belongs to God.—Our great God and Saviour Jesus Christ ... gave himself for us.—God ... gave him to the church as supreme Lord over all things.—Christ loved the church and gave his life for it ... in order to present the church to himself in all its beauty – pure and faultless, without spot or wrinkle or any other imperfection.

I will praise him for what he has done.—Jerusalem rejoices because of what the LORD has done. She is like a bride dressed for her wedding. God has clothed her with salvation and victory.

What else have I in heaven but you? Since I have you, what else could I want on earth? My mind and my body may grow weak, but God is my strength; he is all I ever need.—I say to the LORD, "You are my Lord. You, LORD, are all I have, and you give me all I need; my future is in your hands. How wonderful are your gifts to me; how good they are!"

PS. 119.57.—1 COR. 3.21, 23.—TITUS 2.13, 14.—
EPH. 1.22.—EPH. 5.25, 27.—PS. 34.2.—
ISA. 61.10.—PS. 73.25, 26.—PS. 16.2, 5, 6.

None of us lives for himself only, none of us dies for himself only.

If we live, it is for the Lord that we live, and if we die, it is for the Lord that we die. So whether we live or die, we belong to the Lord.—No one should be looking to his own interests, but to the interests of others.—He bought you for a price. So use your bodies for God's glory.

With my whole being I shall bring honour to Christ, whether I live or die. For what is life? To me, it is Christ. Death, then, will bring more. But if by continuing to live I can do more worthwhile work, then I am not sure which I should choose. I am pulled in two directions. I want very much to leave this life and be with Christ, which is a far better thing.

So far as the Law is concerned ... I am dead – killed by the Law itself – in order that I might live for God. I have been put to death with Christ on his cross, so that it is no longer I who live, but it is Christ who lives in me. This life that I live now, I live by faith in the Son of God, who loved me and gave his life for me.

ROM. 14.7.—ROM. 14.8.—1 COR. 10.24.—
1 COR. 6.20.—PHIL. 1.20–23.—GAL. 2.19, 20.

I have always loved you, so I continue to show you my constant love.

We must thank God at all times for you, brothers, you whom the Lord loves. For God chose you as the first to be saved by the Spirit's power to make you his holy people and by your faith in the truth. God called you to this through the Good News we preached to you; he called you to possess your share of the glory of our Lord Jesus Christ.—He saved us and called us to be his own people, not because of what we have done, but because of his own purpose and grace. He gave us this grace by means of Christ Jesus before the beginning of time.—You saw me before I was born. The days allotted to me had all been recorded in your book, before any of them ever began.

God loved the world so much that he gave his only Son, so that everyone who believes in him may not die but have eternal life.

This is what love is: it is not that we have loved God, but that he loved us and sent his Son to be the means by which our sins are forgiven.

JER. 31.3.—2 THESS. 2.13, 14.—2 TIM. 1.9.—
PS. 139.16.—JOHN 3.16.—1 JOHN 4.10.

AUGUST 24

I know all about their sufferings.

He endured suffering and pain.—Tempted in every way that we are.

He himself took our sickness and carried away our diseases.—Jesus, tired out by the journey, sat down by the well.

Jesus saw her weeping, and he saw how the people who were with her were weeping also; his heart was touched, and he was deeply moved. Jesus wept.—Now he can help those who are tempted, because he himself was tempted and suffered.

The LORD looked down from his holy place on high, he looked down from heaven to earth. He heard the groans of prisoners and set free those who were condemned to die.—God knows every step I take; if he tests me, he will find me pure.—When I am ready to give up, he knows what I should do.

Anyone who strikes you strikes what is most precious to me.—The LORD himself ... saved them. In his love and compassion he rescued them.

EXOD. 3.7.—ISA. 53.3.—HEB. 4.15.—MATT. 8.17.—
JOHN 4.6.—JOHN 11.33, 35.—HEB. 2.18.—
PS. 102.19, 20.—JOB 23.10.—PS. 142.3.—
ZECH. 2.8.—ISA. 63.9.

Think of the rock from which you came, the quarry from which you were dug.

I have been evil from the day I was born.—No one took enough pity on you. When you were born, no one loved you. You were thrown out in an open field. Then I passed by and saw you squirming in your own blood … but I wouldn't let you die.

He pulled me out of a dangerous pit, out of the deadly quicksand. He set me safely on a rock and made me secure. He taught me to sing a new song, a song of praise to our God.

When we were still helpless, Christ died for the wicked at the time that God chose. It is a difficult thing for someone to die for a righteous person. It may even be that someone might dare to die for a good person. But God has shown us how much he loves us – it was while we were still sinners that Christ died for us!—God's mercy is so abundant, and his love for us is so great, that while we were spiritually dead in our disobedience he brought us to life with Christ.

ISA. 51.1.—PS. 51.5.—EZEK. 16.5, 6.—
PS. 40.2, 3.—ROM. 5.6–8.—EPH.2.4, 5.

252

AUGUST 26

*Make an ornament of pure gold and engrave on it
'Dedicated to the LORD'.*

Live a holy life, because no one will see the Lord without
it.—God is Spirit, and only by the power of his Spirit can
people worship him as he really is.—All who serve me must
respect my holiness; I will reveal my glory to my people.—
All of us have been sinful; even our best actions are filthy
through and through.

This is the law of the Temple: All the area surrounding
it on the top of the mountain is sacred and holy.—Your
Temple is holy indeed, for ever and ever.

For their sake I dedicate myself to you, in order that
they, too, may be truly dedicated to you.—We have a great
High Priest who has gone into the very presence of God—
Jesus, the Son of God. Let us have confidence, then, and
approach God's throne, where there is grace. There we
will receive mercy and find grace to help us just when we
need it.

EXOD. 28.36.—HEB. 12.14.—JOHN 4.24.—
LEV. 10.3.—ISA. 64.6.—EZEK. 43.12.—PS. 93.5.—
JOHN 17.19.—HEB. 4.14, 16.

Your word is a lamp to guide me and a light for my path.

I have obeyed your command and have not followed paths of violence. I have always walked in your way and have never strayed from it.

Their teaching will lead you when you travel, protect you at night, and advise you during the day. Their instructions are a shining light; their correction can teach you how to live.—If you wander off the road to the right or the left, you will hear his voice behind you saying, "Here is the road. Follow it."

I am the light of the world. Whoever follows me will have the light of life and will never walk in darkness.—We are ... confident of the message proclaimed by the prophets. You will do well to pay attention to it, because it is like a lamp shining in a dark place.—What we see now is like a dim image in a mirror; then we shall see face to face. What I know now is only partial; then it will be complete – as complete as God's knowledge of me.—They will not need lamps or sunlight, because the Lord God will be their light, and they will rule as kings for ever and ever.

PS. 119.105.—PS. 17.4, 5.—PROV. 6.22, 23.—
ISA. 30.21.—JOHN 8.12.—2 PET. 1.19.—
1 COR. 13.12.—REV. 22.5.

AUGUST 28

*The one who stood before our God and accused our brothers
day and night has been thrown out of heaven.*

Our brothers won the victory over him by the blood of the
Lamb and by the truth which they proclaimed.—Who will
accuse God's chosen people? God himself declares them
not guilty! Who, then, will condemn them? Not Christ
Jesus, who died, or rather, who was raised to life and is at
the right-hand side of God, pleading with him for us!

Christ freed himself from the power of the spiritual
rulers and authorities; he made a public spectacle of
them.—So that through his death he might destroy the
Devil, who has the power over death, and in this way set
free those who were slaves all their lives because of their
fear of death.—In all these things we have complete victory
through him who loved us!—Put on all the armour that
God gives you, so that you will be able to stand up against
the Devil's evil tricks. And accept … the word of God as
the sword which the Spirit gives you.—Thanks be to God
who gives us the victory through our Lord Jesus Christ!

REV. 12.10.—REV. 12.11.—ROM. 8.33, 34.—
COL. 2.15.—HEB. 2.14, 15,—ROM. 8.37.—
EPH. 6.11, 17.—1 COR. 15.57.

Trust in the LORD and you will be happy.

[Abraham's] faith did not leave him, and he did not doubt God's promise; his faith filled him with power, and he gave praise to God. He was absolutely sure that God would be able to do what he had promised.—The people of Judah were victorious over Israel, because they relied on the LORD, the God of their ancestors.

God is our shelter and strength, always ready to help in times of trouble. So we will not be afraid, even if the earth is shaken and mountains fall into the ocean depths.—It is better to trust in the LORD than to depend on man. It is better to trust in the LORD than to depend on human leaders.—The LORD guides a man in the way he should go and protects those who please him. If they fall, they will not stay down, because the LORD will help them up.

Find out for yourself how good the LORD is. Happy are those who find safety with him. Honour the LORD, all his people; those who obey him have all they need.

PROV. 16.20.—ROM. 4.20, 21.—2 CHR. 13.18.—
PS. 46.1, 2.—PS. 118.8, 9.—PS. 37.23, 24.—
PS. 34.8, 9.

AUGUST 30

The king ... held out to her the gold sceptre. [Esther] came up and touched the tip of it.

When he cries out to me for help, I will answer him because I am merciful.

We ourselves know and believe the love which God has for us. God is love, and whoever lives in love lives in union with God and God lives in union with him. Love is made perfect in us in order that we may have courage on Judgement Day; and we will have it because our life in this world is the same as Christ's. There is no fear in love; perfect love drives out all fear. So then, love has not been made perfect in anyone who is afraid, because fear has to do with punishment. We love because God first loved us.

Let us come near to God with a sincere heart and a sure faith, with hearts that have been purified from a guilty conscience and with bodies washed with clean water.— Now, in union with Christ Jesus, you ... have been brought near by the sacrificial death of Christ.—In union with Christ and through our faith in him we have the boldness to go into God's presence with all confidence.—Let us have confidence, then, and approach God's throne, where there is grace. There we will receive mercy and find grace to help us just when we need it.

ESTHER 5.2.—EXOD. 22.27.—1 JOHN 4.16–19.—
HEB. 10.22.—EPH. 2.13.—EPH. 3.12.—HEB. 4.16.

AUGUST 31

*After so many sins, comes the undeserved gift of
"Not guilty!"*

You are stained red with sin, but I will wash you as clean as
snow. Although your stains are deep red, you will be as
white as wool.—I am the God who forgives your sins, and
I do this because of who I am. I will not hold your sins
against you. Let us go to court; bring your accusation!
Present your case to prove you are in the right!—I have
swept your sins away like a cloud. Come back to me; I am
the one who saves you.

God loved the world so much that he gave his only Son,
so that everyone who believes in him may not die but have
eternal life.—The two are not the same, because God's free
gift is not like Adam's sin. It is true that many people died
because of the sin of that one man. But God's grace is much
greater, and so is his free gift to so many people through
the grace of the one man, Jesus Christ.—Some of you were
like that. But you have been purified from sin; you have
been dedicated to God; you have been put right with God
by the Lord Jesus Christ and by the Spirit of our God.

ROM. 5.16.—ISA. 1.18.—ISA. 43.25, 26.—
ISA. 44.22.—JOHN 3.16.—ROM. 5.15.—
1 COR. 6.11.

SEPTEMBER 1

The Spirit produces ... humility.

Poor and humble people will once again find the happiness which the LORD, the holy God of Israel, gives.—Unless you change and become like children, you will never enter the Kingdom of heaven. The greatest in the Kingdom of heaven is the one who humbles himself and becomes like this child.—The ageless beauty of a gentle and quiet spirit, which is of the greatest value in God's sight.—Love ... is not ... conceited or proud.

Strive for ... gentleness.—Take my yoke and put it on you, and learn from me, because I am gentle and humble in spirit.—He was treated harshly, but endured it humbly; he never said a word. Like a lamb about to be slaughtered, like a sheep about to be sheared, he never said a word.—Christ himself suffered for you and left you an example, so that you would follow in his steps. He committed no sin, and no one ever heard a lie come from his lips. When he was insulted, he did not answer back with an insult ... but placed his hopes in God, the righteous Judge.

GAL. 5.22, 23.—ISA. 29.19.—MATT. 18.3, 4.—
1 PET. 3, 4.—1 COR. 13.4.—1 TIM. 6.11.—
MATT. 11.29.—ISA. 53.7.—1 PET. 2.21-23.

Trust in the LORD. Have faith, do not despair. Trust in the LORD.

Don't you know? Haven't you heard? The LORD is the everlasting God; he created all the world. He never grows tired or weary. He strengthens those who are weak and tired.—Do not be afraid – I am with you! I am your God – let nothing terrify you! I will make you strong and help you; I will protect you and save you.—The poor and the helpless have fled to you and have been safe in times of trouble. You give them shelter from storms and shade from the burning heat. Cruel men attack like a winter storm.

When your faith succeeds in facing such trials, the result is the ability to endure. Make sure that your endurance carries you all the way without failing, so that you may be perfect and complete, lacking nothing.—Do not lose your courage, then, because it brings with it a great reward. You need to be patient, in order to do the will of God and receive what he promises.

PS. 27.14.—ISA. 40.28, 29.—ISA. 41.10.—
ISA. 25.4.—JAS 1.3,4.—HEB. 10.35, 36.

260

There must be no yeast or leavened bread anywhere in your land.

To honour the LORD is to hate evil.—Hate what is evil.—Avoid every kind of evil.—Guard against turning back from the grace of God. Let no one become like a bitter plant that grows up and causes many troubles with its poison.

If I had ignored my sins, the Lord would not have listened to me.

You know the saying, "A little bit of yeast makes the whole batch of dough rise." You must remove the old yeast of sin so that you will be entirely pure. Then you will be like a new batch of dough without any yeast, as indeed I know you actually are. For our Passover Festival is ready, now that Christ, our Passover lamb, has been sacrificed. Let us celebrate our Passover, then, not with bread having the old yeast of sin and wickedness, but with the bread that has no yeast, the bread of purity and truth.—Everyone should examine himself first, and then eat the bread and drink from the cup.

Whoever says that he belongs to the Lord must turn away from wrongdoing.—Jesus … is the High Priest that meets our needs. He is holy; he has no fault or sin in him; he has been set apart from sinners.—There is no sin in him.

EXOD. 13.7.—PROV. 8.13.—ROM. 12.9.—
1 THESS. 5.22.—HEB. 12.15.—PS. 66.18.—
1 COR. 5.6-8.—1 COR. 11.28.—
2 TIM. 2.19.—HEB. 7.26.—1 JOHN 3.5.

SEPTEMBER 4

Now be patient, Ruth.

Tell him to keep alert, to stay calm, and not to be frightened or disturbed.—Stop fighting, and know that I am God.— Didn't I tell you that you would see God's glory if you believed?—Human pride will be ended, and human arrogance will be destroyed ... and the LORD alone will be exalted on that day.

Mary ... sat down at the feet of the Lord and listened to his teaching. "Mary has chosen the right thing, and it will not be taken away from her."—Come back and quietly trust in me. Then you will be strong and secure.—Think deeply about this, when you lie in silence on your beds.

Be patient and wait for the LORD to act; don't be worried about those who prosper or those who succeed in their evil plans.

He is not afraid of receiving bad news; his faith is strong, and he trusts in the LORD. He is not worried or afraid.

Faith that is firm is also patient.

RUTH 3.18.—ISA. 7.4.—PS. 46.10.—JOHN 11.40.—
ISA. 2.17.—LUKE 10.39, 42.—ISA. 30.15.—
PS. 4.4.—PS. 37.7.—PS. 112.7, 8.—ISA. 28.16.

Christ is like a single body, which has many parts; it is still one body.

He is the head of his body, the church.—Supreme Lord over all things. The church is Christ's body, the completion of him who himself completes all things everywhere.—We are members of his body.

You have prepared a body for me.—You saw me before I was born. The days allotted to me had all been recorded in your book, before any of them ever began.

They belonged to you, and you gave them to me.— Even before the world was made, God had already chosen us to be his through our union with Christ.—Those whom God had already chosen he also set apart to become like his Son.

We must grow up in every way to Christ, who is the head. Under his control all the different parts of the body fit together, and the whole body is held together by every joint with which it is provided ... the whole body grows and builds itself up through love.

1 COR. 12.12.—COL. 1.18.—EPH. 1.22, 23.—
EPH. 5.30.—HEB. 10.5.—PS. 139.16.—JOHN 17.6—
EPH. 1.4.—ROM. 8.29.—EPH. 4.15, 16.

SEPTEMBER 6

Let us open our hearts to God in heaven and pray.

There is no one like the LORD our God. He lives in the heights above, but he bends down to see the heavens and the earth.—To you, O LORD, I offer my prayer.—I lift up my hands to you in prayer; like dry ground my soul is thirsty for you. Answer me now, LORD! I have lost all hope. Don't hide yourself from me, or I will be among those who go down to the world of the dead. Remind me each morning of your constant love, for I put my trust in you. My prayers go up to you; show me the way I should go.

Your constant love is better than life itself, and so I will praise you. I will give you thanks as long as I live; I will raise my hands to you in prayer.—Make your servant glad, O Lord, because my prayers go up to you. You are good to us and forgiving, full of constant love for all who pray to you.

If you ask me for anything in my name, I will do it.

LAM. 3.41.—PS. 113.5, 6.—PS. 25.1.—
PS. 143.6–8.—PS. 63.3, 4.—PS. 86.4, 5.—
JOHN 14.13.

SEPTEMBER 7

Let your hope keep you joyful.

What you hope for … is kept safe for you in heaven.—If our hope in Christ is good for this life only and no more, then we deserve more pity than anyone else in all the world.—We must pass through many troubles to enter the Kingdom of God.—Whoever does not carry his own cross and come after me cannot be my disciple.—None of you should turn back because of these persecutions. You yourselves know that such persecutions are part of God's will for us.

May you always be joyful in your union with the Lord. I say it again: rejoice!—May God, the source of hope, fill you with all joy and peace by means of your faith in him, so that your hope will continue to grow by the power of the Holy Spirit.—Let us give thanks to the God and Father of our Lord Jesus Christ! Because of his great mercy he gave us new life by raising Jesus Christ from death. This fills us with a living hope.—You love him, although you have not seen him, and you believe in him, although you do not now see him. So you rejoice with a great and glorious joy which words cannot express.—He has brought us by faith into this experience of God's grace, in which we now live. And so we boast of the hope we have of sharing God's glory!

ROM. 12.12.—COL. 1.5.—1 COR. 15.19.—
ACTS 14.22.—LUKE 14.27.—1 THESS. 3.3.—
PHIL. 4.4.—ROM. 15.13.—1 PET. 1.3.—
1 PET. 1.8.—ROM. 5.2.

You have been weighed on the scales and found to be
too light.

The LORD is a God who knows, and he judges all that
people do.—The things that are considered of great value
by man are worth nothing in God's sight.—I do not judge
as man judges. Man looks at the outward appearance, but I
look at the heart.—Do not deceive yourselves; no one
makes a fool of God. A person will reap exactly what he
sows. If he sows in the field of his natural desires, from it
he will gather the harvest of death; if he sows in the field of
the Spirit, from the Spirit he will gather the harvest of
eternal life.

Will a person gain anything if he wins the whole world
but loses his life? Of course not! There is nothing he can
give to regain his life.—All those things that I might count
as profit I now reckon as loss for Christ's sake.

Sincerity and truth are what you require.—You know
my heart. You have come to me at night; you have examined
me completely and found no evil desire in me.

DAN. 5.27.—1 SAM. 2.3.—LUKE 16.15.—
1 SAM. 16.7.—GAL. 6.7, 8.—MATT. 16.26.—
PHIL. 3.7.—PS. 51.6.—PS. 17.3.

He has filled the hungry with good things, and sent the rich away with empty hands.

You say, 'I am rich and well off, I have all I need.' But you do not know how miserable and pitiful you are! You are poor, naked, and blind. I advise you, then, to buy gold from me, pure gold, in order to be rich ... I rebuke and punish all whom I love. Be in earnest, then, and turn from your sins.

Happy are those whose greatest desire is to do what God requires; God will satisfy them fully!—When my people in their need look for water, when their throats are dry with thirst, then I, the LORD, will answer their prayer; I, the God of Israel, will never abandon them.—I am the LORD your God ... open your mouth, and I will feed you.

Why spend money on what does not satisfy? Why spend your wages and still be hungry? Listen to me and do what I say, and you will enjoy the best food of all.—I am the bread of life.

LUKE 1.53.—REV. 3.17-19.—MATT. 5.6.—
ISA. 41.17.—PS. 81.10.—ISA. 55.2.—JOHN 6.35.

I will give them a single purpose in life: to honour me for all time, for their own good and the good of their descendants.

I will give you a new heart and a new mind.—Because the Lord is righteous and good, he teaches sinners the path they should follow. He leads the humble in the right way and teaches them his will. With faithfulness and love he leads all who keep his covenant and obey his commands.

I pray that they may all be one. Father! May they be in us, just as you are in me and I am in you. May they be one, so that the world will believe that you sent me.

I urge you, then ... live a life that measures up to the standard God set when he called you. Be always humble, gentle, and patient. Do your best to preserve the unity which the Spirit gives by means of the peace that binds you together. There is one body and one Spirit, just as there is one hope to which God has called you. There is one Lord, one faith, one baptism; there is one God and Father of all mankind, who is Lord of all, works through all, and is in all.

JER. 32.39.—EZEK. 36.26.—PS. 25.8-10.—
JOHN 17.21.—EPH. 4.1-6.

Do not conform yourselves to the standards of this world,
but let God transform you inwardly by a complete change of
your mind.

Do not follow the majority when they do wrong.

Don't you know that to be the world's friend means to be God's enemy?

How can right and wrong be partners? How can light and darkness live together? How can Christ and the Devil agree? What does a believer have in common with an unbeliever? How can God's temple come to terms with pagan idols?—Do not love the world or anything that belongs to the world. If you love the world, you do not love the Father. The world and everything in it that people desire is passing away; but he who does the will of God lives for ever.

In the past ... you followed the world's evil way; you obeyed the ruler of the spiritual powers in space, the spirit who now controls the people who disobey God.—That was not what you learnt about Christ! You certainly heard about him, and as his followers you were taught the truth that is in Jesus.

ROM. 12.2.—EXOD. 23.2.—JAS 4.4.—
2 COR. 6.14-16.—1 JOHN 2.15, 17.—
EPH. 2.1, 2.—EPH. 4.20, 21.

I have seen how they acted, but I will heal them.

I am the LORD, the one who heals you.

LORD, you have examined me and you know me. You know everything I do; from far away you understand all my thoughts. You see me, whether I am working or resting; you know all my actions.—You place our sins before you, our secret sins where you can see them.—Everything in all creation is exposed and lies open before his eyes.

The LORD says, "Now let's settle the matter. You are stained red with sin, but I will wash you as clean as snow. Although your stains are deep red, you will be as white as wool."—In mercy the angel will say, "Release him! He is not to go down to the world of the dead. Here is the ransom to set him free."—Because of our sins he was wounded, beaten because of the evil we did. We are healed by the punishment he suffered, made whole by the blows he received.—Your faith has made you well.

ISA. 57.18.—EXOD. 15.26.—PS. 139.1-3.—
PS. 90.8.—HEB. 4.13.—ISA. 1.18.—
JOB 33.24.—ISA. 53.5.—MARK 5.34.

Whoever is thirsty should come to me and drink.

How I want to be there! I long to be in the LORD's Temple. With my whole being I sing for joy to the living God.—O God, you are my God, and I long for you. My whole being desires you; like a dry, worn-out, and waterless land, my soul is thirsty for you. Let me see you in the sanctuary; let me see how mighty and glorious you are.

Come, everyone who is thirsty – here is water! Come, you that have no money – buy corn and eat! Come! Buy wine and milk – it will cost you nothing!—The Spirit and the Bride say, "Come!" Everyone who hears this must also say, "Come!" Come, whoever is thirsty; accept the water of life as a gift, whoever wants it.—Whoever drinks the water that I will give him will never be thirsty again. The water that I will give him will become in him a spring which will provide him with life-giving water and give him eternal life.—My blood is the real drink.

Eat, lovers, and drink until you are drunk with love!

JOHN 7.37.—PS. 84.2.—PS. 63.1, 2.—
ISA. 55.1.—REV.22.17.—JOHN 4.14.—
JOHN 6.55.—S. OF S. 5.1.

I am the one who strengthens you.

Let us give thanks to the God and Father of our Lord Jesus Christ, the merciful Father, the God from whom all help comes! He helps us in all our troubles, so that we are able to help others who have all kinds of troubles, using the same help that we ourselves have received from God.—As a father is kind to his children, so the LORD is kind to those who honour him. He knows what we are made of; he remembers that we are dust.—I will comfort you in Jerusalem, as a mother comforts her child.—Leave all your worries with him, because he cares for you.

You, O Lord, are a merciful and loving God, always patient, always kind and faithful.

Another Helper ... the Spirit who reveals the truth about God.—The Spirit ... comes to help us, weak as we are.

He will wipe away all tears from their eyes. There will be no more death, no more grief or crying or pain. The old things have disappeared.

ISA. 51.12.—2 COR.1.3, 4.—PS. 103.13, 14.—
ISA. 66.13.—1 PET. 5.7.—PS. 86.15.—
JOHN 14.16, 17.—ROM. 8.26.—REV. 21.4.

SEPTEMBER 15

*Sin must not be your master; for you do not live under law
but under God's grace.*

What, then? Shall we sin, because we are not under law but
under God's grace? By no means!—As far as the Law is
concerned, you … have died because you are part of the
body of Christ; and now you belong to him who was raised
from death in order that we might be useful in the service
of God.—This does not mean that I don't obey God's law;
I am really under Christ's law.—Death gets its power to hurt
from sin, and sin gets its power from the Law. But thanks
be to God who gives us the victory through our Lord Jesus
Christ!

The law of the Spirit, which bring us life in union with
Christ Jesus, has set me free from the law of sin and
death.—Everyone who sins is a slave of sin. If the Son sets
you free, then you will be really free.

Stand, then, as free people, and do not allow yourselves
to become slaves again.

ROM. 6.14.—ROM. 6.15.—ROM. 7.4.—
1 COR. 9.21.—1 COR. 15.56, 57.—ROM. 8.2.—
JOHN 8.34, 36.—GAL. 5.1.

SEPTEMBER 16

The LORD judges your motives.

The righteous are guided and protected by the LORD, but the evil are on their way to their doom.—The LORD will show us who belongs to him.—Your Father, who sees what you do in private, will reward you.

Examine me, O God, and know my mind; test me, and discover my thoughts. Find out if there is any evil in me and guide me in the everlasting way.—There is no fear in love; perfect love drives out all fear.

O Lord, you know what I long for; you hear all my groans.—When I am ready to give up, he knows what I should do.—God, who sees into our hearts, knows what the thought of the Spirit is; because the Spirit pleads with God on behalf of his people and in accordance with his will.

The solid foundation that God has laid cannot be shaken; and on it are written these words: "The Lord knows those who are his" and "Whoever says that he belongs to the Lord must turn away from wrongdoing."

PROV. 21.2.—PS. 1.6.—NUM. 16.5.—MATT. 6.4.—
PS. 139.23, 24.—1 JOHN 4.18.—PS. 38.9.—
PS. 142.3.—ROM. 8.27.—2 TIM. 2.19.

SEPTEMBER 17

He will not break off a bent reed.

My sacrifice is a humble spirit, O God; you will not reject a humble and repentant heart.—He heals the broken-hearted and bandages their wounds.—I am the high and holy God, who lives for ever. I live in a high and holy place, but I also live with people who are humble and repentant, so that I can restore their confidence and hope. I gave my people life, and I will not continue to accuse them or be angry with them for ever.

I will look for those that are lost, bring back those that wander off, bandage those that are hurt, and heal those that are sick.—Lift up your tired hands, then, and strengthen your trembling knees! Keep walking on straight paths, so that the lame foot may not be disabled, but instead be healed.—God is coming to your rescue.

MATT. 12.20.—PS. 51.17.—PS. 147.3.—
ISA. 57.15, 16.—EZEK. 34.16.—
HEB. 12.12, 13.—ISA. 35.4.

SEPTEMBER 18

Open my eyes, so that I may see the wonderful truths in your law.

Then he opened their minds to understand the Scriptures.—The knowledge about the secrets of the Kingdom of heaven has been given to you, but not to them.—Father, Lord of heaven and earth! I thank you because you have shown to the unlearned what you have hidden from the wise and learned. Yes, Father, this was how you wanted it to happen.—We have not received this world's spirit; instead, we have received the Spirit sent by God, so that we may know all that God has given us.—O God, how difficult I find your thoughts; how many of them there are! If I counted them, they would be more than the grains of sand.—How great are God's riches! How deep are his wisdom and knowledge! Who can explain his decisions? Who can understand his ways? As the scripture says, "Who knows the mind of the Lord? Who is able to give him advice?" For all things were created by him, and all things exist through him and for him. To God be the glory for ever! Amen.

PS. 119.18.—LUKE 24.45.—MATT. 13.11.—
MATT. 11.25, 26.—1 COR 2.12.—
PS. 139.17, 18.—ROM. 11.33, 34, 36.

276

The God of all grace.

In your presence I will pronounce my sacred name. I am the LORD, and I show compassion and pity on those I choose.—In mercy the angel will say, "Release him! He is not to go down to the world of the dead. Here is the ransom to set him free."—By the free gift of God's grace all are put right with him through Christ Jesus, who sets them free. God offered him, so that by his sacrificial death he should become the means by which people's sins are forgiven through their faith in him. God did this in order to demonstrate that he is righteous. In the past he was patient and overlooked people's sins; but in the present time he deals with their sins, in order to demonstrate his righteousness.—Grace and truth came through Jesus Christ.

It is by God's grace that you have been saved through faith. It is not the result of your own efforts, but God's gift.—May God the Father and Christ Jesus our Lord give you grace, mercy, and peace.—Each one of us has received a special gift in proportion to what Christ has given.—Each one, as a good manager of God's different gifts, must use for the good of others the special gift he has received from God.—The grace that God gives is even stronger.

Continue to grow in the grace and knowledge of our Lord and Saviour Jesus Christ. To him be the glory, now and for ever!

1 PET. 5.10.—EXOD. 33.19.—JOB 33.24.—
ROM. 3.24, 25.—JOHN 1.17.—EPH. 2.8.—
1 TIM. 1.2.—EPH. 4.7.—1 PET. 4.10.—
JAS 4.6.—2 PET. 3.18.

Happy is the man who becomes wise – who gains understanding.

The man who finds me finds life, and the LORD will be pleased with him.

The LORD says, "Wise men should not boast of their wisdom, nor strong men of their strength … If anyone wants to boast, he should boast that he knows and understands me. I, the LORD have spoken."—To be wise you must first have reverence for the LORD.

All those things that I might count as profit I now reckon as loss for Christ's sake. Not only those things; I reckon everything as complete loss for the sake of what is so much more valuable, the knowledge of Christ Jesus my Lord. For his sake I have thrown everything away; I consider it all as mere refuse, so that I may gain Christ.—He is the key that opens all the hidden treasures of God's wisdom and knowledge.—I make plans and carry them out. I have understanding, and I am strong.

God has made Christ to be our wisdom. By him we are put right with God; we become God's holy people and are set free.

PROV. 3.13.—PROV. 8.35.—JER. 9.23, 24.—
PROV. 9.10.—PHIL. 3.7, 8.—COL. 2.3.—
PROV. 8.14.—1 COR. 1.30.—PROV. 11.30.

SEPTEMBER 21

We know that in all things God works for good with those who love him.

Men's anger only results in more praise for you; those who survive the wars will keep your festivals.—You plotted evil against me, but God turned it into good.

Everything belongs to you: ... this world, life and death, the present and the future – all these are yours, and you belong to Christ, and Christ belongs to God.—All this is for your sake; and as God's grace reaches more and more people, they will offer to the glory of God more prayers of thanksgiving. For this reason we never become discouraged. Even though our physical being is gradually decaying, yet our spiritual being is renewed day after day. And this small and temporary trouble we suffer will bring us a tremendous and eternal glory, much greater than the trouble.

My brothers, consider yourselves fortunate when all kinds of trials come your way, for you know that when your faith succeeds in facing such trials, the result is the ability to endure. Make sure that your endurance carries you all the way without failing, so that you may be perfect and complete, lacking nothing.

ROM. 8.28.—PS. 76.10.—GEN. 50.20.—
1 COR. 3.21-23.—2 COR. 4.15-17.—JAS 1.2-4.

May he be pleased with my song, for my gladness comes from him.

Like an apple-tree among the trees of the forest, so is my dearest compared with other men. I love to sit in its shadow, and its fruit is sweet to my taste.—No one in heaven is like you, LORD; none of the heavenly beings is your equal.

My lover is handsome and strong; he is one in ten thousand.—One [pearl] that is unusually fine.—The ruler of the kings of the world.

His face is bronzed and smooth; his hair is wavy, black as a raven.—Supreme Lord over all things.—He is the head of his body, the church.

His cheeks are as lovely as a garden that is full of herbs and spices.—He could not stay hidden.

His lips are like lilies, wet with liquid myrrh.—Nobody has ever talked like this man!

He is majestic, like the Lebanon Mountains with their towering cedars.—Look on your servant with kindness.—Give us more blessings, O LORD. Look on us with kindness!

PS. 104.34.—S. OF S. 2.3.—PS. 89.6.—
S. OF S. 5.10.—MATT. 13.46.—REV. 1.5.—
S. OF S. 5.11.—EPH. 1.22.—COL. 1.18.—
S. OF S. 5.13.—MARK 7.24.—S. OF S. 5.13.—
JOHN 7.46.—S. OF S. 5.15.—PS. 31.16.—PS.4.6.

SEPTEMBER 23

You did not leave us in slavery.

My dear friends, do not be surprised at the painful test you are suffering, as though something unusual were happening to you.—Endure what you suffer as being a father's punishment; your suffering shows that God is treating you as his sons. Was there ever a son who was not punished by his father? If you are not punished, as all his sons are, it means you are not real sons, but bastards.

The LORD your God is using him to test you, to see if you love the LORD with all your heart.

The LORD has made a solemn promise, and he will not abandon you, for he has decided to make you his own people.—Can a woman forget her own baby and not love the child she bore? Even if a mother should forget her child, I will never forget you.—Happy is the man who has the God of Jacob to help him and who depends on the LORD his God.

Will God not judge in favour of his own people who cry to him day and night for help? Will he be slow to help them? I tell you, he will judge in their favour and do it quickly.

EZRA 9.9.—1 PET. 4.12.—HEB. 12.7, 8.—
DEUT. 13.3.—1 SAM. 12.22.—ISA. 49.15.—
PS. 146.5.—LUKE 18.7, 8.

As for me, how wonderful to be near God.

I love the house where you live, O LORD, the place where your glory dwells.—One day spent in your Temple is better than a thousand anywhere else; I would rather stand at the gate of the house of my God than live in the homes of the wicked.—Happy are those whom you choose, whom you bring to live in your sanctuary. We shall be satisfied with the good things of your house, the blessings of your sacred Temple.

The LORD is good to everyone who trusts in him.—The LORD is waiting to be merciful to you. He is ready to take pity on you because he always does what is right. Happy are those who put their trust in the LORD.

We have, then, my brothers, complete freedom to go into the Most Holy Place by means of the death of Jesus. He opened for us a new way, a living way ... through his own body. So let us come near to God with a sincere heart and a sure faith, with hearts that have been purified from a guilty conscience and with bodies washed with clean water.

PS. 73.28.—PS. 26.8.—PS. 84.10.—PS. 65.4.—
LAM. 3.25.—ISA. 30.18.—HEB. 10.19, 20, 22.

Make sure that your endurance carries you all the way without failing, so that you may be perfect and complete, lacking nothing.

It may now be necessary for you to be sad for a while because of the many kinds of trials you suffer. Their purpose is to prove that your faith is genuine. Even gold, which can be destroyed, is tested by fire; and so your faith, which is much more precious than gold, must also be tested, so that it may endure. Then you will receive praise and glory and honour on the Day when Jesus Christ is revealed.—We ... boast of our troubles, because we know that trouble produces endurance, endurance brings God's approval, and his approval creates hope.

It is best for us to wait in patience – to wait for him to save us.—You knew that you still possessed something much better, which would last for ever. Do not lose your courage, then, because it brings with it a great reward. You need to be patient, in order to do the will of God and receive what he promises.—May our Lord Jesus Christ himself and God our Father, who loved us and in his grace gave us unfailing courage and a firm hope, encourage you and strengthen you to always do and say what is good.

JAS 1.4.—1 PET. 1.6, 7.—ROM. 5.3, 4.—
LAM. 3.26.—HEB. 10.34-36.—2 THESS. 2.16, 17.

Your God is faithful and true: he does what is right and fair.

God, the righteous Judge.—All of us must appear before Christ, to be judged by him. Each one will receive what he deserves, according to everything he has done, good or bad, in his bodily life.—Every one of us, then, will have to give an account of himself to God.—The person who sins is the one who will die.

The LORD Almighty says, "Wake up, sword, and attack the shepherd who works for me! Kill him."—The LORD made the punishment fall on him, the punishment all of us deserved.—Love and faithfulness will meet; righteousness and peace will embrace.—Mercy triumphs over judgement.—Sin pays its wage – death; but God's free gift is eternal life in union with Christ Jesus our Lord.

The God who saves his people ... there is no other God.—He himself is righteous and ... he puts right everyone who believes in Jesus.—By the free gift of God's grace all are put right with him through Christ Jesus, who sets them free.

DEUT. 32.4.—1 PET. 2.23.—2 COR. 5.10.—
ROM. 14.12.—EZEK. 18.4.—ZECH. 13.7.—
ISA. 53.6.—PS. 85.10.—JAS 2.13.—
ROM. 6.23.—ISA 45.21.—ROM. 3.26.—ROM. 3.24.

Humble yourselves ... under God's mighty hand, so that he will lift you up in his own good time.

The LORD hates everyone who is arrogant; he will never let them escape punishment.

You are our Father, LORD. We are like clay, and you are like the potter. You created us, so do not be too angry with us or hold our sins against us for ever. We are your people; be merciful to us.—LORD, we were like an untamed animal, but you taught us to obey. Bring us back; we are ready to return to you, the LORD our God. We turned away from you, but soon we wanted to return. After you had punished us, we hung our heads in grief. We were ashamed and disgraced, because we sinned when we were young.—It is best to learn this patience in our youth.

Evil does not grow in the soil, not does trouble grow out of the ground. No indeed! Man brings trouble on himself, as surely as sparks fly up from a fire.

1 PET. 5.6.—PROV. 16.5.—ISA. 64.8, 9.—
JER. 31.18, 19.—LAM. 3.27.—JOB 5.6, 7.

SEPTEMBER 28

If they pronounce my name as a blessing upon the people of Israel, I will bless them.

LORD our God, we have been ruled by others, but you alone are our LORD.

All the peoples on earth will see that the LORD has chosen you to be his own people, and they will be afraid of you.—The LORD has made a solemn promise, and he will not abandon you, for he has decided to make you his own people.

Lord, hear us. Lord, forgive us. Lord, listen to us, and act! In order that everyone will know that you are God, do not delay! This city and these people are yours.—Help us, O God, and save us; rescue us and forgive our sins for the sake of our own honour. Why should the nations ask us, "Where is your God?"—The LORD is like a strong tower, where the righteous can go and be safe.

NUM. 6.27.—ISA. 26.13.—DEUT. 28.10.—
1 SAM. 12.22.—DAN. 9.19.—PS. 79.9, 10.—
PROV. 18.10.

This is how we know what love is: Christ gave his life for us.

His love ... can never be fully known.—The greatest love a person can have for his friends is to give his life for them.—You know the grace of our Lord Jesus Christ; rich as he was, he made himself poor for your sake, in order to make you rich by means of his poverty.—Dear friends, if this was how God loved us, then we should love one another.—Be kind and tender-hearted to one another, and forgive one another, as God has forgiven you through Christ.—Be tolerant with one another and forgive one another whenever any of you has a complaint against someone else. You must forgive one another just as the Lord has forgiven you.—For even the Son of Man did not come to be served; he came to serve and to give his life to redeem many people.—Christ himself suffered for you and left you an example, so that you would follow in his steps.

You ... should wash one another's feet. I have set an example for you, so that you will do just what I have done for you.—We too, ought to give our lives for our brothers!

1 JOHN 3.16.—EPH. 3.19.—JOHN 15.13.—
2 COR. 8.9.—1 JOHN 4.11.—EPH. 4.32.—
COL. 3.13.—MARK 10.45.—1 PET. 2.21.—
JOHN 13.14, 15.—1 JOHN 3.16.

God knows every step I take; if he tests me, he will find me pure.

He knows what we are made of.—He takes no pleasure in causing us grief or pain.

The solid foundation that God has laid cannot be shaken; and on it are written these words: "The Lord knows those who are his" and "Whoever says that he belongs to the Lord must turn away from wrongdoing." In a large house there are dishes and bowls of all kinds: some are made of silver and gold, others of wood and clay; some are for special occasions, others for ordinary use. If anyone makes himself clean from all those evil things, he will be used for special purposes, because he is dedicated and useful to his Master, ready to be used for every good deed.

As a metal-worker refines silver and gold, so the LORD's messenger will purify the priests, so that they will bring to the LORD the right kind of offerings.—I ... will purify them as silver is purified ... Then they will pray to me, and I will answer them. I will tell them that they are my people, and they will confess that I am their God.

JOB 23.10.—PS. 103.14.—LAM. 3.33.—
2 TIM. 2.19-21.—MAL. 3.3.—ZECH. 13.9.

OCTOBER 1

The Spirit produces self-control.

Every athlete in training submits to strict discipline, in order to be crowned with a wreath that will not last; but we do it for one that will last for ever. That is why I run straight for the finishing-line; that is why I am like a boxer who does not waste his punches. I harden my body with blows and bring it under complete control, to keep myself from being disqualified after having called others to the contest.

Do not get drunk with wine, which will only ruin you; instead, be filled with the Spirit.

If anyone wants to come with me, he must forget self, carry his cross, and follow me.

We should not be sleeping like the others; we should be awake and sober. It is at night that people sleep; it is at night that they get drunk. But we belong to the day, and we should be sober.—[God's] grace instructs us to give up ungodly living and worldly passions, and to live self-controlled, upright, and godly lives in this world, as we wait for the blessed Day we hope for, when the glory of our great God and Saviour Jesus Christ will appear.

GAL. 5.22.—1 COR. 9.25-27.—EPH. 5.18.—
MATT. 16.24.—1 THESS. 5.6-8.—TITUS 2.12, 13.

OCTOBER 2

The goat is to be driven off into the desert by a man appointed to do it. The goat will carry all their sins away with him into some uninhabited land.

As far as the east is from the west, so far does he remove our sins from us.—When that time comes, no sin will be found in Israel and no wickedness in Judah, because I will forgive those people whose lives I have spared. I, the LORD, have spoken.—You will ... send [our sins] to the bottom of the sea! There is not other god like you, O LORD; you forgive the sins of your people.

All of us were like sheep that were lost, each of us going his own way. But the LORD made the punishment fall on him, the punishment all of us deserved.—My devoted servant ... will bear the punishment of many ... And so I will give him a place of honour, a place among great and powerful men. He willingly gave his life and shared the fate of evil men. He took the place of many sinners and prayed that they might be forgiven.—There is the Lamb of God, who takes the away the sin of the world!

LEV. 16.21, 22.—PS. 103.12.—JER. 50.20.—
MIC. 7.19, 18.—ISA. 53.6.—ISA. 53.11, 12.—
JOHN 1.29.

OCTOBER 3

He loves us, and by his sacrificial death he has freed us from our sins.

Water cannot put it out; no flood can drown it. Love is as powerful as death.—The greatest love a person can have for his friends is to give his life for them.

Christ himself carried our sins in his body to the cross, so that we might die to sin and live for righteousness. It is by his wounds that you have been healed.—By the sacrificial death of Christ we are set free, that is, our sins are forgiven. How great is the grace of God!

You have been purified from sin; you have been dedicated to God; you have been put right with God by the Lord Jesus Christ and by the Spirit of our God.—You are the chosen race, the King's priests, the holy nation, God's own people, chosen to proclaim the wonderful acts of God, who called you out of darkness into his own marvellous light.—My brothers, because of God's great mercy to us I appeal to you: Offer yourselves as a living sacrifice to God, dedicated to his service and pleasing to him. This is the true worship that you should offer.

REV 1.5.—S. OF S. 8.7, 6.—JOHN 15.13.—
1 PET. 2.24.—EPH. 1.7.—1 COR. 6.11.—
1 PET. 2.9.—ROM. 12.1.

OCTOBER 4

*Moses' face was shining because he had been speaking with
the LORD but he did not know it.*

To you alone, O LORD, to you alone, and not to us, must
glory be given.—When, Lord did we ever see you hungry
and feed you, or thirsty and give you a drink?—Be humble
towards one another, always considering others better than
yourselves.—Put on the apron of humility.

As they looked on, a change came over Jesus: his face
was shining like the sun, and his clothes were dazzling
white.—All those sitting in the Council fixed their eyes on
Stephen and saw that his face looked like the face of an
angel.—I gave them the same glory you gave me.—All of
us … reflect the glory of the Lord with uncovered faces;
and that same glory, coming from the Lord, who is the
Spirit, transforms us into his likeness in an ever greater
degree of glory.

You are like light for the whole world. A city built on a
hill cannot be hidden. No one lights a lamp and puts it under
a bowl; instead he puts it on the lampstand, where it gives
light for everyone in the house.

EXOD. 34.29.—PS. 115.1.—MATT. 25.37.—
PHIL. 2.3.—1 PET. 5.5.—MATT. 17.2.—
ACTS 6.15.—JOHN 17.22.—2 COR.3.18.—
MATT. 5.14, 15.

Call to me when trouble comes; I will save you, and you will praise me.

Why am I so sad? Why am I so troubled? I will put my hope in God, and once again I will praise him, my saviour and my God.—You will listen, O LORD, to the prayers of the lowly; you will give them courage.—You are good to us and forgiving, full of constant love for all who pray to you.

Jacob said to his family ... "We are going to leave here and go to Bethel, where I will build an altar to the God who helped me in the time of my trouble and who has been with me everywhere I have gone."

I love the LORD, because he hears me; he listens to my prayers. He listens to me every time I call to him. The danger of death was all round me; the horrors of the grave closed in on me ... Then I called to the LORD.

PS. 50.15.—PS. 42.11.—PS. 10.17.—
PS. 86.5.—GEN. 35.2, 3.—PS. 116.1–4.

The Lord, our Almighty God, is King!

I know ... that you can do everything you want.—What is impossible for man is possible for God.—He looks on the people of the earth as nothing; angels in heaven and people on earth are under his control. No one can oppose his will or question what he does.—No one can escape from my power; no one can change what I do.—My Father! All things are possible for you.

"Do you believe that I can heal you?" "Yes, sir!" they answered. Then Jesus touched their eyes and said, "Let it happen, then, just as you believe!"—"Sir, if you want to, you can make me clean." Jesus stretched out his hand and touched him. "I do want to," he answered. "Be clean!"—"Mighty God."—I have been given all authority in heaven and on earth.

Some trust in their war-chariots and others in their horses, but we trust in the power of the LORD our God.—Be determined and confident, and don't be afraid ... We have more power and our side than he has on his.

REV. 19.6.—JOB 42.2.—LUKE 18.27.—
DAN. 4.35.—ISA. 43.13.—MARK 14.36.—
MATT. 9.28, 29.—MATT. 8.2, 3.—ISA. 9.6.—
MATT. 28.18.—PS. 20.7.—2 CHR. 32.7.

He leads the humble in the right way.

Happy are those who are humble.

I realized another thing, that in this world fast runners do not always win the race, and the brave do not always win the battle. Wise men do not always earn a living, intelligent men do not always get rich, and capable men do not always rise to high positions.—You may make your plans, but God directs your actions.

LORD, I look up to you, up to heaven, where you rule. As a servant depends on his master, as a maid depends on her mistress, so we will keep looking to you, O LORD our God.—Set me free from my distress; then in the assembly of your people I will praise you.

You are our God! Punish them, for we are helpless in the face of this large army that is attacking us. We do not know what to do, but we look to you for help.

If any of you lacks wisdom, he should pray to God, who will give it to him; because God gives generously and graciously to all.

When ... the Spirit comes, who reveals the truth about God, he will lead you into all the truth.

PS. 25.9.—MATT. 5.5.—ECCLES. 9.11.—
PROV. 16.9.—PS. 123.1, 2.—PS. 142.7.—
2 CHR. 20.12.—JAS 1.5.—JOHN 16.13.

I will not be afraid. What can anyone do to me?

Who … can separate us from the love of Christ? Can trouble do it, or hardship or persecution or hunger or poverty or danger or death? No, in all these things we have complete victory through him who loved us!

Do not be afraid of those who kill the body but cannot afterwards do anything worse. I will show you whom to fear: fear God, who, after killing, has the authority to throw into hell. Believe me, he is the one you must fear!

Happy are those who are persecuted because they do what God requires; the Kingdom of heaven belongs to them! Happy are you when people insult you and persecute you and tell all kinds of evil lies against you because you are my followers. Be happy and glad, for a great reward is kept for you in heaven.—I reckon my own life to be worth nothing to me; I only want to complete my mission and finish the work that the Lord Jesus gave me to do.—I will announce your commands to kings and I will not be ashamed.

HEB. 13.6.—ROM. 8.35, 37.—LUKE 12.4, 5.—
MATT. 5.10–12.—ACTS 20.24.—PS. 119.46.

*You are a God who forgives; you are gracious and loving ...
your mercy is great.*

The Lord is not slow to do what he has promised, as some think. Instead, he is patient with you, because he does not want anyone to be destroyed, but wants all to turn away from their sins.—Look on our Lord's patience as the opportunity he is giving you to be saved.

God was merciful to me in order that Christ Jesus might show his full patience in dealing with me, the worst of all sinners, as an example for all those who would later believe in him and receive eternal life.—Everything written in the Scriptures was written to teach us, in order that we might have hope through the patience and encouragement which the Scriptures give us.

Perhaps you despise his great kindness, tolerance, and patience. Surely you know that God is kind, because he is trying to lead you to repent.—Let your broken heart show your sorrow; tearing your clothes is not enough. Come back to the LORD your God. He is kind and full of mercy; he is patient and keeps his promise; he is always ready to forgive and not punish.

NEH. 9.17.—2 PET. 3.9.—2 PET. 3.15.—
1 TIM. 1.16.—ROM. 15.4.—ROM. 2.4.—JOEL 2.13.

Every family in heaven and on earth.

One God and Father of all mankind, who is Lord of all, works through all, and is in all.—It is through faith that all of you are God's sons in union with Christ Jesus.—This plan, which God will complete when the time is right, is to bring all creation together, everything in heaven and on earth, with Christ as head.

Jesus is not ashamed to call them his brothers.—Look! Here are my mother and my brothers! Whoever does what my Father in heaven wants him to do is my brother, my sister, and my mother.—Go to my brothers and tell them that I am returning to him who is my Father and their Father, my God and their God.

I saw underneath the altar the souls of those who had been killed because they had proclaimed God's word and has been faithful in their witnessing. Each of them was given a white robe, and they were told to rest a little while longer, until the complete number of their fellow-servants and brothers had been killed, as they had been.—Only in company with us would they be made perfect.

EPH. 3.15.—EPH. 4.6.—GAL. 3.26.—EPH. 1.10.—
HEB. 2.11.—MATT. 12.49, 50.—JOHN 20.17.—
REV. 6.9, 11.—HEB. 11.40.

Do not stay away from me! Trouble is near.

How much longer will you forget me, LORD? For ever? How much longer will you hide yourself from me? How long must I endure trouble? How long will sorrow fill my heart day and night?—Don't hide yourself from me! Don't be angry with me; don't turn your servant away. You have been my help; don't leave me, don't abandon me, O God, my saviour.

When they call to me, I will answer them; when they are in trouble, I will be with them. I will rescue them and honour them.—He is near to those who call to him, who call to him with sincerity. He supplies the needs of those who honour him; he hears their cries and saves them.

When I go, you will not be left all alone; I will come back to you.—I will be with you always, to the end of the age.

God is our shelter and strength, always ready to help in times of trouble.—I wait patiently for God to save me. I depend on God alone; I put my hope in him.

PS. 22.11.—PS. 13.1, 2.—PS. 27.9.—PS. 91.15.—
PS. 145.18, 19.—JOHN 14.18.—MATT. 28.20.—
PS. 46.1.—PS. 62.1, 5.

God was making all mankind his friends through Christ. God did not keep an account of their sins.

It was by God's own decision that the Son has in himself the full nature of God. Through the Son, then, God decided to bring the whole universe back to himself.—Love and faithfulness will meet; righteousness and peace will embrace.

I alone know the plans I have for you, plans to bring you prosperity and not disaster.—The LORD says, "Now, let's settle the matter. You are stained red with sin, but I will wash you as clean as snow. Although your stains are deep red, you will be as white as wool."

There is no other god like you, O LORD; you forgive the sins of your people.

Make peace with God.—Keep on working with fear and trembling to complete your salvation, because God is always at work in you to make you willing and able to obey his own purpose.—You will give us prosperity, LORD; everything that we achieve is the result of what you do.

2 COR. 5.19.—COL. 1.19, 20.—PS. 85.10.—
JER. 29.11.—ISA. 1.18.—MIC. 7.18.—
JOB 22.21.—PHIL. 2.12, 13.—ISA. 26.12.

God has heard your prayers ever since the first day you decided to humble yourself in order to gain understanding.

I am the high and holy God, who lives for ever. I live in a high and holy place, but I also live with people who are humble and repentant, so that I can restore their confidence and hope.—My sacrifice is a humble spirit, O God; you will not reject a humble and repentant heart.—Even though you are so high above, you care for the lowly, and the proud cannot hide from you.—Humble yourselves, then, under God's mighty hand, so that he will lift you up in his own good time.—God resists the proud, but gives grace to the humble. So then, submit to God.

You are good to us and forgiving, full of constant love for all who pray to you. Listen, LORD, to my prayer; hear my cries for help. I call to you in times of trouble, because you answer my prayers.

DAN. 10.12.—ISA. 57.15.—PS. 51.17.—
PS. 138.6.—1 PET. 5.6.—JAS 4.6, 7.—PS. 86.5–7.

Christ died and rose to life in order to be the Lord of the living and of the dead.

The LORD says, "It was my will that he should suffer; his death was a sacrifice to bring forgiveness. And so he will see his descendants; he will live a long life, and through him my purpose will succeed. After a life of suffering, he will again have joy; he will know that he did not suffer in vain. My devoted servant, with whom I am pleased, will bear the punishment of many and for his sake I will forgive them."—Was it not necessary for the Messiah to suffer these things and then to enter his glory?—We recognize that one man died for everyone, which means that all share in his death. He died for all, so that those who live should no longer live for themselves, but only for him who died and was raised to life for their sake.

All the people of Israel, then, are to know for sure that this Jesus, whom you crucified, is the one that God has made Lord and Messiah!—He had been chosen by God before the creation of the world and was revealed in these last days for your sake. Through him you believe in God.

ROM. 14.9.—ISA. 53.10, 11.—LUKE 24.26.—
2 COR. 5.14, 15.—ACTS 2.36.—1 PET. 1.20, 21.

OCTOBER 15

You are my refuge, O God.

The Lord is my protector; he is my strong fortress. My God is my protection, and with him I am safe. He protects me like a shield; he defends me and keeps me safe. He is my saviour; he protects me and saves me from violence.—The LORD protects and defends me; I trust in him. He gives me help and makes me glad; I praise him with joyful songs.

From east to west everyone will fear him, and his great power. He will come like a rushing river, like a strong wind.—Let us be bold, then, and say, "The Lord is my helper, I will not be afraid. What can anyone do to me?"

The LORD is my light and my salvation; I will fear no one. The LORD protects me from all danger; I will never be afraid.

As the mountains surround Jerusalem, so the LORD surrounds his people now and for ever.—You have always been my help. In the shadow of your wings I sing for joy.

You are my refuge and defence; guide me and lead me as you have promised.

PS. 59.9.—2 SAM. 22.2, 3.—PS. 28.7.—
ISA. 59.19.—HEB. 13.6.—PS. 27.1.—
PS. 125.2.—PS. 63.7.—PS. 31.3.

Work hard and do not be lazy. Serve the Lord with a heart full of devotion.

Work hard at whatever you do, because there will be no action, no thought, no knowledge, no wisdom in the world of the dead – and that is where you are going.—Whatever you do, work at it with all your heart, as though you were working for the Lord and not for men. Remember that the Lord will give you as a reward what he has kept for his people. For Christ is the real Master you serve.—Remember that the Lord will reward everyone, whether slave or free, for the good work he does.

As long as it is day, we must keep on doing the work of him who sent me; night is coming when no one can work.—Didn't you know that I had to be in my Father's house?—My devotion to your house, O God, burns in me like a fire.

My brothers, try even harder to make God's call and his choice of you a permanent experience; if you do so, you will never abandon your faith.—Our great desire is that each one of you keep up his eagerness to the end, so that the things you hope for will come true. We do not want you to become lazy, but to be like those who believe and are patient, and so receive what God has promised.—Run … in such a way as to win the prize.

ROM. 12.11.—ECCLES. 9.10.—COL. 3.23, 24.—
EPH. 6.8.—JOHN 9.4.—LUKE 2.49.—JOHN 2.17.—
2 PET. 1.10.—HEB. 6.11.—1 COR. 9.24.

Because of you they rejoice all day long, and they praise you for your goodness.

Only through me are victory and strength to be found; but all who hate me will suffer disgrace. I, the LORD, will rescue all the descendants of Jacob, and they will give me praise.— You that are righteous, be glad and rejoice because of what the LORD has done. You that obey him, shout for joy!

Now God's way of putting people right with himself has been revealed. It has nothing to do with law, even though the Law of Moses and the prophets gave their witness to it. God puts people right through their faith in Jesus Christ. God does this to all who believe in Christ. In this way God shows that he himself is righteous and that he puts right everyone who believes in Jesus.—You love him, although you have not seen him, and you believe in him, although you do not now see him. So you rejoice with a great and glorious joy which words cannot express.

May you always be joyful in your union with the Lord. I say it again: rejoice!

PS. 89.16.—ISA. 45. 24, 25.—PS.32.11.—
ROM. 3.21, 22, 26.—1 PET. 1.8.—PHIL. 4.4.

*One of the soldiers ... plunged his spear into Jesus' side,
and at once blood and water poured out.*

This is the blood that seals the covenant which the LORD
made with you.—The life of every living thing is in the
blood, and that is why the LORD has commanded that all
blood be poured out on the altar to take away the people's
sins.—The blood of bulls and goats can never take away
sins.

Jesus said, "This is my blood which is poured out for
many, my blood which seals God's covenant."—When
Christ ... entered once and for all into the Most Holy Place
... he took his own blood and obtained eternal salvation
for us.—Peace through his Son's sacrificial death on the
cross.

You know what was paid to set you free ... It was not
something that can be destroyed, such as silver or gold; it
was the costly sacrifice of Christ, who was like a lamb
without defect or flaw.

I will sprinkle clean water on you and make you clean
from all your idols.—Let us come near to God with a
sincere heart and a sure faith, with hearts that have been
purified from a guilty conscience and with bodies washed
with clean water.

JOHN 19.34.—EXOD. 24.8.—LEV. 17.11.—
HEB. 10.4.—MARK 14.24.—HEB. 9.12.—
COL. 1.20.—1PET. 1.18, 19.—
EZEK. 36.25.—HEB. 10.22.

OCTOBER 19

The LORD will keep you safe. He will not let you fall into a trap.

Men's anger only results in more praise for you; those who survive the wars will keep your festivals.—The LORD controls the mind of a king as easily as he directs the course of a stream.—When you please the LORD, you can make your enemies into friends.

I wait eagerly for the LORD's help, and in his word I trust. I wait for the Lord more eagerly than watchmen wait for the dawn – than watchmen wait for the dawn.—I prayed to the LORD, and he answered me; he freed me from all my fears.

God has always been your defence; his eternal arms are your support. He drove out your enemies as you advanced, and told you to destroy them all.—I will bless the person who puts his trust in me.

In view of all this, what can we say? If God is for us, who can be against us?

PROV. 3.26.—PS. 76.10.—PROV. 21.1.—
PROV. 16.7.—PS. 130.5, 6.—PS. 34.4.—
DEUT. 33.27.—JER. 17.7.—ROM. 8.31.

OCTOBER 20

My inner being delights in the law of God.

How I love your law! I think about it all day long.—You spoke to me, and I listened to every word. Your words filled my heart with joy and happiness.—I love to sit in its shadow, and its fruit is sweet to my taste.—I always do what God commands; I follow his will, not my own desires.

How I love to do your will, my God! I keep your teaching in my heart.—My food ... is to obey the will of the one who sent me and to finish the work he gave me to do.

The laws of the LORD are right, and those who obey them are happy. The commands of the LORD are just and give understanding to the mind. They are more desirable than the finest gold; they are sweeter than the purest honey.—Do not deceive yourselves by just listening to his word; instead, put it into practice. Whoever listens to the word but does not put it into practice is like a man who looks in a mirror and sees himself as he is.

ROM. 7.22.—PS. 119.97.—JER. 15.16.—
S. OF S. 2.3.—JOB 23.12.—PS. 40.8.—
JOHN 4.34.—PS. 19.8, 10.—JAS 1.22, 23.

308

Out of the fullness of his grace he has blessed us all, giving us one blessing after another.

This is my own dear Son, with whom I am pleased.—See how much the Father has loved us! His love is so great that we are called God's children.

His Son ... is the one whom God has chosen to possess all things at the end.—Since we are his children, we will possess the blessings he keeps for his people, and we will also possess with Christ what God has kept for him; for if we share Christ's suffering, we will also share his glory.

The Father and I are one. The Father is in me and ... I am in the Father.—My Father and their Father, my God and their God.—I in them and you in me, so that they may be completely one.

The church is Christ's body, the completion of him who himself completes all things everywhere.

All these promises are made to us, my dear friends. So then, let us purify ourselves from everything that makes body or soul unclean, and let us be completely holy by living in awe of God.

JOHN 1.16.—MATT. 17.5—1 JOHN 3.1.—HEB. 1.2.—
ROM. 8.17.—JOHN 10.30, 38.—JOHN 20.17.—
JOHN 17.23.—EPH. 1.23.—2 COR. 7.1.

I have complete confidence, O God!

The LORD is my light and my salvation; I will fear no one. The LORD protects me from all danger; I will never be afraid.

You, LORD, give perfect peace to those who keep their purpose firm and put their trust in you.—He is not afraid of receiving bad news; his faith is strong, and he trusts in the LORD. He is not worried or afraid; he is certain to see his enemies defeated.

When I am afraid, O LORD Almighty, I put my trust in you.—In times of trouble he will shelter me; he will keep me safe in his Temple and make me secure on a high rock. So I will triumph over my enemies around me. With shouts of joy I will offer sacrifices in his Temple; I will sing, I will praise the LORD.

After you have suffered for a little while, the God of all grace, who calls you to share his eternal glory in union with Christ, will himself perfect you and give you firmness, strength, and a sure foundation. To him be the power for ever!

PS. 108.1.—PS. 27.1.—ISA. 26.3.—
PS. 112.7, 8.—PS. 27.5, 6.—1 PET. 5.10, 11.

OCTOBER 23

A person's true life is not made up of the things he owns, no matter how rich he may be.

The little that a good man owns is worth more than the wealth of all the wicked.—Better to be poor and fear the LORD than to be rich and in trouble.—Religion does not make a person very rich, if he is satisfied with what he has. If we have food and clothes, that should be enough for us.

Let me be neither rich nor poor. So give me only as much food as I need. If I have more, I might say that I do not need you. But if I am poor, I might steal and bring disgrace on my God.—Give us today the food we need.

I tell you not to be worried about the food and drink you need in order to stay alive, or about clothes for your body. After all, isn't life worth more than food? And isn't the body worth more than clothes?—"When I sent you out that time without purse, bag, or shoes, did you lack anything?" "Not a thing," they answered.—Keep your lives free from the love of money, and be satisfied with what you have. For God has said, "I will never leave you; I will never abandon you."

LUKE 12.15.—PS. 37.16.—PROV. 15.16.—
1 TIM.6.6, 8.—PROV. 30.8, 9.—MATT. 6.11.—
MATT. 6.25.—LUKE 22.35.—HEB. 13.5.

I thought I had been banished from your presence and would never see your holy Temple again.

The people of Jerusalem said, "The LORD has abandoned us! He has forgotten us." So the LORD answers, "Can a woman forget her own baby and not love the child she bore? Even if a mother should forget her child, I will never forget you."

I have forgotten what health and peace and happiness are. I have not much longer to live; my hope in the LORD is gone.—Wake up, Lord! Why are you asleep? Rouse yourself! Don't reject us for ever!—Israel, why ... do you complain that the Lord doesn't know your troubles or care if you suffer injustice?—"I turned away angry for only a moment, but I will show you my love for ever." So says the LORD who saves you.

Why am I so sad? Why am I so troubled? I will put my hope in God, and once again I will praise him, my saviour and my God.—We are often troubled, but not crushed; sometimes in doubt, but never in despair; there are many enemies, but we are never without a friend; and though badly hurt at times, we are not destroyed.

JONAH 2.4.—ISA. 49.14, 15.—LAM. 3.17, 18.—
PS. 44.23.—ISA. 40.27.—ISA. 54.8.—
PS. 43.5.—2 COR. 4.8, 9.

OCTOBER 25

I will be with you always, to the end of the age.

Whenever two of you on earth agree about anything you pray for, it will be done for you by my Father in heaven. For where two or three come together in my name, I am there with them.—Whoever accepts my commandments and obeys them is the one who loves me. My Father will love whoever loves me; I too will love him and reveal myself to him.

"Lord, how can it be that you will reveal yourself to us and not to the world?" "Whoever loves me will obey my teaching. My Father will love him, and my Father and I will come to him and live with him."

To him who is able to keep you from falling, and to bring you faultless and joyful before his glorious presence—to the only God our Saviour, through Jesus Christ our Lord, be glory, majesty, might, and authority, from all ages past, and now, and for ever and ever! Amen.

MATT. 28.20.—MATT. 18.19, 20.—JOHN 14.21.—
JOHN 14.22, 23.—JUDE 24, 25.

313

The LORD is king.

I am the LORD; why don't you fear me? Why don't you tremble before me? I placed the sand as the boundary of the sea, a permanent boundary that it cannot cross. The sea may toss, but it cannot go beyond it; the waves may roar, but they cannot break through.—Judgement does not come from the east or from the west, from the north or from the south; it is God who is the judge, condemning some and acquitting others.

He controls the times and the seasons; he makes and unmakes kings; it is he who gives wisdom and understanding.—You are going to hear the noise of battles close by and the news of battles far away; but do not be troubled.

If God is for us, who can be against us?—For only a penny you can buy two sparrows, yet not one sparrow falls to the ground without your Father's consent. As for you, even the hairs of your head have all been counted. So do not be afraid; you are worth much more than many sparrows!

PS. 99.1.—JER. 5.22.—PS. 75.6, 7.—DAN. 2.21.—
MATT. 24.6.—ROM. 8.31.—MATT. 10.29-31.

He himself took our sickness and carried away our diseases.

The priest shall order two ritually clean birds to be brought, together with a piece of cedar-wood, a red cord, and a sprig of hyssop. Then the priest shall order one of the birds to be killed over a clay bowl containing fresh spring water. He shall take the other bird and dip it, together with the cedar-wood, the red cord, and the hyssop, in the blood of the bird that was killed. He shall sprinkle the blood seven times on the person who is to be purified from his skin-disease, and then he shall pronounce him clean. He shall let the live bird fly away over the open fields.

There was a man who was suffering from a dreaded skin-disease. When he saw Jesus, he threw himself down and begged him, "Sir, if you want to, you can make me clean!"—Jesus was filled with pity, and stretched out his hand and touched him. "I do want to," he answered. "Be clean!" At once the disease left the man, and he was clean.

MATT. 8.17.—LEV. 14.4–7.—LUKE 5.12.—
MARK 1.41, 42.

He is astonished to see that there is no one to help the oppressed. So he will use his own power to rescue them.

You do not want sacrifices and offerings; you do not ask for animals burnt whole on the altar or for sacrifices to take away sins. Instead, you have given me ears to hear you, and so I answered, "Here I am; your instructions for me are in the book of the Law. How I love to do your will, my God! I keep your teaching in my heart."—I am willing to give up my life, in order that I may receive it back again. No one takes my life away from me. I give it up of my own free will. I have the right to give it up, and I have the right to take it back.

I, the LORD, the God who saves his people. There is no other god. Turn to me now and be saved, people all over the world! I am the only God there is.—In all the world there is no one else whom God has given who can save us.

You know the grace of our Lord Jesus Christ; rich as he was, he made himself poor for your sake, in order to make you rich by means of his poverty.

ISA. 59.16.—PS. 40.6–8.—JOHN 10.17, 18.—
ISA. 45.21, 22.—ACTS 4.12.—2 COR. 8.9.

Everything about him enchants me.

May he be pleased with my song.—My lover ... is one in ten thousand.—I chose a valuable stone, which I am placing as the cornerstone ... and whoever believes in him will never be disappointed.—You are the most handsome of men; you are an eloquent speaker.—God raised him to the highest place above and gave him the name that is greater than any other name.—It was by God's own decision that the Son has in himself the full nature of God.

You love him, although you have not seen him, and you believe in him, although you do not now see him. So you rejoice with a great and glorious joy which words cannot express.

I reckon everything as complete loss for the sake of what is so much more valuable, the knowledge of Christ Jesus my Lord. For his sake I have thrown everything away; I consider it all as mere refuse, so that I may gain Christ and be completely united with him. I no longer have a righteousness of my own, the kind that is gained by obeying the Law. I now have the righteousness that is given through faith in Christ, the righteousness that comes from God and is based on faith.

S. OF S. 5.16.—PS. 104.34.—S. OF S. 5.10.—
1 PET. 2.6.—PS. 45.2.—PHIL. 2.9.—COL. 1.19.—
1 PET. 1.8.—PHIL. 3.8, 9.

OCTOBER 30

It is best for us to wait in patience – to wait for him to save us.

Has God forgotten to be merciful? Has anger taken the place of his compassion?—I was afraid and thought that he had driven me out of his presence. But he heard my cry, when I called to him for help.

Will God not judge in favour of his own people who cry to him day and night for help? Will he be slow to help them? I tell you, he will judge in their favour and do it quickly.—Trust the LORD and he will make it right.—Be patient and wait for the LORD to act; don't be worried about those who prosper or those who succeed in their evil plans.

You will not have to fight this battle. Just take up your positions and wait; you will see the LORD give you victory.

Let us not become tired of doing good; for if we do not give up, the time will come when we will reap the harvest.—See how patient a farmer is as he waits for his land to produce precious crops. He waits patiently for the autumn and spring rains.

LAM. 3.26.—PS. 77.9.—PS. 31.22.—
LUKE 18.7, 8.—PROV. 20.22.—PS. 37.7.—
2 CHR. 20.17.—GAL. 6.9.—JAS 5.7.

This message from the LORD: "You will succeed, not by military might or by your own strength, but by my spirit."

Can anyone tell the LORD what to do? Who can teach him or give him advice?

God purposely chose what the world considers nonsense in order to shame the wise, and he chose what the world considers weak in order to shame the powerful. He chose what the world looks down on and despises, and thinks is nothing, in order to destroy what the world thinks is important. This means that no one can boast in God's presence.

The wind blows wherever it wishes; you hear the sound it makes, but you do not know where it comes from or where it is going. It is like that with everyone who is born of the Spirit.—They did not become God's children by natural means, that is, by being born as the children of a human father; God himself was their Father.

I am still with you, so do not be afraid.—The battle depends on God, not on you.

The LORD does not need swords or spears to save his people. He is victorious in battle.

ZECH. 4.6.—ISA. 40.13.—1 COR. 1.27–29.—
JOHN 3.8.—JOHN 1.13.—HAG. 2.5.—
2 CHR. 20.15.—1 SAM. 17.47.

NOVEMBER 1

The man who listens to me will be happy — the man who stays at my door every day, waiting at the entrance to my home.

As a servant depends on his master, as a maid depends on her mistress, so we will keep looking to you, O LORD our God, until you have mercy on us.

For all time to come, this burnt-offering is to be offered in my presence at the entrance of the Tent of my presence. That is where I will meet my people and speak to you.—In every place that I set aside for you to worship me, I will come to you and bless you.

Where two or three come together in my name, I am there with them.

The time is coming and is already here, when by the power of God's Spirit people will worship the Father as he really is, offering him the true worship that he wants. God is Spirit, and only by the power of his Spirit can people worship him as he really is.

Pray on every occasion, as the Spirit leads.—Pray at all times.

PROV. 8.34.—PS. 123.2.—EXOD. 29.42.—
EXOD. 20.24.—MATT. 18.20.—JOHN 4.23, 24.—
EPH. 6.18.—1 THESS. 5.17.

At all times make it your aim to do good.

It was to this that God called you, for Christ himself suffered for you and left you an example, so that you would follow in his steps. He committed no sin, and no one ever heard a lie come from his lips. When he was insulted, he did not answer back with an insult; when he suffered, he did not threaten, but placed his hopes in God, the righteous Judge.—Think of what he went through; how he put up with so much hatred from sinners! So do not let yourselves become discouraged and give up.

Let us rid ourselves of everything that gets in the way, and of the sin which holds on to us so tightly, and let us run with determination the race that lies before us. Let us keep our eyes fixed on Jesus, on whom our faith depends from beginning to end. He did not give up because of the cross! On the contrary, because of the joy that was waiting for him, he thought nothing of the disgrace of dying on the cross, and he is now seated at the right-hand side of God's throne.

In conclusion, my brothers, fill your minds with those things that are good and that deserve praise: things that are true, noble, right, pure, lovely, and honourable.

1 THESS. 5.15.—1 PET. 2.21–23.—HEB. 12.3.—
HEB. 12.1, 2.—PHIL. 4.8.

*The LORD's ways are right, and righteous people live by
following them, but sinners stumble and fall because they
ignore them.*

This stone is of great value for you that believe; but for
those who do not believe ... "This is the stone that will
make people stumble, the rock that will make them fall."—
The LORD protects honest people, but destroys those who
do wrong.

Listen ... if you have ears!—May those who are wise
think about these things; may they consider the LORD's
constant love.—The eyes are like a lamp for the body. If
your eyes are sound, your whole body will be full of light;
but if your eyes are no good, your body will be in darkness.—Whoever is willing to do what God wants will know
whether what I teach comes from God or whether I speak
on my own authority.—The person who has something will
be given more, so that he will have more than enough.

He who comes from God listens to God's words. You,
however, are not from God, and that is why you will not
listen.—You are not willing to come to me in order to have
life.—My sheep listen to my voice; I know them, and they
follow me.

HOS. 14.9.—1 PET. 2.7, 8.—PROV. 10.29.—
MATT. 11.15.—PS. 107.43.—MATT. 6.22.—
JOHN 7.17.—MATT. 13.12.—JOHN 8.47.—
JOHN 5.40.—JOHN 10.27.

NOVEMBER 4

It may now be necessary for you to be sad for a while because of the many kinds of trials you suffer.

My dear friends, do not be surprised at the painful test you are suffering, as though something unusual were happening to you. Rather be glad that you are sharing Christ's sufferings, so that you may be full of joy when his glory is revealed.—The encouraging words which God speaks to you as his sons ... "My son, pay attention when the Lord corrects you, and do not be discouraged when he rebukes you."—When we are punished, it seems to us at the time something to make us sad, not glad. Later, however, those who have been disciplined by such punishment reap the peaceful reward of a righteous life.

Our High Priest is not one who cannot feel sympathy for our weaknesses. On the contrary, [he] ... was tempted in every way that we are, but did not sin.—Now he can help those who are tempted, because he himself was tempted and suffered.—God keeps his promise, and he will not allow you to be tested beyond your power to remain firm.

1 PET. 1.6.—1 PET. 4.12, 13.—HEB. 12.5.—
HEB. 12.11.—HEB. 4.15.—HEB. 2.18.—
1 COR. 10.13.

Take the finest spices ... and make a sacred anointing oil.

It must not be poured on ordinary men, and you must not use the same formula to make any mixture like it. It is holy, and you must treat it as holy.—One Spirit.—There are different kinds of spiritual gifts, but the same Spirit gives them.

Your God ... has poured out more happiness on you than on any other king.—Jesus of Nazareth ... God poured out on him the Holy Spirit and power.—God gives him the fullness of his Spirit.

Out of the fullness of his grace he has blessed us all.—His Spirit teaches you about everything, and what he teaches is true, not false. Obey the Spirit's teaching, then, and remain in union with Christ.—It is God himself who has set us apart, who has placed his mark of ownership upon us, and who has given us the Holy Spirit in our hearts as the guarantee of all that he has in store for us.

The Spirit produces love, joy, peace, patience, kindness, goodness, faithfulness, humility, and self-control. There is no law against such things as these.

EXOD. 30.23, 25.—EXOD. 30.32.—EPH. 4.4.—
1 COR. 12.4.—PS. 45.7.—ACTS 10.38.—
JOHN 3.34.—JOHN 1.16.—1 JOHN 2.27.—
2 COR. 1.21, 22.—GAL. 5.22, 23.

*Your real life is Christ and when he appears, then you too
will appear with him and share his glory!*

I am the resurrection and the life. Whoever believes in me
will live, even though he dies.—God has given us eternal
life, and this life has its source in his Son. Whoever has the
Son has this life; whoever does not have the Son of God
does not have life.

There will be the shout of command, the archangel's
voice, the sound of God's trumpet, and the Lord himself
will come down from heaven. Those who have died believing in Christ will rise to life first; then we who are living at
that time will be gathered up along with them in the clouds
to meet the Lord in the air. And so we will always be with
the Lord. So then, encourage one another with these
words.—When Christ appears, we shall be like him, because we shall see him as he really is.—When buried, it is
ugly and weak; when raised, it will be beautiful and strong.

After I go and prepare a place for you, I will come back
and take you to myself, so that you will be where I am.

COL. 3.4.—JOHN 11.25.—1 JOHN 5.11, 12.—
1 THESS. 4.16–18.—1 JOHN 3.2.—
1 COR. 15.43.—JOHN 14.3.

*They must thank the L*ORD *for his constant love, for the*
wonderful things he did for them.

Find out for yourself how good the LORD is. Happy are
those who find safety with him.—How wonderful are the
good things you keep for those who honour you!

They are the people I made for myself, and they will
sing my praises!—God had already decided that through
Jesus Christ he would make us his sons – this was his
pleasure and purpose. Let us praise God for his glorious
grace, for the free gift he gave us in his dear Son! Let us,
then, who were the first to hope in Christ, praise God's
glory!

How good and beautiful [his] land will be!—He is good
to everyone and has compassion on all he made. All your
creatures, LORD, will praise you, and all your people will give
you thanks. They will speak of the glory of your royal power
and tell of your might, so that everyone will know your
mighty deeds and the glorious majesty of your kingdom.

PS. 107.8.—PS. 34.8.—PS. 31.19.—ISA. 43.21.—
EPH. 1.5, 6, 12.—ZECH. 9.17.—PS. 145.9-12.

We belong to the day, and we should be sober. We must wear faith and love as a breastplate, and our hope of salvation as a helmet.

Have your minds ready for action. Keep alert and set your hope completely on the blessing which will be given you when Jesus Christ is revealed.—Stand ready, with truth as a belt tight round your waist, with righteousness as your breastplate. At all times carry faith as a shield; for with it you will be able to put out all the burning arrows shot by the Evil One. And accept salvation as a helmet, and the word of God as the sword which the Spirit gives you.

The Sovereign LORD will destroy death for ever! He will wipe away the tears from everyone's eyes and take away the disgrace his people have suffered throughout the world. The LORD himself has spoken! When it happens, everyone will say, "He is our God! We have put our trust in him, and he has rescued us. He is the LORD! We have put our trust in him, and now we are happy and joyful because he has saved us."

To have faith is to be sure of the things we hope for, to be certain of the things we cannot see.

1 THESS. 5.8.—1 PET. 1.13.—EPH. 6.14, 16, 17.—
ISA. 25.8, 9.—HEB. 11.1.

NOVEMBER 9

I have given help to a famous soldier; I have given the throne to one I chose from the people.

I alone am the LORD, the only one who can save you.— There is one God, and there is one who brings God and mankind together, the man Christ Jesus.—In all the world there is no one else whom God has given who can save us.

Mighty God.—Of his own free will he gave up all he had, and took the nature of a servant. He became like man and appeared in human likeness. He was humble and walked the path of obedience all the way to death—his death on the cross. For this reason God raised him to the highest place above and gave him the name that is greater than any other name.—We do see Jesus, who for a little while was made lower than the angels, so that through God's grace he should die for everyone. We see him now crowned with glory and honour because of the death he suffered.—Since the children … are people of flesh and blood, Jesus himself became like them and shared their human nature.

PS. 89.19.—ISA. 43.11.—1 TIM. 2.5.—ACTS 4.12.—
ISA. 9.6.—PHIL. 2.7-9.—HEB. 2.9.—HEB. 2.14.

328

Your lives will produce all kinds of good deeds, and you will grow in your knowledge of God.

My brothers, because of God's great mercy to us I appeal to you: Offer yourselves as a living sacrifice to God, dedicated to his service and pleasing to him. This is the true worship that you should offer. Do not conform yourselves to the standards of this world, but let God transform you inwardly by a complete change of your mind. Then you will be able to know the will of God – what is good and is pleasing to him and is perfect.—At one time you surrendered yourselves entirely as slaves to impurity and wickedness for wicked purposes. In the same way you must now surrender yourselves entirely as slaves of righteousness for holy purposes.—It does not matter at all whether or not one is circumcised; what does matter is being a new creature. As for those who follow this rule in their lives, may peace and mercy be with them.

My father's glory is shown by your bearing much fruit; and in this way you become my disciples.—You did not choose me; I chose you and appointed you to go and bear much fruit, the kind of fruit that endures.

COL. 1.10.—ROM. 12.1, 2.—ROM. 6.19.—
GAL. 6.15, 16.—JOHN 15.8.—JOHN 15.16.

He led them safely, and they were not afraid.

I walk the way of righteousness; I follow the paths of justice.

I will send an angel ahead of you to protect you as you travel and to bring you to the place which I have prepared.—It was not an angel, but the LORD himself who saved them. In his love and compassion he rescued them. He had always taken care of them in the past.

Your people did not conquer the land with their swords; they did not win it by their own power; it was by your power and your strength, by the assurance of your presence, which showed that you loved them.—He led his people and brought honour to his name.

LORD, I have so many enemies! Lead me to do your will; make your way plain for me to follow.—Send your light and your truth; may they lead me and bring me back to Zion, your sacred hill, and to your Temple, where you live. Then I will go to your altar, O God; you are the source of my happiness. I will play my harp and sing praise to you, O God, my God.

PS. 78.53.—PROV. 8.20.—EXOD. 23.20.—
ISA. 63.9.—PS. 44.3.—ISA. 63.14.—PS. 5.8.—
PS. 43.3, 4.

The sadness that is used by God brings a change of heart that leads to salvation – and there is no regret in that!

Peter remembered what Jesus had told him: "Before the cock crows, you will say three times that you do not know me." He went out and wept bitterly.—If we confess our sins to God, he will keep his promise and do what is right: he will forgive us our sins and purify us from all our wrongdoing.—The blood of Jesus, his Son, purifies us from every sin.

My sins have caught up with me, and I can no longer see; they are more than the hairs of my head, and I have lost my courage. Save me, LORD! Help me now!

Trust in your God and return to him. Be loyal and just, and wait patiently for your God to act.

My sacrifice is a humble spirit, O God; you will not not reject a humble and repentant heart.—He heals the broken-hearted.—The LORD has told us what is good. What he requires of us is this: to do what is just, to show constant love, and to live in humble fellowship with our God.

2 COR. 7.10.—MATT. 26.75.—1 JOHN 1.9.—
1 JOHN 1.7.—PS. 40.12, 13.—HOS. 12.6.—
PS. 51.17.—PS. 147.3.—MIC. 6.8.

NOVEMBER 13

Christ loved the church and gave his life for it. He did this to dedicate the church to God by his word, after making it clean by washing it in water.

Your life must be controlled by love, just as Christ loved us and gave his life for us as a sweet-smelling offering and sacrifice that pleases God.

For through the living and eternal word of God you have been born again as the children of a parent who is immortal, not mortal.—Dedicate them to yourself by means of the truth; your word is truth.—No one can enter the Kingdom of God unless he is born of water and the Spirit.—It was not because of any good deeds that we ourselves had done, but because of his own mercy that he saved us, through the Holy Spirit, who gives us new birth and new life by washing us.—Your promise gave me life.

The law of the LORD is perfect; it gives new strength. The commands of the LORD are trustworthy, giving wisdom to those who lack it. The laws of the LORD are right, and those who obey them are happy. The commands of the LORD are just and give understanding to the mind.

EPH. 5.25, 26.—EPH. 5.2.—1 PET. 1.23.—
JOHN 17.17.—JOHN 3.5.—TITUS 3.5.—
PS. 119.50.—PS. 19.7, 8.

You are my saviour and my God – hurry to my aid!

The LORD guides a man in the way he should go and protects those who please him. If they fall, they will not stay down, because the LORD will help them up.—Reverence for the LORD gives confidence and security to a man and his family.—Why should you fear mortal man, who is no more enduring than grass? Have you forgotten the LORD who made you?

I will be with you to protect you.—Be determined and confident. Do not be afraid of them. Your God, the LORD himself, will be with you. He will not fail you or abandon you.

I will sing about your strength; every morning I will sing aloud of your constant love. You have been a refuge for me, a shelter in my time of trouble.—You are my hiding place; you will save me from trouble. I sing aloud of your salvation, because you protect me.

PS. 40.17.—PS. 37.23, 24.—PROV. 14.16.—
ISA. 51.12, 13.—JER. 1.8.—DEUT. 31.6.—
PS. 59.16.—PS. 32.7.

*God is to be trusted, the God who called you to have
fellowship with his Son Jesus Christ, our Lord.*

Let us hold on firmly to the hope we profess, because we
can trust God to keep his promise.—As God himself has
said, "I will make my home with my people and live among
them; I will be their God, and they shall be my people."—
The fellowship that we have with the Father and with his
Son Jesus Christ.—Rather be glad that you are sharing
Christ's sufferings so that you may be full of joy when his
glory is revealed.

I pray that Christ will make his home in your hearts
through faith. I pray that you may have your roots and
foundation in love, so that you, together with all God's
people, may have the power to understand how broad and
long, how high and deep, is Christ's love. Yes, may you
come to know his love – although it can never be fully
known – and so be completely filled with the very nature of
God.

If anyone declares that Jesus is the Son of God, he lives
in union with God and God lives in union with him.—
Whoever obeys God's commands lives in union with God
and God lives in union with him.

1 COR. 1.9.—HEB. 10.23.—2 COR. 6.16.—
1 JOHN 1.3.—1 PET. 4.13.—EPH. 3.17-19.—
1 JOHN 4.15.—1 JOHN 3.24.

NOVEMBER 16

Dedicate them to yourself by means of the truth; your word is truth.

You have been made clean already by the teaching I have given you.—Christ's message in all its richness must live in your hearts.

How can a young man keep his life pure? By obeying your commands. With all my heart I try to serve you; keep me from disobeying your commandments.

You will become wise, and your knowledge will give you pleasure. Your insight and understanding will protect you.

I follow faithfully the road he chooses, and never wander to either side. I always do what God commands; I follow his will, not my own desires.—I understand more than all my teachers, because I meditate on your instructions.—If you obey my teaching, you are really my disciples; you will know the truth, and the truth will set you free.

JOHN 17.17.—JOHN 15.3.—COL. 3.16.—
PS. 119.9, 10.—PROV. 2.10, 11.—JOB 23.11, 12.—
PS. 119.99.—JOHN 8.31, 32.

NOVEMBER 17

How deep are your thoughts!

We have always prayed for you ... we ask God to fill you with the knowledge of his will, with all the wisdom and understanding that his Spirit gives.—I pray that you may have your roots and foundation in love, so that you, together with all God's people, may have the power to understand how broad and long, how high and deep, is Christ's love. Yes, may you come to know his love—although it can never be fully known—and so be completely filled with the very nature of God.

How great are God's riches! How deep are his wisdom and knowledge! Who can explain his decisions? Who can understand his ways?—"My thoughts," says the LORD, "are not like yours, and my ways are different from yours. As high as the heavens are above the earth, so high are my ways and thoughts above yours."—You have done many things for us, O LORD our God; there is no one like you! You have made many wonderful plans for us. I could never speak of them all – their number is so great!

PS. 92.5.—COL. 1.9.—EPH. 3.17–19.—
ROM. 11.33.—ISA. 55.8, 9.—PS. 40.5.

NOVEMBER 18

He took them away with a cruel wind from the east.

Let the LORD himself be the one to punish us, for he is merciful.—I will come to you and save you. I will not let you go unpunished; but when I punish you, I will be fair.—He does not keep on rebuking; he is not angry for ever. He does not punish us as we deserve or repay us according to our sins and wrongs. He knows what we are made of; he remembers that we are dust.—I will be merciful to them, as a father is merciful to the son who serves him.

God keeps his promise, and he will not allow you to be tested beyond your power to remain firm; at the time you are put to the test, he will give you the strength to endure it, and so provide you with a way out.—Satan has received permission to test all of you, to separate the good from the bad, as a farmer separates the wheat from the chaff. But I have prayed for you … that your faith will not fail.

The poor and the helpless have fled to you and have been safe in times of trouble. You give them shelter from storms and shade from the burning heat.

ISA. 27.8.—2 SAM. 24.14—JER. 30.11.—
PS. 103.9, 10, 14.—MAL. 3.17.—1 COR. 10.13.—
LUKE 22.31, 32.—ISA. 25.4.

You will know the false prophets by what they do.

Let no one deceive you, my children! Whoever does what is right is righteous, just as Christ is righteous.—No spring of water pours out sweet water and bitter water from the same opening. A fig-tree, my brothers, cannot bear olives; a grapevine cannot bear figs, nor can a salty spring produce sweet water. Is there anyone among you who is wise and understanding? He is to prove it by his good life, by his good deeds performed with humility and wisdom.—Your conduct among the heathen should be so good that when they accuse you of being evildoers, they will have to recognize your good deeds and so praise God on the Day of his coming.

To have good fruit you must have a healthy tree; if you have a poor tree, you will have bad fruit. A tree is known by the kind of fruit it bears.—A good person brings good things out of his treasure of good things; a bad person brings bad things out of his treasure of bad things.

Is there anything I failed to do for [my vineyard]?

MATT. 7.20.—1 JOHN 3.7.—JAS 3.11–13.—
1 PET. 2.12.—MATT. 12.33.—MATT. 12.35.—
ISA. 5.4.

NOVEMBER 20

We are in darkness now, but the LORD will give us light.

When you pass through deep waters, I will be with you; your troubles will not overwhelm you. When you pass through fire, you will not be burnt; the hard trials that come will not hurt you. For I am the LORD your God, the holy God of Israel, who saves you.—I will lead my blind people by roads they have never travelled. I will turn their darkness into light and make rough country smooth before them. These are my promises, and I will keep them without fail.

Even if I go through the deepest darkness, I will not be afraid, LORD, for you are with me. Your shepherd's rod and staff protect me.—When I am afraid, O LORD Almighty, I put my trust in you. I trust in God and am not afraid; I praise him for what he has promised. What can a mere human being do to me?—The LORD is my light and my salvation; I will fear no one. The LORD protects me from all danger; I will never be afraid.

MIC. 7.8.—ISA. 43.2, 3.—ISA. 42.16.—
PS. 23.4.—PS. 56.3, 4.—PS. 27.1.

I will never turn away anyone who comes to me.

When he cries out to me for help, I will answer him because I am merciful.—I will not completely abandon or destroy them. That would put an end to my covenant with them, and I am the LORD their God.—I will honour the covenant I made with you when you were young, and I will make a covenant with you that will last for ever.

The LORD says, "Now, let's settle the matter. You are stained red with sin, but I will wash you as clean as snow. Although your stains are deep red, you will be as white as wool."—Let the wicked leave their way of life and change their way of thinking. Let them turn to the LORD, our God; he is merciful and quick to forgive.—"Remember me, Jesus, when you come as King!" Jesus said to him, "I promise you that today you will be in Paradise with me."

He will not break off a bent reed or put out a flickering lamp.

JOHN 6.37.—EXOD. 22.27.—LEV. 26.44.—
EZEK. 16.60.—ISA. 1.18.—ISA. 55.7.—
LUKE 23.42, 43.—ISA. 42.3.

Pray in the power of the Holy Spirit.

God is Spirit, and only by the power of his Spirit can people worship him as he really is.—All of us … are able to come in the one Spirit into the presence of the Father.

My Father, if it is possible, take this cup of suffering from me! Yet not what I want, but what you want.

The Spirit … comes to help us, weak as we are. For we do not know how we ought to pray; the Spirit himself pleads with God for us in groans that words cannot express. And God, who sees into our hearts, knows what the thought of the Spirit is; because the Spirit pleads with God on behalf of his people and in accordance with his will.—We have courage in God's presence, because we are sure that he hears us if we ask him for anything that is according to his will.—When … the Spirit comes, who reveals the truth about God, he will lead you into all the truth.

Pray on every occasion, as the Spirit leads. For this reason keep alert and never give up; pray always for all God's people.

JUDE 20.—JOHN 4.24.—EPH. 2.18.—
MATT. 26.39.—ROM. 8.26, 27.—1 JOHN 5.14.—
JOHN 16.13.—EPH. 6.18.

NOVEMBER 23

*Whoever listens to me will have security. He will be safe,
with no reason to be afraid.*

O Lord, you have always been our home.—Whoever goes
to the LORD for safety, whoever remains under the protection of the Almighty.—His faithfulness will protect and
defend you.

Your life is hidden with Christ in God.—Anyone who
strikes you strikes what is most precious to me.—Don't be
afraid! Stand your ground, and you will see what the LORD
will do to save you today. The LORD will fight for you, and
there is no need for you to do anything.—God is our shelter
and strength, always ready to help in times of trouble.

Jesus spoke to them at once. "Courage!" he said. "It is
I. Don't be afraid!"—Why are you alarmed? Why are these
doubts coming up in your minds? Look at my hands and
my feet, and see that it is I myself. Feel me, and you will
know, for a ghost doesn't have flesh and bones, as you can
see I have.—I know whom I have trusted, and I am sure
that he is able to keep safe until that Day what he has
entrusted to me.

PROV. 1.33.—PS. 90.1.—PS. 91.1.—PS. 91.4.—
COL. 3.3.—ZECH. 2.8.—EXOD. 14.13, 14.—
PS. 46.1.—MATT. 14.27.—LUKE 24.38, 39.—
2 TIM. 1.12.

NOVEMBER 24

My mother and brothers are those who hear the word of God and obey it.

He purifies people from their sins, and both he and those who are made pure all have the same Father. That is why Jesus is not ashamed to call them his brothers. He says to God, "I will tell my brothers what you have done; I will praise you in their meeting."—When we are in union with Christ Jesus, neither circumcision nor the lack of it makes any difference at all; what matters is faith that works through love.—You are my friends if you do what I command you.—How happy are those who hear the word of God and obey it!

Not everyone who calls me 'Lord, Lord' will enter the Kingdom of heaven, but only those who do what my Father in heaven wants them to do.—My food ... is to obey the will of the one who sent me.

If ... we say that we have fellowship with him, yet at the same time live in the darkness, we are lying both in our words and in our actions.—Whoever obeys his word is the one whose love for God has really been made perfect. This is how we can be sure that we are in union with God.

LUKE 8.21.—HEB. 2.11, 12.—GAL. 5.6.—
JOHN 15.14.—LUKE 11.28.—MATT. 7.21.—
JOHN 4.34.—1 JOHN 1.6.—1 JOHN 2.5.

*You were set free from sin and became the slaves of
righteousness.*

You cannot serve both God and money.—When you were
the slaves of sin, you were free from righteousness. What
did you gain from doing the things that you are now
ashamed of? The result of those things is death! But now
you have been set free from sin and are the slaves of God.
Your gain is a life fully dedicated to him, and the result is
eternal life.

Christ has brought the Law to an end, so that everyone
who believes is put right with God.

Whoever wants to serve me must follow me, so that my
servant will be with me where I am. And my Father will
honour anyone who serves me.—Take my yoke and put it
on you, and learn from me, because I am gentle and humble
in spirit; and you will find rest. For the yoke I will give you
is easy, and the load I will put on you is light.

LORD our God, we have been ruled by others, but you
alone are our LORD.—I will eagerly obey your commands,
because you will give me more understanding.

ROM. 6.18.—MATT. 6.24.—ROM. 6.20-22.—
ROM. 10.4.—JOHN 12.26.—MATT. 11.29, 30.—
ISA. 26.13.—PS. 119.32.

NOVEMBER 26

The LORD is pleased with you.

The LORD who created you says, "Do not be afraid—I will save you. I have called you by name – you are mine."—Can a woman forget her own baby and not love the child she bore? Even if a mother should forget her child, I will never forget you … I can never forget you! I have written your name on the palms of my hands.

The LORD guides a man in the way he should go and protects those who please him.—Pleased with the human race.—He takes pleasure in those who honour him, in those who trust in his constant love.—"They will be my people," says the LORD Almighty. "On the day when I act, they will be my very own. I will be merciful to them, as a father is merciful to the son who serves him."

At one time you were far away from God and were his enemies because of the evil things you did and thought. But now, by means of the physical death of his Son, God has made you his friends, in order to bring you, holy, pure, and faultless, into his presence.

ISA. 62.4.—ISA. 43.1.—ISA. 49.15, 16.—
PS. 37.23.—PROV. 8.31.—PS. 147.11.—
MAL. 3.17.—COL. 1.21, 22.

I gave them the same glory you gave me.

I saw the Lord. He was sitting on his throne, high and exalted, and his robe filled the whole Temple. Round him flaming creatures were standing. They were calling out to each other: "Holy, holy, holy! The LORD Almighty is holy! His glory fills the world."—Isaiah said this because he saw Jesus' glory and spoke about him.—Sitting on the throne was a figure that looked like a man. It shone all over with a bright light that had in it all the colours of the rainbow. This was the dazzling light that shows the presence of the LORD.

"Please, let me see the dazzling light of your presence." [The LORD answered,] "I will not let you see my face, because no one can see me and stay alive."—No one has ever seen God. The only Son, who is the same as God and is at the Father's side, he has made him known.—The God who said, "Out of darkness the light shall shine!" is the same God who made his light shine in our hearts, to bring us the knowledge of God's glory shining in the face of Christ.

JOHN 17.22.—ISA. 6.1–3.—JOHN 12.41.—
EZEK. 1.26, 28.—EXOD. 33.18, 20.—
JOHN 1.18.—2 COR. 4.6.

NOVEMBER 28

As the body without the spirit is dead, so also faith without actions is dead.

Not everyone who calls me 'Lord, Lord' will enter the Kingdom of heaven, but only those who do what my Father in heaven wants them to do.—Try to live a holy life, because no one will see the Lord without it.—Do your best to add goodness to your faith; to your goodness add knowledge; to your knowledge add self-control; to your self-control add endurance; to your endurance add godliness; to your godliness add brotherly affection and love. These are the qualities you need, and if you have them in abundance, they will make you active and effective in your knowledge of our Lord Jesus Christ. But whoever does not have them is so shortsighted that he cannot see and has forgotten that he has been purified from his past sins. So then, my brothers, try even harder to make God's call and his choice of you a permanent experience; if you do so, you will never abandon your faith.

It is by God's grace that you have been saved through faith. It is not the result of your own efforts, but God's gift, so that no one can boast about it.

JAS 2.26.—MATT. 7.21.—HEB. 12.14.—
2 PET. 1.5-10.—EPH. 2.8.

347

We shall be satisfied with the good things of your house.

I have asked the LORD for one thing; one thing only do I want: to live in the LORD's house all my life, to marvel there at his goodness, and to ask for his guidance.

Happy are those whose greatest desire is to do what God requires; God will satisfy them fully!—He has filled the hungry with good things, and sent the rich away with empty hands.

He satisfies those who are thirsty and fills the hungry with good things.—I am the bread of life ... he who comes to me will never be hungry; he who believes in me will never be thirsty.

How precious, O God, is your constant love! We find protection under the shadow of your wings. We feast on the abundant food you provide; you let us drink from the river of your goodness. You are the source of all life, and because of your light we see the light.

PS. 65.4.—PS. 27.4.—MATT. 5.6.—LUKE 1.53.—
PS. 107.9—JOHN 6.35.—PS. 36.7–9.

348

NOVEMBER 30

May the Lord himself, who is our source of peace, give you peace at all times and in every way. The Lord be with you all.

Peace be yours from God, who is, who was, and who is to come.—God's peace, which is far beyond human understanding, will keep your hearts and minds safe in union with Christ Jesus.

The LORD himself stood among them and said to them, "Peace be with you."—Peace is what I leave with you; it is my own peace that I give you. I do not give it as the world does. Do not be worried and upset; do not be afraid.

The Helper ... the Spirit, who reveals the truth about God.—The Spirit produces love, joy, peace.—God's Spirit joins himself to our spirits to declare that we are God's children.

The LORD said, "I will go with you, and I will give you victory." Moses replied, "If you do not go with us, don't make us leave this place. How will anyone know that you are pleased with your people and with me if you do not go with us?"

2 THESS. 3.16.—REV. 1.4.—PHIL. 4.7.—
LUKE 24.36.—JOHN 14.27.—JOHN 15.26.—
GAL. 5.22.—ROM. 8.16.—EXOD. 33.14-16.

*Like a shelter from the wind and a place to hide
from storms.*

He had to become like his brothers in every way.—The
LORD Almighty says, "… the shepherd who works for
me!"—The Father and I are one.

Whoever goes to the LORD for safety … remains under
the protection of the Almighty.—His glory will shade the
city from the heat of the day and make it a place of safety,
sheltered from the rain and storm.—The LORD will guard
you; he is by your side to protect you. The sun will not hurt
you during the day, nor the moon during the night.

In despair and far from home I call to you! Take me to
a safe refuge.—You are my hiding place; you will save me
from trouble.—The poor and the helpless have fled to you
and have been safe in times of trouble. You give them
shelter from storms and shade from the burning heat.

ISA. 32.2.—HEB. 2.17.—ZECH. 13.7.—
JOHN 10.30.—PS. 91.1.—ISA. 4.6.—
PS. 121.5, 6.—PS. 61.2.—PS. 32.7.—ISA. 25.4.

DECEMBER 2

*You have had the Holy Spirit poured out on you by Christ,
and so all of you know the truth.*

You know about Jesus of Nazareth and how God poured
out on him the Holy Spirit and power.—It was by God's
own decision that the Son has in himself the full nature of
God.—Out of the fullness of his grace he has blessed us all,
giving us one blessing after another.

You welcome me as an honoured guest.—Christ has
poured out his Spirit on you. As long as his Spirit remains
in you, you do not need anyone to teach you. For his Spirit
teaches you about everything, and what he teaches is true,
not false. Obey the Spirit's teaching, then, and remain in
union with Christ.

The Helper, the Holy Spirit, whom the Father will send
in my name, will teach you everything and make you remember all that I have told you.

The Spirit also comes to help us, weak as we are. For
we do not know how we ought to pray; the Spirit himself
pleads with God for us in groans that words cannot express.

1 JOHN 2.20.—ACTS 10.38.—COL. 1.19.—
JOHN 1.16.—PS. 23.5.—1 JOHN 2.27.—
JOHN 14.26.—ROM. 8.26.

DECEMBER 3

I would turn to God and present my case to him.

Is anything too hard for the LORD?—Give yourself to the LORD; trust in him, and he will help you.—Don't worry about anything, but in all your prayers ask God for what you need, always asking him with a thankful heart.—Leave all your worries with him, because he cares for you.

King Hezekiah took the letter from the messengers and read it. Then he went to the Temple, placed the letter there in the presence of the LORD, and prayed.

Even before they finish praying to me, I will answer their prayers.—The prayer of a good person has a powerful effect.

I love the LORD, because he hears me; he listens to my prayers. He listens to me every time I call to him.

JOB 5.8.—GEN. 18.14.—PS. 37.5.—PHIL. 4.6.—
1 PET. 5.7.—ISA. 37.14, 15.—ISA. 65.24.—
JAS 5.16.—PS. 116.1, 2.

DECEMBER 4

Where can wisdom be found?

If any of you lacks wisdom, he should pray to God, who will give it to him; because God gives generously and graciously to all. But when you pray, you must believe and not doubt at all.—Trust in the LORD with all your heart. Never rely on what you think you know. Remember the LORD in everything you do, and he will show you the right way.—The only God.—Never let yourself think that you are wiser than you are; simply obey the LORD and refuse to do wrong.

"Sovereign LORD, I don't know how to speak; I am too young." But the LORD said to me, "Do not say that you are too young, but go to the people I send you to, and tell them everything I command you to say. Do not be afraid of them, for I will be with you to protect you. I, the LORD, have spoken!"

The Father will give you whatever you ask him for in my name. Until now you have not asked for anything in my name; ask and you will receive, so that your happiness may be complete.—If you believe, you will receive whatever you ask for in prayer.

JOB 28.12.—JAS 1.5, 6.—PROV. 3.5, 6.—
1 TIM. 1.17.—PROV. 3.7.—JER. 1.6–8.—
JOHN 16.23, 24.—MATT. 21.22.

DECEMBER 5

My punishment was good for me, because it made me learn your commands.

Even though he was God's Son, he learnt through his sufferings to be obedient.—If we share Christ's suffering, we will also share his glory. I consider that what we suffer at this present time cannot be compared at all with the glory that is going to be revealed to us.

God knows every step I take; if he tests me, he will find me pure. I follow faithfully the road he chooses, and never wander to either side.

Remember how the LORD your God led you on this long journey through the desert these past forty years, sending hardships to test you, so that he might know what you intended to do and whether you would obey his commands. Remember that the LORD your God corrects and punishes you just as a father disciplines his children. So then, do as the LORD has commanded you: live according to his laws and obey him.

PS. 119.71.—HEB. 5.8.—ROM. 8.17, 18.—
JOB 23.10, 11.—DEUT. 8.2, 5, 6.

354

God is always at work in you.

There is nothing in us that allows us to claim that we are capable of doing this work. The capacity we have comes from God.—No one can have anything unless God gives it to him.—No one can come to me unless the Father who sent me draws him to me; and I will raise him to life on the last day.—I will give them a single purpose in life: to honour me for all time.

Do not be deceived, my dear brothers! Every good gift and every perfect present comes from heaven; it comes down from God, the Creator of the heavenly lights, who does not change or cause darkness by turning. By his own will he brought us into being through the word of truth, so that we should have first place among all his creatures.

God has made us what we are, and in our union with Christ Jesus he has created us for a life of good deeds, which he has already prepared for us to do.

You will give us prosperity, LORD; everything that we achieve is the result of what you do.

PHIL. 2.13.—2 COR. 3.5.—JOHN 3.27.—
JOHN 6.44.—JER. 32.39.—JAS 1.16–18.—
EPH. 2.10.—ISA. 26.12.

*Christ was without sin, but for our sake God made him
share our sin in order that in union with him we might
share the righteousness of God.*

The LORD made the punishment fall on him.—Christ himself carried our sins in his body to the cross, so that we might die to sin and live for righteousness. It is by his wounds that you have been healed.—Just as all people were made sinners as the result of the disobedience of one man, in the same way they will all be put right with God as the result of the obedience of the one man.

When the kindness and love of God our Saviour was revealed, he saved us. It was not because of any good deeds that we ourselves had done, but because of his own mercy that he saved us, through the Holy Spirit, who gives us new birth and new life by washing us. God poured out the Holy Spirit abundantly on us through Jesus Christ our Saviour, so that by his grace we might be put right with God and come into possession of the eternal life we hope for.— There is no condemnation now for those who live in union with Christ Jesus.

'The LORD Our Salvation.'

2 COR. 5.21.—ISA. 53.6—1 PET. 2.24.—
ROM. 5.19.—TITUS 3.4-7.—ROM. 8.1.—JER. 23.6.

Let love make you serve one another.

My brothers, if anyone is caught in any kind of wrongdoing, those of you who are spiritual should set him right; but you must do it in a gentle way. And keep an eye on yourselves, so that you will not be tempted, too. Help to carry one another's burdens, and in this way you will obey the law of Christ.

My brothers, if one of you wanders away from the truth and another one brings him back again, remember this: whoever turns a sinner back from his wrong way will save that sinner's soul from death and bring about the forgiveness of many sins.—Now that by your obedience to the truth you have purified yourselves and have come to have a sincere love for your fellow-believers, love one another earnestly with all your heart.—Be under obligation to no one – the only obligation you have is to love one another. Whoever does this has obeyed the Law.—Love one another warmly as Christian brothers, and be eager to show respect for one another.—All of you must put on the apron of humility, to serve one another; for the scripture says, "God resists the proud, but shows favour to the humble."

We who are strong in the faith ought to help the weak to carry their burdens. We should not please ourselves.

GAL. 5.13.—GAL. 6.1, 2.—JAS 5.19, 20.—
1 PET. 1.22.—ROM. 13.8.—ROM. 12.10.—
1 PET. 5.5.—ROM. 15.1.

DECEMBER 9

Do what is right and fair; that pleases the LORD more than bringing him sacrifices.

The LORD has told us what is good. What he requires of us is this: to do what is just, to show constant love, and to live in humble fellowship with our God.—Which does the LORD prefer: obedience or offerings and sacrifices? It is better to obey him than to sacrifice the best sheep to him.—Man must love God with all his heart and with all his mind and with all his strength; and he must love his neighbour as he loves himself. It is more important to obey these two commandments than to offer animals and other sacrifices to God.

Trust in your God and return to him. Be loyal and just, and wait patiently for your God to act.—Mary ... sat down at the feet of the Lord and listened to his teaching. "Mary has chosen the right thing, and it will not be taken away from her."

God is always at work in you to make you willing and able to obey his own purpose.

PROV. 21.3.—MIC. 6.8.—1 SAM. 15.22.—
MARK 12.33.—HOS. 12.6.—LUKE 10.39, 42.—
PHIL. 2.13.

No one can snatch them away from the Father's care.

I know whom I have trusted, and I am sure that he is able to keep safe until that Day what he has entrusted to me.— The Lord will rescue me from all evil and take me safely into his heavenly Kingdom.—We have complete victory through him who loved us! For I am certain that nothing can separate us from his love: neither death nor life, neither angels nor other heavenly rulers or powers, neither the present nor the future, neither the world above nor the world below – there is nothing in all creation that will ever be able to separate us from the love of God which is ours through Christ Jesus our Lord.—Your life is hidden with Christ in God.

God chose the poor people of this world to be rich in faith and to possess the kingdom which he promised to those who love him.

May our Lord Jesus Christ himself and God our Father, who loved us and in his grace gave us unfailing courage and a firm hope, encourage you and strengthen you to always do and say what is good.

JOHN 10.29.—2 TIM. 1.12.—2 TIM. 4.18.—
ROM. 8.37–39.—COL. 3.3.—JAS 2.5.—
2 THESS. 2.16, 17.

Do not let what you regard as good get a bad name.

Avoid every kind of evil.—Our purpose is to do what is right, not only in the sight of the Lord, but also in the sight of man.—God wants you to silence the ignorant talk of foolish people by the good things you do.

If any of you suffers, it must not be because he is a murderer or a thief or a criminal or a meddler in other people's affairs. However, if you suffer because you are a Christian, don't be ashamed of it, but thank God that you bear Christ's name.

My brothers, you were called to be free. But do not let this freedom become an excuse for letting your physical desires control you. Instead, let love make you serve one another.—Be careful ... not to let your freedom of action make those who are weak in the faith fall into sin.—If anyone should cause one of these little ones to lose his faith in me, it would be better for that person to have a large millstone tied round his neck and be drowned in the deep sea.—Whenever you did this for one of the least important of these brothers of mine, you did it for me!

ROM. 14.16.—1 THESS. 5.22.—2 COR. 8.21.—
1 PET. 2.15.—1 PET. 4.15, 16.—GAL. 5.13.—
1 COR. 8.9.—MATT. 18.6.—MATT. 25.40.

The LORD ... is with you.

Do not be afraid—I am with you! I am your God—let nothing terrify you! I will make you strong and help you; I will protect you and save you.—Give strength to hands that are tired and to knees that tremble with weakness. Tell everyone who is discouraged, "Be strong and don't be afraid! God is coming to your rescue, coming to punish your enemies."—The LORD your God is with you; his power gives you victory. The LORD will take delight in you, and in his love he will give you new life. He will sing and be joyful over you.—Trust in the LORD. Have faith, do not despair. Trust in the LORD.

I heard a loud voice speaking from the throne: "Now God's home is with mankind! He will live with them, and they shall be his people. God himself will be with them, and he will be their God. He will wipe away all tears from their eyes. There will be no more death, no more grief or crying or pain."

ZEPH. 3.15.—ISA. 41.10.—ISA. 35.3, 4.—
ZEPH. 3.17.—PS. 27.14.—REV. 21.3, 4.

Be strong through the grace that is ours in union with Christ Jesus.

May you be made strong with all the strength which comes from his glorious power.—Since you have accepted Christ Jesus as Lord, live in union with him. Keep your roots deep in him, build your lives on him, and become stronger in your faith as you were taught. And be filled with thanksgiving.— They will be like trees that the LORD himself has planted. They will all do what is right, and God will be praised for what he has done.—You ... are built upon the foundation laid by the apostles and prophets, the cornerstone being Christ Jesus himself. He is the one who holds the whole building together and makes it grow into a sacred temple dedicated to the Lord. In union with him you too are being built together with all the others into a place where God lives through his Spirit.

I commend you to the care of God and to the message of his grace, which is able to build you up and give you the blessings God has for all his people.—Your lives will be filled with the truly good qualities which only Jesus Christ can produce, for the glory and praise of God.

Run your best in the race of faith.—Don't be afraid of your enemies.

2 TIM. 2.1.—COL. 1.11.—COL. 2.6, 7.—ISA. 61.3.—
EPH. 2.20–22.—ACTS 20.32.—PHIL. 1.11—
1 TIM. 6.12.—PHIL. 1.28.

Offer him glorious praise!

They are the people I made for myself, and they will sing my praises!—I will purify them from the sins that they have committed against me, and I will forgive their sins and their rebellion. Jerusalem will be a source of joy, honour, and pride to me; and every nation in the world will fear and tremble when they hear about the good things that I do.— Let us, then, always offer praise to God as our sacrifice through Jesus, which is the offering presented by lips that confess him as Lord.

I will praise you with all my heart, O Lord my God; I will proclaim your greatness for ever. How great is your constant love for me! You have saved me from the grave itself.—LORD, who among the gods is like you? Who is like you, wonderful in holiness? Who can work miracles and mighty acts like yours?—I will praise God with a song; I will proclaim his greatness by giving him thanks.—[They were] … singing the song of Moses, the servant of God, and the song of the Lamb; "Lord God Almighty, how great and wonderful are your deeds!"

PS. 66.2.—ISA. 43.21.—JER. 33.8, 9.—
HEB. 13.15.— PS. 86.12, 13.—EXOD. 15.11.—
PS. 69.30.—REV. 15.3.

363

*Help to carry one another's burdens, and in this way you
will obey the law of Christ.*

Look out for one another's interests, not just for your own.
The attitude you should have is the one that Christ Jesus
had: He ... took the nature of a servant.—Even the Son of
Man did not come to be served; he came to serve and to
give his life to redeem many people.—He died for all, so
that those who live should no longer live for themselves,
but only for him who died and was raised to life for their
sake.

Jesus saw her weeping, and he saw how the people who
were with her were weeping also; his heart was touched, and
he was deeply moved. Jesus wept.—Be happy with those
who are happy, weep with those who weep.

You must all have the same attitude and the same
feelings; love one another as brothers, and be kind and
humble with one another. Do not pay back evil with evil or
cursing with cursing; instead, pay back with a blessing,
because a blessing is what God promised to give you when
he called you.

GAL. 6.2.—PHIL. 2.4, 5, 7.—MARK 10.45.—
2 COR. 5.15.—JOHN 11.33, 35.—ROM. 12.15.—
1 PET. 3.8, 9.

He had always loved those in the world who were his own,
and he loved them to the very end.

I pray for them. I do not pray for the world but for those
you gave me, for they belong to you. All I have is yours, and
all you have is mine; and my glory is shown through them.
I do not ask you to take them out of the world, but I do ask
you to keep them safe from the Evil One. Just as I do not
belong to the world, they do not belong to the world.

I love you just as the Father loves me; remain in my
love.—The greatest love a person can have for his friends
is to give his life for them. And you are my friends if you
do what I command you.—Now I give you a new commandment: love one another. As I have loved you, so you
must love one another.

God, who began this good work in you, will carry it on
until it is finished on the Day of Christ Jesus.—Christ loved
the church and gave his life for it. He did this to dedicate
the church to God by his word, after making it clean by
washing it in water.

JOHN 13.1.—JOHN 17.9, 10, 15, 16.—JOHN 15.9.—
JOHN 15.13, 14.—JOHN 13.34.—PHIL. 1.6.—
EPH. 5.25, 26.

Keep us alive, and we will praise you.

What gives life is God's Spirit.—The Spirit also comes to help us, weak as we are. For we do not know how we ought to pray; the Spirit himself pleads with God for us in groans that words cannot express. And God, who sees into our hearts, knows what the thought of the Spirit is; because the Spirit pleads with God on behalf of his people and in accordance with his will.—Pray on every occasion, as the Spirit leads, For this reason keep alert and never give up.

I will never neglect your instructions, because by them you have kept me alive.—The words I have spoken to you bring God's life-giving Spirit.—The written law brings death, but the Spirit gives life.—If you remain in me and my words remain in you, then you will ask for anything you wish, and you shall have it.—We have courage in God's presence, because we are sure that he hears us if we ask him for anything that is according to his will.

No one can confess "Jesus is Lord," unless he is guided by the Holy Spirit.

PS. 80.18.—JOHN 6.63.—ROM. 8.26, 27.—
EPH. 6.18.—PS. 119.93.—JOHN 6.63.—
2 COR. 3.6.— JOHN 15.7.—1 JOHN 5.14.—
1 COR. 12.3.

DECEMBER 18

Let us have confidence ... and approach God's throne, where there is grace. There we will receive mercy and find grace to help us just when we need it.

Don't worry about anything, but in all your prayers ask God for what you need, always asking him with a thankful heart. And God's peace, which is far beyond human understanding, will keep your hearts and minds safe in union with Christ Jesus.—The Spirit that God has given you does not make you slaves and cause you to be afraid; instead, the Spirit makes you God's children, and by the Spirit's power we cry out to God, "Father! my Father!"

I did not require the people of Israel to look for me in a desolate waste.—We have, then, my brothers, complete freedom to go into the Most Holy Place by means of the death of Jesus. He opened for us a new way, a living way, through the curtain – that is, through his own body. We have a great priest in charge of the house of God. So let us come near to God with a sincere heart and a sure faith, with hearts that have been purified from a guilty conscience and with bodies washed with clean water.—Let us be bold, then, and say, "The Lord is my helper, I will not be afraid. What can anyone do to me?"

HEB. 4.16.—PHIL. 4.6, 7.—ROM. 8.15.—
ISA. 45.19.—HEB. 10.19–22.—HEB. 13.6.

DECEMBER 19

Light shines in the darkness for good men.

All of you that honour the LORD and obey the words of his servant, the path you walk may be dark indeed, but trust in the LORD, rely on your God.—If they fall, they will not stay down, because the LORD will help them up.—Their instructions are a shining light; their correction can teach you how to live.

Our enemies have no reason to gloat over us. We have fallen, but we will rise again. We are in darkness now, but the LORD will give us light. We have sinned against the LORD, so now we must endure his anger for a while. But in the end he will defend us and right the wrongs that have been done to us. He will bring us out to the light; we will live to see him save us.

The eyes are like a lamp for the body. If your eyes are sound, your whole body will be full of light; but if your eyes are no good, your body will be in darkness. So if the light in you is darkness, how terribly dark it will be!

PS. 112.4.—ISA. 50.10.—PS. 37.24.—PROV. 6.23.—
MIC. 7.8, 9.—MATT. 6.22, 23.

*Even before the world was made, God had already chosen
us to be his through our union with Christ.*

So that we would be holy and without fault before him.

God chose you as the first to be saved by the Spirit's
power to make you his holy people and by your faith in the
truth … he called you to possess your share of the glory of
our Lord Jesus Christ.—Those whom God had already
chosen he also set apart to become like his Son, so that the
Son would be the first among many brothers. And so those
whom God set apart, he called; and those he called, he put
right with himself, and he shared his glory with them.—You
were chosen according to the purpose of God the Father
and were made a holy people by his Spirit, to obey Jesus
Christ and be purified by his blood.

I will give you a new heart and a new mind. I will take
away your stubborn heart of stone and give you an obedient
heart.—God did not call us to live in immorality, but in
holiness.

EPH. 1.4.—EPH. 1.4.—2 THESS. 2.13, 14.—
ROM. 8.29, 30.—1 PET. 1.2.—EZEK. 36.26.—
1 THESS. 4.7.

Your days of grief will come to an end.

The world will make you suffer.—We know that up to the present time all of creation groans with pain, like the pain of childbirth. But it is not just creation alone which groans; we who have the Spirit as the first of God's gifts also groan within ourselves, as we wait for God to make us his sons and set our whole being free.—While we live in this earthly tent, we groan with a feeling of oppression; it is not that we want to get rid of our earthly body, but that we want to have the heavenly one put on over us, so that what is mortal will be transformed by life.

These are the people who have come safely through the terrible persecution. They have washed their robes and made them white with the blood of the Lamb. That is why they stand before God's throne and serve him day and night in his temple. He who sits on the throne will protect them with his presence. Never again will they hunger or thirst; neither sun nor any scorching heat will burn them, because the Lamb, who is in the centre of the throne, will be their shepherd, and he will guide them to springs of life-giving water. And God will wipe away every tear from their eyes.

ISA. 60.20.—JOHN 16.33.—ROM. 8.22, 23.—
2 COR. 5.4.—REV. 7.14-17.

You put your faith into practice.

What God wants you to do is to believe in the one he sent.

So it is with faith; if it is alone and includes no actions, then it is dead.—Faith ... works through love.—If he sows in the field of his natural desires, from it he will gather the harvest of death; if he sows in the field of the Spirit, from the Spirit he will gather the harvest of eternal life.—God has made us what we are, and in our union with Christ Jesus he has created us for a life of good deeds, which he has already prepared for us to do.—He gave himself for us, to rescue us from all wickedness and to make us a pure people who belong to him alone and are eager to do good.

Our brothers, we must thank God at all times for you. It is right for us to do so, because your faith is growing so much and the love each of you has for the others is becoming greater. That is why we always pray for you. We ask our God to make you worthy of the life he has called you to live. May he fulfil by his power all your desire for goodness and complete your work of faith.—God is always at work in you to make you willing and able to obey his own purpose.

1 THESS. 1.3.—JOHN 6.29.—JAS 2.17.—GAL. 5.6.—
GAL. 6.8.—EPH. 2.10.—TITUS 2.14.—
2 THESS. 1.3, 11.—PHIL. 2.13.

DECEMBER 23

*If the enemies of my people want my protection, let them
make peace with me.*

I alone know the plans I have for you, plans to bring you
prosperity and not disaster.—"There is no safety for sinners," says the LORD.

Now, in union with Christ Jesus, you who used to be
far away have been brought near by the sacrificial death of
Christ. For Christ himself has brought us peace.

It was by God's own decision that the Son has in
himself the full nature of God. Through the Son, then, God
decided to bring the whole universe back to himself—
Christ Jesus … God offered him, so that by his sacrificial
death he should become the means by which people's sins
are forgiven through their faith in him. In this way God
shows that he himself is righteous and that he puts right
everyone who believes in Jesus.—If we confess our sins to
God, he will keep his promise and do what is right: he will
forgive us our sins and purify us from all our wrongdoing.

Trust in the LORD for ever; he will always protect us.

ISA. 27.5.—JER. 29.11.—ISA. 48.22.—
EPH. 2.13, 14.—COL. 1.19, 20.—ROM. 3.24–26.—
1 JOHN 1.9.—ISA. 26.4.

If you live according to your human nature, you are going to die; but if by the Spirit you put to death your sinful actions, you will live.

What human nature does is quite plain. It shows itself in immoral, filthy, and indecent actions; ... and ... other things like these. I warn you now as I have before: those who do these things will not possess the Kingdom of God. But the Spirit produces love, joy, peace, patience, kindness, goodness, faithfulness, humility, and self-control. There is no law against such things as these. And those who belong to Christ Jesus have put to death their human nature with all its passions and desires. The Spirit has given us life; he must also control our lives.

God has revealed his grace for the salvation of all mankind. That grace instructs us to give up ungodly living and worldly passions, and to live self-controlled, upright, and godly lives in this world, as we wait for the blessed Day we hope for, when the glory of our great God and Saviour Jesus Christ will appear. He gave himself for us, to rescue us from all wickedness.

ROM. 8.13.—GAL. 5.19, 21–25.—TITUS 2.11–14.

The kindness and love of God our Saviour was revealed.

I continue to show you my constant love.

God showed his love for us by sending his only Son into the world, so that we might have life through him. This is what love is: it is not that we have loved God, but that he loved us and sent his Son to be the means by which our sins are forgiven.

When the right time finally came, God sent his own Son. He came as the son of a human mother and lived under the Jewish Law, to redeem those who were under the Law, so that we might become God's sons.—The Word became a human being and, full of grace and truth, lived among us. We saw his glory, the glory which he received as the Father's only Son.—How great is the secret of our religion: he appeared in human form.

Since the children … are people of flesh and blood, Jesus himself became like them and shared their human nature. He did this so that through his death he might destroy the Devil, who has the power over death.

TITUS 3.4.—JER. 31.3.—1 JOHN 4.9, 10.—
GAL. 4.4, 5.—JOHN 1.14.—1 TIM.3.16.—HEB. 2.14.

*Stand firm and steady. Keep busy always in your work for
the Lord.*

You know that nothing you do in the Lord's service is ever
useless.—Since you have accepted Christ Jesus as Lord, live
in union with him. Keep your roots deep in him, build your
lives on him, and become stronger in your faith, as you were
taught. And be filled with thanksgiving.—Whoever holds
out to the end will be saved.—The seeds that fell in good
soil stand for those who hear the message and retain it in a
good and obedient heart, and they persist until they bear
fruit.

You stand firm in the faith.

As long as it is day, we must keep on doing the work of
him who sent me; night is coming when no one can work.

If he sows in the field of his natural desires, from it he
will gather the harvest of death; if he sows in the field of the
Spirit, from the Spirit he will gather the harvest of eternal
life. So let us not become tired of doing good; for if we do
not give up, the time will come when we will reap the
harvest. So then, as often as we have the chance, we should
do good to everyone, and especially to those who belong
to our family in the faith.

1 COR. 15.58.—1 COR. 15.58.—COL. 2.6, 7.—
MATT. 24.13.—LUKE 8.15.—2 COR. 1.24.—
JOHN 9.4.— GAL. 6.8-10.

We fix our attention, not on things that are seen ... what can be seen lasts only for a time, but what cannot be seen lasts for ever.

There is no permanent city for us here on earth.—You knew that you still possessed something much better, which would last for ever.

Do not be afraid, little flock, for your Father is pleased to give you the Kingdom.

It may now be necessary for you to be sad for a while because of the many kinds of trials you suffer.—In the grave wicked men stop their evil, and tired workmen find rest at last.

While we live in this earthly tent, we groan with a feeling of oppression.—He will wipe away all tears from their eyes. There will be no more death, no more grief or crying or pain. The old things have disappeared.

What we suffer at this present time cannot be compared at all with the glory that is going to be revealed to us.—This small and temporary trouble we suffer will bring us a tremendous and eternal glory, much greater than the trouble.

2 COR. 4.18.—HEB. 13.14.—HEB. 10.34.—
LUKE 12.32.—1 PET. 1.6.—JOB. 3.17.—
2 COR. 5.4.—REV. 21.4.—ROM. 8.18.—2 COR. 4.17.

Your sins are forgiven.

I will forgive their sins and I will no longer remember their wrongs.—God is the only one who can forgive sins!

I am the God who forgives your sins, and I do this because of who I am. I will not hold your sins against you.—Happy are those whose sins are forgiven, whose wrongs are pardoned. Happy is the man whom the LORD does not accuse of doing wrong.—There is no other god like you, O LORD; you forgive the sins of your people.

God has forgiven you through Christ.—The blood of Jesus, his Son, purifies us from every sin. If we say that we have no sin, we deceive ourselves, and there is no truth in us. But if we confess our sins to God, he will keep his promise and do what is right: he will forgive us our sins and purify us from all our wrongdoing.

As far as the east is from the west, so far does he remove our sins from us.—Sin must not be your master; for you do not live under law but under God's grace. You were set free from sin and became the slaves of righteousness.

MARK 2.5.—JER. 31.34.—MARK 2.7.—ISA. 43.25.—
PS. 32.1, 2.—MIC. 7.18.—EPH. 4.32.—
1 JOHN 1.7-9.—PS. 103.12.—ROM. 6.14, 18.

Try to find out what the Lord wants you to do.

God wants you to be holy. Make peace with God ... if you do, then he will bless you.—Eternal life means knowing you, the only true God, and knowing Jesus Christ, whom you sent.

We know that the Son of God has come and has given us understanding, so that we know the true God. We live in union with the true God – in union with his Son Jesus Christ.

We have always prayed for you ... We ask God to fill you with the knowledge of his will, with all the wisdom and understanding that his Spirit gives.—[I] ask the God of our Lord Jesus Christ, the glorious Father, to give you the Spirit who will make you wise and reveal God to you, so that you will know him. I ask that your minds may be opened to see his light, so that you will know what is the hope to which he has called you, how rich are the wonderful blessings he promises his people, and how very great is his power at work in us who believe.

EPH. 5.17.—1 THESS. 4.3.—JOB 22.21.—
JOHN 17.3.—1 JOHN 5.20.—COL. 1.9.—
EPH. 1.17–19.

Faultless on the Day of our Lord Jesus Christ.

At one time you were far away from God and were his enemies because of the evil things you did and thought. But now, by means of the physical death of his Son, God has made you his friends, in order to bring you, holy, pure, and faultless, into his presence. You must, of course, continue faithful on a firm and sure foundation, and must not allow yourselves to be shaken from the hope you gained when you heard the gospel.—So that you may be innocent and pure as God's perfect children, who live in a world of corrupt and sinful people. You must shine among them like stars lighting up the sky.

So, my friends, as you wait for that Day, do your best to be pure and faultless in God's sight and to be at peace with him.—Then you will be free from all impurity and blame on the Day of Christ.

Tp him who is able to keep you from falling, and to bring you faultless and joyful before his glorious presence – to the only God our Saviour, through Jesus Christ our Lord, be glory, majesty, might, and authority, from all ages past, and now, and for ever and ever!

1 COR. 1.8.—COL. 1.21-23.—PHIL. 2.15.—
2 PET. 3.14.—PHIL. 1.10.—JUDE 24, 25.

He brought you safely all the way to this place, just as a father would carry his son.

I carried you as an eagle carries her young on her wings, and brought you here to me.—In his love and compassion he rescued them. He had always taken care of them in the past.—Like an eagle teaching its young to fly, catching them safely on its spreading wings, the LORD kept Israel from falling. The LORD alone led his people.

I am your God and will take care of you until you are old and your hair is grey. I made you and will care for you; I will give you help and rescue you.—This God is our God for ever and ever; he will lead us for all time to come.

Leave your troubles with the LORD, and he will defend you; he never lets honest men be defeated.—I tell you not to be worried about the food and drink you need in order to stay alive, or about clothes for your body. Your father in heaven knows that you need all these things.

The LORD has helped us all the way.

DEUT. 1.31.—EXOD. 19.4.—ISA. 63.9.—
DEUT. 32.11, 12.—ISA. 46.4.—PS. 48.14.—
PS. 55.22.—MATT. 6.25, 32.—1 SAM. 7.12.

COLLINS GEM

Other Gem titles that may interest you include:

Gem Dictionary of the Bible
Contains over 2,700 entries covering the people, places, objects and ideas in the Old and New Testaments **£3.50**

Gem Bible Guide
A compact guide to the content and meaning of all 66 books in the Bible **£2.99**

New Testament and Psalms
The Good News New Testament and Psalms in compact form (GNB93) **£5.50**

Gem Quotations
A fascinating selection of quotations drawn from over 900 authors **£3.50**

Gem Flags
Up-to-date, full-colour guide to over 200 flags of the world, explaining their history and significance **£3.50**

Gem Ready Reference
A unique compilation of information from the world of measures, with quick-reference conversion tables and helpful illustrations **£2.99**

COLLINS GEM

Bestselling Collins Gem titles include:

Gem English Dictionary (£3.50)

Gem Calorie Counter (£2.99)

Gem Thesaurus (£2.99)

Gem French Dictionary (£3.50)

Gem German Dictionary (£3.50)

Gem Basic Facts Mathematics (£2.99)

Gem Birds (£3.50)

Gem Babies' Names (£2.99)

Gem Card Games (£3.50)

Gem World Atlas (£3.50)

All Collins Gems are available from your local bookseller or can be ordered direct from the publishers.

In the UK, contact Mail Order, Dept 2M, HarperCollins Publishers, Westerhill Rd, Bishopbriggs, Glasgow, G64 2QT, listing the titles required and enclosing a cheque or p.o. for the value of the books plus £1.00 for the first title and 25p for each additional title to cover p&p. Access and Visa cardholders can order on 041-772 2281 (24 hr).

In Australia, contact Customer Services, HarperCollins Distribution, Yarrawa Rd, Moss Vale 2577 (tel. [048] 68 0300). **In New Zealand**, contact Customer Services, HarperCollins Publishers, 31 View Rd, Glenfield, Auckland 10 (tel. [09] 444 3740). **In Canada**, contact your local bookshop.

All prices quoted are correct at time of going to press.